A CELEBRATION OF POETS

WEST
GRADES K-3
SPRING 2010

creativeCOMMUNICATION
A CELEBRATION OF TODAY'S WRITERS

A CELEBRATION OF POETS
WEST
GRADES K-3
SPRING 2010

AN ANTHOLOGY COMPILED BY CREATIVE COMMUNICATION, INC.

Published by:

creativeCOMMUNICATION
A CELEBRATION OF TODAY'S WRITERS

1488 NORTH 200 WEST · LOGAN, UTAH 84341
TEL. 435-713-4411 · WWW.POETICPOWER.COM

ISBN: 978-1-60050-380-1

FOREWORD

I am often asked why we create a book of the best entries to our contest. We started this project when the internet was in its infancy. It was a time when the written word was less electronic and recorded the old fashioned way: written on paper. Now in 2010, with email being the primary form of personal communication and classroom assignments often existing only between computers, this project takes on new meaning. We often say that our project helps record literature that would have been lost in the bottom of a locker or a backpack. However, with electronic books becoming increasingly popular, our books also create a historical and permanent record. We create an actual book that can be handed down and read and re-read for generations.

I also reflect upon the letters from poets, parents and teachers I receive each year. This year the most meaningful letter came from a teacher who had a student that was not interested in school and was a member of a gang. This student had received little recognition in school. However, she wrote a poem, sent it into our contest, and it was accepted to be published. With this small bit of recognition, the teacher stated that this student quit her gang, changed what she was wearing to school, and now has an interest in writing.

Why do we create a book of the best entries? We create a book to motivate and inspire today's student writers. We create a book to record poems that would be lost to history. We create a book, and in the process, change lives.

Enjoy what these students have created.

Thomas Worthen, Ph.D.
Editor
Creative Communication

WRITING CONTESTS!

Enter our next POETRY contest!

Enter our next ESSAY contest!

Why should I enter?

Win prizes and get published! Each year thousands of dollars in prizes are awarded throughout North America. The top writers in each division receive a monetary award and a free book that includes their published poem or essay. Entries of merit are also selected to be published in our anthology.

Who may enter?

There are four divisions in the poetry contest. The poetry divisions are grades K-3, 4-6, 7-9, and 10-12. There are three divisions in the essay contest. The essay divisions are grades 3-6, 7-9, and 10-12.

What is needed to enter the contest?

To enter the poetry contest send in one original poem, 21 lines or less. To enter the essay contest send in one original non-fiction essay, 250 words or less, on any topic. Each entry must include the student's name, grade, address, city, state, and zip code, and the student's school name and school address. Students who include their teacher's name may help their teacher qualify for a free copy of the anthology. Contest changes and updates are listed at www.poeticpower.com.

How do I enter?

Enter a poem or essay online: **or**   Mail your entry to:
www.poeticpower.com   Creative Communication
                                     1488 North 200 West
                                     Logan, UT 84341

When is the deadline?

Poetry contest deadlines are December 2nd, April 5th and August 16th. Essay contest deadlines are October 19th, February 15th and July 19th. Students can enter one poem and one essay for each spring, summer, and fall contest deadline.

Are there benefits for my school?

Yes. We award $12,500 each year in grants to help with Language Arts programs. Schools qualify to apply for a grant by having 15 or more accepted entries.

Are there benefits for my teacher?

Yes. Teachers with five or more students published receive a free anthology that includes their students' writing.

For more information please go to our website at
www.poeticpower.com,
email us at editor@poeticpower.com or call 435-713-4411.

TABLE OF CONTENTS

STATES INCLUDED IN THIS EDITION:

Alaska
California
Hawaii
Idaho
Montana
New Mexico
Oregon
Texas
Utah
Wyoming

Spring 2010 Poetic Achievement Honor Schools

* Teachers who had fifteen or more poets accepted to be published

The following schools are recognized as receiving a "Poetic Achievement Award." This award is given to schools who have a large number of entries of which over fifty percent are accepted for publication. With hundreds of schools entering our contest, only a small percent of these schools are honored with this award. The purpose of this award is to recognize schools with excellent Language Arts programs. This award qualifies these schools to receive a complimentary copy of this anthology. In addition, these schools are eligible to apply for a Creative Communication Language Arts Grant. Grants of two hundred and fifty dollars each are awarded to further develop writing in our schools.

Annunciation Orthodox School
Houston, TX
    Maxine Adams
    Sharon Alexander*
    Lise Lanceley*
    Kiki Przewlocki*
    Marian Rosse
    Sarah Williams

Baldwin Stocker Elementary
School
Arcadia, CA
    Jennifer Aoki*
    Denise Landis*
    Clarissa Phillips*

C W Cline Primary School
Friendswood, TX
    Sharon Sullivan*

Cache Valley Learning Center
Logan, UT
    Frances Caplan
    Anne Desjardins
    Heidi Smith*
    Marianne Young

Carlthorp School
Santa Monica, CA
    Laura Bickel*
    Dr. Leslie Johnson
    Nicola Meyer
    Lis Tarvin

CLASS Academy
Portland, OR
Cortney Benvenuto-Nipp
Mr. Butler
Teresa Cantlon
Kaylie Crispen
Matt Dougherty
Ashley Scuderi

Coeur d'Alene Avenue
Elementary School
Venice, CA
Joyce Koff*

Dixie Sun Elementary School
St George, UT
Ms. Berglund
Joy Duncan*
Diana Hormaza
Diane Lee
Brooke Porter
Anne Rogers

Elder Creek Elementary School
Sacramento, CA
Vivian Chung*

Faith Academy of Bellville
Bellville, TX
Shirley A. Mize*

Fort Worth Country Day School
Fort Worth, TX
Manuel Alvear
Kim Buck
Karen Davis
Darlene Ignagni*
Edwena Thompson*
Mary Kay Varley
Anne-Lise Woods*

Goethe International Charter
School
Los Angeles, CA
Cynthia Lopez
Jessica Tyerman

Henry Haight Elementary
School
Alameda, CA
Joan Braze
Jessica Fisher
Scott Hixon
Nicole Jones
Danielle Ullendorff
Bill Weinreb

Heritage Elementary School
St George, UT
Linda Spainhower*
Carrie Webb*

Horn Academy
Bellaire, TX
Lisa Miller*
Shirley A. Wright

Iolani School
Honolulu, HI
Dorsey Gibson
Dr. Michael F. LaGory
Mrs. Okino*
Mrs. Shim*

Islamic School of Muslim
Educational Trust
Portland, OR
Katie Escobar
Vi Pham*
Ava Sujana
Youssef Zirari

Islamic School of San Diego
San Diego, CA
Aisha Boulil*
Fardusa Sharif

Jackson Elementary School
Sanger, CA
Debbie Galloway*
Chris Mimura*
Mrs. O'Donnell
Mr. Tomlinson*
Mrs. Westover

Juliet Morris Elementary
School
Cypress, CA
Mindy Pfafflin*

Kentwood Elementary School
Los Angeles, CA
Ms. Buckly
Roberta Guarnieri*
Karen Mc Broom

Keone'ula Elementary School
Ewa Beach, HI
Tasha Firestone
Aimee K. Matsuura*
Lindsey Richards

Laurence School
Valley Glen, CA
Kim Milman*

Legacy Christian Academy
Alamogordo, NM
Theresa Bean
Yvonne Horgan
Ms. McKee
Christina Stewart

Lockeford Elementary School
Lockeford, CA
Lark Lieb*

Lolo Elementary School
Lolo, MT
Jennifer Christensen*

Longfellow Elementary School
Houston, TX
Mr. Berry
Georgia King
Teri Marsh*

Lorenzo De Zavala Elementary
School
Baytown, TX
Denise Morgan*

Montessori Learning Institute
Houston, TX
MyLe Nguyen Vo
Lekha Worah

Mosaic Academy
Aztec, NM
Sarah Rankin*

Notre Dame Academy
Elementary School
Los Angeles, CA
Pat Genovese*

Oak Park Elementary School
San Diego, CA
Mick Rabin*

Old Town Elementary School
Round Rock, TX
Caroline Coffin*
Staci Raya

Our Lady of the Rosary School
Paramount, CA
    Sr. Ellen Mary Conefrey
    Mr. Delgado
    Mary Frankart
    Sr. Brigid Mary
        McGuire
    Maricruz Soto

P H Greene Elementary School
Webster, TX
    Virginia Gamache*
    Brandy Magdos

Plum Creek Elementary School
Lockhart, TX
    Keitha Hernandez*

Providence Hall
Herriman, UT
    Alicia Barton*

Reid School
Salt Lake City, UT
    Kathleen Barlow
    Lucie Chamberlain
    Cheri Israelsen
    Meagan Jones
    Angela Preble
    Stephanie Taylor

Robert L Stevens Elementary
School
Santa Rosa, CA
    Amber Moran*

Robinson Elementary School
Robinson, TX
    Amanda Bright*

Round Rock Christian
Academy
Round Rock, TX
    Andrea Cermak*

Russian Jack Elementary
School
Anchorage, AK
    John Pace*

Scholars Academy
San Jose, CA
    Janice Brcich*
    Sonu Dhawan
    Anjna Kaul
    Shailaja Nayak
    Rina Roy
    Pooja Tyagi

Selwyn College Preparatory
School
Denton, TX
    Connie Miller*

Sierra Hills Elementary School
Meadow Vista, CA
    Ann Linkugel*

Spring Creek Elementary
School
Laramie, WY
    Koren Burling
    Linda Cavalli
    Andrea Hayden

St Aloysius Parochial School
Tulare, CA
    April Beck*

St James Episcopal School
Del Rio, TX
    Julie Hedman*
    Morgan Scully
    Carol Sunderland
    Zanna Watkins

St John's Episcopal Day School
McAllen, TX
    Beverly Moore*

St Joseph Catholic School
Auburn, CA
    Cecilia Holmes
    Kristen Mendonsa
    Gayle Moore
    JoAnn O'Donnell
    Robert Socik
    Georgia Stempel
    Jamie Zalud

St Mary Elementary School
Palmdale, CA
    Rowena Catalla*

St Mary of Assumption School
Santa Maria, CA
    Ellen Muldoon*

St Pius X Catholic School
Corpus Christi, TX
    Adele Farrell
    Kathi Urbis*
    Emily Wenzel

St Raphael School
Santa Barbara, CA
    Ms. Breton
    Barbara Malvinni*
    Diane McClenathen*

The Mirman School
Los Angeles, CA
    Dr. Julia Candace
    Corliss*
    Veronica Gonzales*
    Bonnie Muler*
    Tracy Walker*
    Marjorie Zinman

Thomas Edison Charter School
- North
North Logan, UT
    Stephani Bennion*
    Tanya Bidstrup*
    Jamie Lewis
    Emili Wall*

Three Rivers Elementary
School
Three Rivers, TX
    Jennifer Self*

Tracy Learning Center -
Primary Charter School
Tracy, CA
    Jill Grabert*
    Ladonna Means*
    Lori Rodieck
    Carolyn Woods*

Wagon Wheel Elementary
School
Trabuco Canyon, CA
    Mrs. Casebeir
    Jill LeFevre*
    Dionne Petzold*

Wasatch Elementary School
Provo, UT
    Marie Mattinson*

Wilchester Elementary School
Houston, TX
Erica Finley*
Mrs. Luong
Beverly McKenty*

Winona Elementary and
Intermediate School
Winona, TX
Kristy Davis*

Wonderland Avenue
Elementary School
Los Angeles, CA
Zachary Earl*

Woodcrest School
Tarzana, CA
Carol Bittner*
Anna Feinberg
Patricia Fernandez
Mrs. Martin*
Mr. Menager
Luanne Paglione*
Mrs. Rubin
Michelle Tran

Language Arts Grant Recipients 2009-2010

After receiving a "Poetic Achievement Award" schools are encouraged to apply for a Creative Communication Language Arts Grant. The following is a list of schools who received a two hundred and fifty dollar grant for the 2009-2010 school year.

Arrowhead Union High School, Hartland, WI
Blessed Sacrament School, Seminole, FL
Booneville Jr High School, Booneville, AR
Buckhannon-Upshur Middle School, Buckhannon, WV
Campbell High School, Ewa Beach, HI
Chickahominy Middle School, Mechanicsville, VA
Clarkston Jr High School, Clarkston, MI
Covenant Life School, Gaithersburg, MD
CW Rice Middle School, Northumberland, PA
Eason Elementary School, Waukee, IA
East Elementary School, Kodiak, AK
Florence M Gaudineer Middle School, Springfield, NJ
Foxborough Regional Charter School, Foxborough, MA
Gideon High School, Gideon, MO
Holy Child Academy, Drexel Hill, PA
Home Choice Academy, Vancouver, WA
Jeff Davis Elementary School, Biloxi, MS
Lower Alloways Creek Elementary School, Salem, NJ
Maple Wood Elementary School, Somersworth, NH
Mary Walter Elementary School, Bealeton, VA
Mater Dei High School, Evansville, IN
Mercy High School, Farmington Hills, MI
Monroeville Elementary School, Monroeville, OH

Language Arts Grant Winners cont.

Nautilus Middle School, Miami Beach, FL
Our Lady Star of the Sea School, Grosse Pointe Woods, MI
Overton High School, Memphis, TN
Pond Road Middle School, Robbinsville, NJ
Providence Hall Charter School, Herriman, UT
Reuben Johnson Elementary School, McKinney, TX
Rivelon Elementary School, Orangeburg, SC
Rose Hill Elementary School, Omaha, NE
Runnels School, Baton Rouge, LA
Santa Fe Springs Christian School, Santa Fe Springs, CA
Serra Catholic High School, Mckeesport, PA
Shadowlawn Elementary School, Green Cove Springs, FL
Spectrum Elementary School, Gilbert, AZ
St Edmund Parish School, Oak Park, IL
St Joseph Institute for the Deaf, Chesterfield, MO
St Joseph Regional Jr High School, Manchester, NH
St Mary of Czestochowa School, Middletown, CT
St Monica Elementary School, Garfield Heights, OH
St Vincent De Paul Elementary School, Cape Girardeau, MO
Stevensville Middle School, Stevensville, MD
Tashua School, Trumbull, CT
The New York Institute for Special Education, Bronx, NY
The Selwyn School, Denton, TX
Tonganoxie Middle School, Tonganoxie, KS
Westside Academy, Prince George, BC
Willa Cather Elementary School, Omaha, NE
Willow Hill Elementary School, Traverse City, MI

Grades K-1-2-3
Top Ten Winners

List of Top Ten Winners for Grades K-3; listed alphabetically

Kevanna Babyak, Grade 2
Carlyle C Ring Elementary School, NY

Taylor Bond, Grade 3
Elmer Elson Elementary School, AB

Matthew Geurtsen, Grade 1
St Zachary Elementary School, IL

Evangeline Gilmer, Kindergarten
Mary Burgess Neal Elementary School, MD

Samantha Jabra, Grade 3
St Joseph School, NJ

Taryn Jackson, Grade 3
Midland Academy of Advanced and Creative Studies, MI

Alexandra Lorentzatos, Grade 3
Wilchester Elementary School, TX

Sydney May, Grade 3
C Hunter Ritchie Elementary School, VA

Bonnie Nguyen, Grade 3
Oak Park Elementary School, CA

Mackenzie Stewart, Grade 1
St Mark's Day School, TX

All Top Ten Poems can be read at www.poeticpower.com

Note: The Top Ten poems were finalized through an online voting system. Creative Communication's judges first picked out the top poems. These poems were then posted online. The final step involved thousands of students and teachers who registered as the online judges and voted for the Top Ten poems. We hope you enjoy these selections.

Sports

Sports are fun.
The more you play, the stronger you get.
The game starts; the lights turn on.
When you're on the field, the crowd goes wild for you.
When you score, you are the star.
The game finishes; the lights turn off.
And the moment ends.

Mussa Mahamed, Grade 3
Islamic School of San Diego, CA

Wild Horses

Beautiful mane
pretty body formation
big hooves
long fast legs
very pretty mammals
cute foals
gallop fast

Piper Green Teigeler, Grade 3
Thomas Edison Charter School - North, UT

Comedy to Tragedy

Comedy,
Light, amusing,
Laughing, smiling, acting,
Entertainment, mischief, loss, heartache,
Worrying, wishing, crying,
Heavy, sad,
Tragedy.

Ashlee Pike, Grade 3
Tracy Learning Center - Primary Charter School, CA

My Cousins

Some cousins are nice and some are not.
Some don't care about me,
Some do a lot.
Some are special,
Some are not.
Some are funny,
Some make me laugh a lot.

Nuzhat Maisha Hoque, Grade 2
Islamic School of Muslim Educational Trust, OR

Christmas

C hrist is born
H earts gathering
R oast beef
I ncredible prayers being said
S tars twinkling in the night
T iny steps of a small one
M others caring for the family
A child sleeping
S ongs of the happiness Christmas will bring

Isaiah McElderry, Grade 3
Lolo Elementary School, MT

Nature

Wind howls as it blows.
Snow laughs as it drifts down from the sky.
Flowers dance in the wind.
Mountains look over the Earth.
Sand tickles your feet.
Rain speaks as it falls.
Grass sways as it blows in the wind.
Birds sing in the trees.
Nature is always moving.

Lauren Yee, Grade 2
CLASS Academy, OR

Ocean

Ocean
Blue water, waves
Making waves all the time
Makes me peaceful when I'm swimming
Water

Clarisse Ocampo, Grade 2
Tracy Learning Center - Primary Charter School, CA

Spring

Spring is finally here.
I can see the pretty yellow sun.
I can hear the rabbits chewing on carrots.
I can smell the red roses growing in the garden.
I can taste mommy's special pumpkin pie.
I feel happy because it's spring time.

Delbar Nonahal, Grade 2
Woodcrest School, CA

Where I'm From

I am from black belts, uniforms, and blue mats.
I am from palm trees in my front yard.
I am from pine trees in the tall forests.
From stickbugs that crawl in my glass tank.
I am from my grandma's kimchi and from rice in a bowl.
I am from artistic parents and nice grandparents.
I am from "Clean your room!" and "Brush your teeth!"
I am from stickbugs that stick on my finger.
I am from Rachel and Peter.
I am from pushing my friend in the pool.
I am from past pictures, present schools, and future jobs.

Brian Im, Grade 3
Juliet Morris Elementary School, CA

Earth

Earth is our planet.
We live on it.
Earth is beautiful.
Everyone loves it.
Only Earth has life.
No other planets have…
Air we breathe,
Water we drink, and
the fresh breeze we enjoy.
We should take care of our planet…
Earth!

Haadiya Ansari, Grade 3
Islamic School of Muslim Educational Trust, OR

J Boy

Janus
It means cool, fun and hard working.
It is the number 3,000
It is like the flame in the fire.
It is hip hopping to cool dance moves.
It is the memory of my best friend Chasen
Who taught me how to break dance
Who taught me to be caring and a risk taker
When he makes me take care of people
And just the things that are hard.
My name is Janus.

Janus Gapusan, Grade 2
Keone'ula Elementary School, HI

A Wonderful Zoo
Two golden gates are opening swiftly in the early morning
The furry, fierce lion is walking quickly in its giant cage
Half a dozen scary tigers are sleeping peacefully near a deep moat
A huge, slow elephant is eating joyfully in the cold afternoon
Many fast zebras are running swiftly in a grassy area
Four tall giraffes are stretching slowly on a large rock
Five sleepy, beautiful girls are watching carefully on a brown bench
Three likeable, joyful boys are laughing enjoyably at the little monkey house
Seven pairs of calm parents are talking happily in the warm sun
Some cheerful, friendly people are chatting excitedly near a large shop
A huge number of spiky lionfish are swimming awkwardly under a huge leaf
Dozens of colorful clownfish are resting happily in the clean water
All of the friendly people leaving quickly out of the large zoo
The endless, starry sky shining gracefully on the miraculous animals

Samantha Chung, Grade 3
The Mirman School, CA

Happy Summer
Summer is a season that kids do not have to go to school,
They can stay home all day.
Summer is a season where
It is scorching hot!

The kids are having fun and
They are really excited.
The kids saw butterflies
Flying around and around.

The sun rose from a night's sleep
And the kids splash in the pool
Like crazy monkeys.
Summer is the best season ever!

Leon Pham, Grade 3
Wilchester Elementary School, TX

Christmas Is in the Air
You can smell it in the baking turkey.
You can taste it in the delicious ham.
You can hear it in the tunes of carols.
You can see it in the funny snowman.
You can feel the Christmas cheer in the air.

Enrico Hernandez, Grade 3
A E Arnold Elementary School, CA

St. Patrick's Day Guide
At the end of a spectrum, it has been told,
Of little green men, and a cauldron of gold.
The 17th of March is when you might find,
A leprechaun, but he's not always very kind.
You may have to bargain, or get something sold,
If you want the pot, that's all full of gold.
Please follow these instructions,
To prevent any abductions.
1. Walk so quietly that you cannot even hear yourself.
2. Make sure nobody is following you.
3. Don't take the whole pot of gold, because
I'll bet you anything that you wouldn't be able to carry it.
4. Stuff your pockets with gold coins.
5. Tighten your pants so they don't fall down.

Luke Reno, Grade 3
Providence Hall, UT

Pizza
I really like pizza!
Sweet crusty crust,
Nice saucy sauce,
Chewy cheesy cheese.
So warm in my mouth
When I open the box, hot steam hits my face
It smells great!
I cut the pizza
Pick up a nice big piece
It flops in my hand
I take a big bite.
The warm cheese heats my mouth
I chew and swallow
It's perfect!

Aaron Berger, Grade 3
Wonderland Avenue Elementary School, CA

Is Like...
An apple is a red circle
A mouse is like a tiny animal that lives in a hole
A cupcake is like a hill with frosting
Cotton candy is like a fluffy pink or blue cloud
A mountain is like an ice-cream hill

Katie Tran, Grade 3
Elder Creek Elementary School, CA

Dolls

I like to play with them
I have a lot at my house
I bring them into my living room to play with them
I count with them, play school with them, and read with them
Bring them to my grandma's and play
Watch TV with them and sleep with them
I love my dolls

Rakaylyn Burk, Kindergarten
Legacy Christian Academy, NM

Hunter-Gatherers

A tidal wave of rain is near by in the state of Queensland
While the wind whistles roughly.
All the marsupials keep their young in their pouch
To protect from harsh hail.
And suddenly, the rain stopped and the sun came out.
The sun gazes above one's head and beneath aborigines
That hunt and gather.
If you come, you will have fun.

Justin Tierney, Grade 3
CLASS Academy, OR

I Am a Particle

I am an atom,
Made of many particles.
I am an electron,
Whirling with an atom's energy.
I am a neutron,
Boring and neutral.
I am a particle.
The world would be nothing if it weren't for me.

Duncan Howell, Grade 3
CLASS Academy, OR

The Sun!!

The sun is so bright!
It's too bad it doesn't come out at night.
Beneath the sun you might need a sweater.
Well, a T-shirt might be better.
That sun is so bright!

Sofia Al-Bawani, Grade 3
Islamic School of Muslim Educational Trust, OR

Short Week

It was Monday at school and my friend told me
there was no Friday at school next week.
So now there is no Friday.

It was still Monday after school and my brother told me
that football was cancelled Thursday next week.
So now there is no Thursday.

It was Monday night and my dad told me
the store was closed Wednesday next week.
So now there is no Wednesday.

It was 12:00 at night on Monday and in my dream
someone told me that I would be sick Tuesday next week.
So now there is no Tuesday.

It was now Saturday and my sister told me
that ballet was cancelled Monday this week.
So now there is no Monday.

So there is Saturday and Sunday
oh what a relief,
I love having a very short week!!

Adison LoPiccolo, Grade 3
St. Joseph Catholic School, CA

Big Mac

I am a Big Mac.
I live in McDonalds.
Lunch time is hard because I have to round up the french fries
In the fryer.
I have talks with the milkshakes at night.
And fun with the pancakes in the morning.
Winter is so cold, I need to warm up by the grill.
I have to sleep in the freezer in summer
Because it is so hot.
What's this?
A cave?
It's dark in here.
What are these white things?
Gulp.

Derrick Jensen, Grade 3
CLASS Academy, OR

My House

My
House makes
me feel relaxed and

welcome. I go upstairs

and start to read my crumbly
pages of my book. My

House is where I am open to new

possibilities on the doors I have not opened.

Sarah Mitchell, Grade 3
Old Town Elementary School, TX

The Wild Zoo

Happy children are entering excitedly into the wild zoo
Their tiny feet move quickly to see the
massive animals before the bright day ends
To the right, enormous crocodiles feast
exquisitely on their prey
To the left, long giraffes are raising their
necks upward towards the sky
The massive lions roaring loudly from the blocks away,
Colorful birds tweeting lightly through the air and
Cute seals splashing water quickly to the crowd
I end my day with wet clothes from the seals
Making me miserable after the whole day

Bryan Montenegro, Grade 3
The Mirman School, CA

Blue Is

Blue is Uranus in the night sky,
Blue sounds like a long waterfall crashing down,
Blue feels like a Warrior's jersey,
Blue looks like the morning sky,
Blue is ice in winter,
Blue is Neptune,
Blue is the jeans on you,
Blue feels like a cold ice pack,
These are all blue to me!

Ty Riveras, Grade 3
Marguerite Hahn Elementary School, CA

Tree

I saw a bird in a tree, singing its song, looking at me.
In the tree there was a bee, an angry bee looking at me.
In the tree there was a bug, a big bug, his name was Jug.
I saw a nest, in the tree, with 2 birds looking at me.
I saw a branch with 7 twigs and 18 leaves.
I climbed to the top tip! tip! of the tree.
I love that tree because it is mine.
If you see a tree, don't cut it down.

Riley Rosenbluh, Grade 3
Aveson Charter School, CA

Snowflake

Beautiful jewels falling from the heavens
A pretty flower blooming
A delicious glass of eggnog trickling down my throat
A bunch of butterflies floating down to Earth
A very fluffy pillow where I rest my weary head
A colorful kite flying high above
Rays of light plunging down from the sky
An eagle soaring way up high

Cody Boland, Grade 3
Lolo Elementary School, MT

Feelings

Sometimes I feel so tired like I just ran for three days.
Sometimes I feel like a star shining brighter than the others.
Sometimes I feel lost in a different world and I can't get out.
Sometimes I feel so mad, like a volcano exploding.
Sometimes I feel so happy like I'm jumping up and down!
Sometimes I feel invisible, like I'm the only person in the room.
There are a lot of feelings in this world,
and these are only some of those feelings.

Laura Althaus, Grade 2
Longfellow Elementary School, TX

A Cat Named Fred

I once had a cat named Fred.
He liked to sleep on my bed.
He gave me quite a fright,
He jumped so high one night,
He landed on my head (and I rolled out of bed!)

Ethan Stewart-Duke, Grade 3
St John's Episcopal School, TX

Ethan Loves His Sister

Ethan
It means funny, kind and respectful,
It is the number sixteen
It is like flowers all around me.
It is when me and my sister went to Chuck-E-Cheese's
It is the memory of my sister.
Bowling ball getting stuck in my sisters hand when she was about to throw.
Who taught me to be nice to other people and respect other people
When she makes me laugh.
It means to respect others.

Ethan Prieto, Grade 2
Keone'ula Elementary School, HI

Michelle

Michelle
It means active, smart and generous.
It is the number 1
It is like a beautiful rose.
It is having a great time with Cory at the end of the day playing tag.
It is the memory of Cory having a royal time with me
Who taught me to be great and special
When he makes me feel like a lovely rose.
My name is Michelle
It means to always believe in yourself.

Michelle Winczner, Grade 2
Keone'ula Elementary School, HI

Texas

The motto is friendship.
It's the lone star state.
It's original name was TEJAS.
There are seas of blue bonnets in the spring.
Cattle grazing,
Indians roaming,
Coyotes wailing,
Cowboys lassoing,
Rodeo.
That's TEXAS!!!

Wes Waitkus, Grade 3
Wilchester Elementary School, TX

What Is Hannah?
Is Hannah a Montana?
Does she live next to Savannah?
Is she a beaver or a retriever?
Does she hibernate in the winter?
If she does she's the real winner.
Is she a mammal?
Is she a camel?
Wait! Is a camel a mammal?
Is she a person whose nickname is Ms. Jerkson?
Is she a caterpillar whose nickname is Miller?
Is she a dog whose nickname is Spikey Mikey?
Is she a type of toy or the name of a plane?
No-o-o-o silly milly, she's my dog, Hannah!

Joy Nichols, Grade 3
Kingwood Montessori School, TX

The Zoo
The iron gates opened while happy animals walked in to see mad screaming
people in cages.
Joyful animals happily walk around the humongous zoo smiling at the crazy folks.
Angry humans were being yelled at by the cheerful animals.
Some smart human beings quickly found a way out of the steel cages.
Alarmed animals ran fast into the huge cages because smiling people chased them
into the humongous cages.
Pleased people excitedly laughed at the crying animals because they were in
gold cages.
The zoo's strong gates opened, and the confused people look at them.
Sneaky animals came out of the silver cages and ran out of the enormous zoo.
As the huge gates closed, the mad people ran after the laughing animals.

Andrew Sington, Grade 3
The Mirman School, CA

Witch Stew
Bubbler, bubble, hiss, bang
Boiling broth and bat tailed soup
Wobble, slobber, liquid, goo
You put a shoe, a sock, and a rotten tooth
Gnarly, ow, tickle, itch
Stir it round and make it rich
Mush, stink, sizzle, and caboom!
They are making witch stew for you!

Suzy Park, Grade 3
Wonderland Avenue Elementary School, CA

Cherry Blossom

C herries they will bring.
H eaping baskets full of bright red berries.
E xcept during the summer, spring, and winter.
R ed isn't always the color.
R eddish pink, black, and when ripening,
Y ellow is green.

B ut now they bring bees,
L ots of them, collecting pollen.
O f course they want some of the
S weet and sticky nectar too.
S ometimes if you look closely you will see
O rb-like green things at the base of
M ost flowers coming towards the end of summer.

Lexi Echols, Grade 3
Cache Valley Learning Center, UT

The One Hundred Dollar Bill

Just today I was given a one hundred dollar bill.
So I went shopping with my really silly Uncle Phil.
These prices are so really good, they are low and they are high!
The high ones are the greatest ones, these dollars are worth a try!
Board games, markers, toy cars, magnets, Super Mario too!
Paint tubes, Legos, laptops, baseballs, a DS colored blue.
I would buy a thing for fun, I'd give money to the clerk.
And with one hundred dollars, she would get up and just perk.
So, I just said, "I want no toy, I decided I want food."
I went to buy some yums, I didn't want to be rude.
Cookies, Ruffles, Cheerios, doughnuts, delicious ice cream, YUM!
It all went down the hatch, right down to the last crumb.
Toys or food, I could not choose so I had a good idea!
In my bank account it goes, I gave it to teller Mia.

Sam Rose, Grade 3
Bilquist Elementary School, OR

Kimia

K ind to others!
I love my family!
M any things are interesting to me!
I love reading and math.
A lways thinks about other people's feelings.

Kimia Shirvani, Kindergarten
Woodcrest School, CA

Paramount Purple

Purple looks like a jewel, shining in a sunlit room.
Purple sounds like a kite, whipping fiercely in the wind.
Purple smells like a flower, swaying in the peaceful breeze.
Purple tastes like a grape, juicy and ripe.
Purple feels like a ribbon, tied up in your hair.

Peyton Ashby, Grade 3
Providence Hall Charter School, UT

Students

Students
Small, smart
Laughing, running, learning
They are nice and very loving
Children

Kathleen Field, Grade 2
Tracy Learning Center - Primary Charter School, CA

Garbage

Garbage
Smelly, stinky
Dumping, walking, smelling
People cannot stand the stench
Stinky

Kade Lovell, Grade 2
Tracy Learning Center - Primary Charter School, CA

Kids

kids
little people
amusing, playing, working
creative, quick, talkative, talented
children

Mariana Rodriguez, Grade 3
Lorenzo De Zavala Elementary School, TX

Mrs. Means

Mrs. Means
Beautiful, nice
Teaching, writing, typing
Friendly and colorful
Teacher

Marcus Martinez, Grade 3
Tracy Learning Center - Primary Charter School, CA

Love My Uncle
Dillon

It means crazy, funny and fun to play with.
My number is 1,000.
It is the color of grass.
It is when I went to the Big Island.
It is the memory of my uncle
Who taught me he is my uncle.
My uncle taught me how to be serious.
My name is Dillon
It means to not be crazy all the time.

Dillon Matsu, Grade 2
Keone'ula Elementary School, HI

Sith Lords
S layers of the Jedi,
I ncredibly bad.
T he separatist alliance,
H ideous enemies of the Jedi.

L ords of evil and darkness,
O ' mighty enemies of the Jedi.
R ulers of fear and death
D ark lords of the Sith.
S ith lords.

William Flessner, Grade 3
Thomas Edison Charter School - North, UT

New Baby
One sunny day
A baby was on the way,
I ran to my mom's phone
I called 911 for the ambulance
I rode with my mom.
A pretty, beautiful baby was in the hands of the doctor.
Now I held my baby brother
He started to cry.
Mom named him David Alexander Leija
I have a real baby brother.

Annette Leija, Grade 3
Three Rivers Elementary School, TX

My Dog Riley
She has green eyes,
And white fur like a part of a bald eagle,
But she can't spread her wings and soar.

She rocks like good music,
She is the best animal.
Even thought she can't play music,
If she could, that would be cool.

I was so excited when I got her,
I wanted Riley the most,
I was glad I didn't get the other dog,
That was a good call.

Riley is so, so silly,
She is better than all other mammals,
She is better than bunnies, cats, and more.
That is why Riley is the best!

Troy Durant, Grade 3
Wilchester Elementary School, TX

The Rainbow
Rainbow was born
From her mother and her father:
Rainy and Sunny.

Rainbow's other relatives are:
Red, Orange, Yellow, Green,
Blue, Indigo and Purple.

Rainbow's favorite relative is Blue,
Her cousin.

Rainbow's favorite holiday is Valentine's Day
When her parents visit her.

Her most favorite food is chocolate.

Rainbow's home is a cozy cottage in the sky
Where they all live.

Sahana Jayaraman, Grade 3
CLASS Academy, OR

Oh Poison Ivy

Ivy, Ivy, Ivy
I wish to eat,
   but you're poison for a tasty treat.
I'm not trying to upset you like that.
I am obsessed with you.

But your bumpy lump
   makes me want to throw up.
But when people tell me you're good and sweet
   when I take a nibble a poison dark taste
falls into my mouth when I start to erase.

Now I have lumpy bumps
   all over my face.
That's when I go to sleep.
I gather everyone to my bed and see
   if a bump appears on my feet.

So paint away every bump and feeling.
Now I'm healing.
So long bumps of poison ivy and lumpy bum feet.

Zachary White, Grade 2
Greenleaf Elementary School, CA

Why Poetry?

Forget it.
You must be kidding.
My hair is limp.
I need to go to the doctor.
I'm nodding without brain signals!
SNAP! AAAH! There's termites eating my desk!
I'm tuning out!
I have the measles!
My mom is coming to take me home.
I have to go to the dentist.
Time's up? Uh-oh!
All I have is a dumb list of excuses.
You like it? Really?
No kidding?
Thanks a lot.
Would you like to hear another one?

Sarah Semaan, Grade 3
Juliet Morris Elementary School, CA

Zoo Day

The fast gates that are opening are too quick for the excited
people to see.
The gray monkeys are greeting the smart families while they
come into the enormous zoo where no one is trapped.
The joyful children are happily playing, feeding, and reading
inside the huge zoo, and they are doing it with the smart and
noisy animals working behind a juicy apple tree.
Thrilled parents are quietly talking about the funny animals
and laughing hysterically.
The black gorillas and loud elephants are bringing in some
funny named instruments — saxophone, trumpets, clarinet, and
clapper sticks.
All the other colorful animals are making hyper blast sounds
and were excited like other overly proud people.
Everyone, except the pleased parents, were overly loud that
more than 10 unhappy boys and girls were hoarse.
Within the group of mute, sad people, the glad animals are
loudly laughing that they lost their intense voices.
Everyone hears nothing!!!
Everyone starts to leave to go outside the crazy zoo, and the
red gates close behind the not so noisy people.

Analea Beckman, Grade 2
The Mirman School, CA

I Know the Movies

I know the movies
The smell of the popcorn
The smell of the candy
I know the movies
I hear the people laughing
I hear the people screaming
I know the movies
I see the people walking in
I see the movie
I know the movies
I taste the sour gummy candy
I taste the yummy nachos
I know the movies
I feel the squishy gummy worms in my mouth
I feel the buttery popcorn on my fingers
I know the movies

Thomas Zepeda, Grade 3
Horn Academy, TX

The Crack of a Bat

I get up to bat,
With the wind in my face.
I've practiced and practiced,
I stare at the pitcher,
I see determination in his eyes,
I was going to…
Make a crack in the bat!
Finally he began to pitch.
I swing the piece of wood
And I closed my eyes.
I heard an enormous "CRACK!"
It was the most incredible!
The most astonishing!
The most beautiful sound I ever heard!
As I saw the ball sail over the fence,
My team was yelling "RUN MATTHEW RUN!"
As I sprinted around the bases,
My team cheered at the plate.
I jumped in the crowd,
As we won the game!

Matthew Daiy, Grade 3
D P Morris Elementary School, TX

Black and Orange

Black and orange are Halloween colors,
Black is the night, and orange is the
jack 'o' lantern that gives you a fright,
Orange is the color of an EXPLOSION!
and black is the color of dead leaves.
Orange is the color of fire,
And black is the color of the smoke it makes.
Orange is the color of wars,
And black represents the sadness it makes.
Black is the color of darkness,
And orange is the color of light,
that penetrates darkness.
Orange is the color of joy,
And black is the color of sadness.
Black and orange are opposite colors,
And in very few places do they go together.
What I am saying I know is very true.

Georgo Joeckel, Grade 3
Thomas Edison Charter School - North, UT

Thank You
Thank you God for giving me friends
Thank you God for giving me family
Thank you God for giving me light to see at night
Thank you God for giving me my school and a home
Thank you God for giving me my pets, food, and clothes
Thank you for giving me my mom and dad and my brothers and sisters
Thank you God

Ethan Wagner, Grade 2
Legacy Christian Academy, NM

What My Family Means to Me
What my family means to me.
Is the sun that brightens my day.
What my family means to me.
Is the rays that chased the clouds away.
What my family means to me is the smile they bring to my face.
What my family is to me is a love that cannot be replaced.
That is what my family means to me.

Olivia Bowers, Grade 3
Warren Elementary School, OR

The Color Yellow
The color yellow is the color of the Sun.
It brings the shine of a beautiful Daisy.
When the stars bring their light, it reminds me of yellow.

Yellow is the color that brings joy to my life.
When it's sunset, I say yellow spreads its wings across the sky.
I am very thankful for yellow.

Leila Soliman, Grade 3
Islamic School of San Diego, CA

Three Happy Mice
Three mice flew around my house
Happily goofing around the kitchen
Jumping and running

Until the house owner came
And three happy mice
cant goof around no longer.

Mayam Loren Timbol, Grade 2
Welby Way and Gifted/High Achieving Magnet School, CA

Wild Horses
Ancient relatives gallop through the stars,
In America they run
Through the plains of Neverland
Colts so young and brave
As the tide comes crashing they drink
The American horse so wild and free
Stallions together as they breathe
More babies come to Earth as young.

Sophie Burningham, Grade 3
Thomas Edison Charter School - North, UT

Mom and Dad
Mom
Nice, beautiful
Laughing, walking, writing
Purse, shoes, wallet, car
Driving, working, eating
Handsome, awesome
Dad

Jose Diaz, Grade 2
Tracy Learning Center - Primary Charter School, CA

Free Like Nature
Birds fly,
Birds build their nests in any tree,
Squirrels climb and jump,
Squirrels hide nuts all over the neighborhood,
Fish swim
Fish have the whole ocean,
Me?
I have my whole backyard.

Arnav Ranade, Kindergarten
Scholars Academy, CA

Christmas Is in the Air
You can smell it in the piney air.
You can taste it in the yummy snickerdoodle cookies.
You can hear it in the chimes ringing.
You can see it in the beautiful wreath.
You can feel it in the smooth ornaments.

Joshua Suh, Grade 3
A E Arnold Elementary School, CA

I Know the Movies

I know the movies
The buttery popcorn
The sweet icee
I know the movies
The soft seats
The plastic arm rest
The hard ground
I know the movies
The people saying "shh"
The people laughing
The loudness
I know the movies
The people watching
My friend watching
The boy watching too
I know the movies
The smell of salt
The smell of butter
The smell of sweets
I know the movies
Aidan Clark, Grade 3
Horn Academy, TX

Rain

Pat, pat as the rain hits my umbrella,
splash! As I step in the puddle,
rain comes from above
where clouds are dark
like darkness.
Rain comes with lightning!
But when rain wants a friend,
snow is rain's friend.

Rain is awesome in my world
but some of you could not
like rain as much as other people.
Rain is tears in your eyes
rain comes when clouds are dark
rain,
rain,
it's all about rain.
Daniel Joung, Grade 3
Wilchester Elementary School, TX

Sea

Oh, sweet Poseidon when I go to sea
all your powers
come to me.

The breeze comes not to seas,
but to cool me down
when I go down
I turn that frown upside down.

So,
go explore so much
more.

That
is Sea.
Preston Meek, Grade 3
Old Town Elementary School, TX

Swimming

One, two, three!
Here we go, let's swim.
Let's swim down, let's swim up
I like swimming.
You can go to the top,
and swim all around.
You can go back and forth
and swim down.
Swimming lets you meet new friends.
Get up and swim
and try a dive,
When it's a hot day,
you can get goggles
and a swimsuit, and swim all around.
Let's swim now!!
Tessa Crouch, Grade 3
St. Joseph Catholic School, CA

Hamburgers

Hamburgers are good
With soda and chocolate
It is a great food.
Jacob Vampola, Grade 3
St Raphael School, CA

Spelling

Spelling is my favorite subject, it is easy
I almost always get a 105
I don't really practice but still I love spelling
My mom says I have a gift that I can use later on
And that's why I love spelling

Tristan Brabson, Grade 2
Legacy Christian Academy, NM

Life

life
hard challenge
motivating, running, spinning
difficult, good, lengthy, colorful
path

Jackson May, Grade 3
Lorenzo De Zavala Elementary School, TX

Grave in Heaven

One day I went to the grave in heaven.
Where I saw my dog
I touched her but I didn't feel a thing.
I fell down in tears of sorrow
I wish my dog wasn't in heaven.

Jake Lekhtgolts, Grade 3
Wonderland Avenue Elementary School, CA

Cheetahs

cheetahs
fast animals
hunting, running, killing
quick, spotted, furry, vicious
mammals

Everett Crutchfield, Grade 3
Lorenzo De Zavala Elementary School, TX

Dancing Dirty Dogs

Dancing dirty dogs in a drain
It was the main rain drain in Spain
Some dogs got washed out
They began to shout
It drove the nice neighbors insane

Kathy Lee, Grade 3
Wonderland Avenue Elementary School, CA

Spring

Spring showers so much in sunny days
Those plants grow or blossom
Some students see that spring
Is very warm and cool
It is windy as fall
We will watch
Wild animals and plants sometimes
Then it is hot summer

Iris Lee, Grade 3
Wonderland Avenue Elementary School, CA

The Sun

I am the most important star in the solar system.
My flares are roller coaster tracks!
Beware! My 10,000 degree Fahrenheit temperature
will scorch you if you get too close.
Without me, you wouldn't be here right now!
Martian the Warrior is no match for me.
Civilization will perish without me in 5 billion years.
I am the sun!

Eric Chen, Grade 3
Saigling Elementary School, TX

Ocean

Buoying boats
Colorful coral
Pecking pelicans
Sandy seashore
Rough rocks
Salty sea
Fishing fisherman
Outrageous ocean

Patrick Yoon, Grade 3
Wonderland Avenue Elementary School, CA

Chinchillas

Chinchillas are small.
Chinchillas are fast and furious like a runner.
Chinchillas are rodents.
Chinchillas have very soft fur.
Chinchillas are amazing.

Nathaniel Crain, Grade 3
Annunciation Orthodox School, TX

Snow

Snow falls and the ground turns white,
Just yesterday it was a different sight,
Now people wear scarves and gloves to go out,
If you listen you can hear the kids shout,
They scream and throw snow at each other,
You can hear yells from the kids' mother,
Today was a perfect day,
Oh snow, please don't go away

Sarah Kim, Grade 3
Wonderland Avenue Elementary School, CA

Feathers

Fall from birds in the sky
that float on twinkling water
ready for you to pick up.
Feathers, as soft and as beautiful
as a baby's blanket.
As delicate as your mom's glass vase.
When I look at it my heart sees one ballerina,
two birds chirping, and Romeo and Juliet dancing.

Brooke Butler, Grade 3
Old Town Elementary School, TX

Haiti

I read about a girl named Katie,
She really cared about Haiti.
I heard she cried all night long.
Then she sang a folk song.
Then, she cried again
For all the children, women, and men.
She hoped and prayed that the world stay safe and sound...
Then a better future would be found.

Luna Dolce Milito, Grade 3
Wonderland Avenue Elementary School, CA

Christmas Is in the Air

You can smell it in the fresh Christmas wreath.
You can taste it in the crisp cookies.
You can hear it in the singing carolers.
You can see it in the bright and twinkling lights.
You can feel it in the smooth glassy ornaments.

Rebekah Lee, Grade 3
A E Arnold Elementary School, CA

Fall

Leaves fall from the trees
Wind is blowing a little
It is time for coats

Jaden Thompson, Grade 2
Tracy Learning Center - Primary Charter School, CA

Sun

As bright as can be.
The rays glaze over the sea.
It puts glory in me.

Lauren Gandall, Grade 3
Tracy Learning Center - Primary Charter School, CA

Sea Shell

Hearing the ocean
The waves push it to sea shore
Shining from the sun

Maci Voller, Grade 3
Tracy Learning Center - Primary Charter School, CA

Cook

I knew a cook.
The cook had a book.
He put his apron on a hook.

Katie Chambers, Grade 3
Tracy Learning Center - Primary Charter School, CA

River

Shining and growing
Ducks swim quietly and fast
The moon reflects off

Camille Cifra, Grade 3
Tracy Learning Center - Primary Charter School, CA

Forest

Great green trees grow big.
A howler monkey can climb.
A loud sound is heard.

Quinn Herrick, Grade 3
Tracy Learning Center - Primary Charter School, CA

Spring

I love spring
and flowery things.
I love daisies,
lazy, and crazy kids.
When it is spring
I love everything.

Sofia Rizzi, Kindergarten
Notre Dame Academy Elementary School, CA

My Panda

I love to watch the pandas dine on lush bamboo.
Sometimes they're just sitting there
As if they had nothing else to do.
Sometimes they're sleeping, eating or playing.
I don't care what they do,
Only as long as it's my panda dining on lush bamboo.

Jackson Gledhill, Grade 3
Wasatch Elementary School, UT

The Earth

The earth is cool.
The earth has water and land,
There are whales, sharks, and dolphins in the water all the time,
here are lions, polar bears, dogs, cats, wolves, tigers, buffalos, and
dragons on land all the time.
The state I live in is Oregon.

Halima Yusuf, Grade 2
Islamic School of Muslim Educational Trust, OR

Friends

Funny, fast
Running, jumping, laughing
Playing with me a lot today
Children

Everett Conner, Grade 2
Tracy Learning Center - Primary Charter School, CA

Lightning

Electricity
Thunder cloud, zigzag, loud, light
Power, fluorescent

Harpreet Dhadalia, Grade 2
Tracy Learning Center - Primary Charter School, CA

I Wish I Were A...

I wish I were a leprechaun so I could find a pot of gold at the end of a rainbow.
I wish I were a whale because I would be the biggest animal in the world.
I wish I were a scientist so I could make a big explosion.
I wish I were a baseball player.
I wish I were a basketball player.
I wish I were a teacher so I could tell the students they could play outside for the
    whole day.

Jay West, Grade 2
Annunciation Orthodox School, TX

I Wish...

I wish I were a purple tulip dancing through
the afternoon sunshine in the country hills.
I wish I were a golden bunny. I would be hopping through
a beautiful meadow, and I would make sad children happy.
I wish I were a pink smooth oval stone. I would be a good
luck stone and people would rub me and have good luck.
I wish I were.

Clara Sophie Haymon, Grade 2
Annunciation Orthodox School, TX

All About Kate Larrick

I am strong and rare as a bald eagle,
Beautiful as a water lily,
Gentle as the color pink,
Loving and kind as a heart,
Friendly as the number two,
Brilliant, enduring, and valuable as a diamond,
And clean as the breeze.

Kate Larrick, Grade 1
Baldwin Stocker Elementary School, CA

Missouri, Amazing Missouri

The color of Missouri is blue when we fly with the bluebirds. It sounds like
laughter and happiness coming from Fred's Train Restaurant. It tastes like
sweet ice cream cones for they were invented here. The smell of Missouri is the
fragrance of the state flower, white hawthorn blossoms. It makes you feel cold
inside when it starts to snow. When you are here, you will see a gate over the
Mississippi River. Go under it and it will lead you to the west, for it is the Gateway
Arch, the Gateway to the West. Oh, beautiful Missouri.

Georgia Elgohary, Grade 3
Annunciation Orthodox School, TX

Dogs
dogs
cute animals
playing, barking, running
soft, adorable, fun, playful
pets

Abbie Payne, Grade 3
Lorenzo De Zavala Elementary School, TX

Shoes
I always have to tie my shoe
It's something that I have to do
I ask my mother
I ask my brother
Except they have to tie theirs too!

Sam Frank, Grade 3
Wonderland Avenue Elementary School, CA

The Mood Egg
The egg is sparkling gold and bronze.
When I am happy it has a tint of rose.
When I am glum the egg is green.
If the egg is broken darkness will spread.
The citizens of Earth will be yelling what a dread.

Christian Carr, Grade 3
Thomas Edison Charter School - North, UT

Daniel
Daniel
Nice, handsome
Caring, loving, helping
He is very friendly
Dad

Yeanna Jang, Grade 3
Wonderland Avenue Elementary School, CA

Why I Enjoy Going to School
I always enjoy going to school,
To see my teacher who is cool,
He teaches me how to study,
Oh my, oh my, he is a great buddy,
I'm always going to follow his rule.

Janet Lee, Grade 3
Wonderland Avenue Elementary School, CA

Rainbow and Tornado
Rainbow
Colorful, beautiful
Spreading, widening, reaching
Rain, storm, wind, dust
Whistling, spinning, turning
Loud, fast
Tornado

Alyssa Barba, Grade 2
Tracy Learning Center - Primary Charter School, CA

Girl and Boy
Girl
Nice, pretty
Loving, helping, caring
Comb, brush, football, dog
Scoring, playing, running
Naughty, messy
Boy

Melissa Romero, Grade 2
Tracy Learning Center - Primary Charter School, CA

Sunny and Cloudy
Sunny
Hot, warm
Burning, tanning, flashing
Morning, school, fog clouds
Floating, moving, hiding
Puffy, white
Cloudy

Aryanna Shokoor, Grade 3
Tracy Learning Center - Primary Charter School, CA

Cats!
Do you know a kindle is a group of kittens? All kittens are born with blue eyes!
A cat's sense is better than dogs. Cats can run up to thirty miles an hour!
Cats can jump up to 7 times their height! A cat holding its tail high means it's
happy or it's greeting you. When you see a cat with its whiskers forward,
it means it's feeling friendly. If its whiskers are back, watch out!
That's a sign that cat could be feeling defensive or aggressive.
If a cat blinks at you, it means it loves you and likes you to blink back!

Sydney Kendall, Grade 3
Providence Hall, UT

Teddy Bear

Teddy bear
I want you,
I really do,
I miss you,
I wish you were here,
I cannot go to sleep.
Lying down in bed,
Wishing you were here,
There you are,
Now I can go to sleep.

Kaisey Mellott, Grade 2
Robert L Stevens Elementary School, CA

CORY

Cory...
It means fast, strong, and smart.
It is the number 16.
It is like the sun setting.
It is when I went to Seattle's bakery.
It is the memory of my Grandpapa
Who taught me to read and write
When he sent me all his books.
My name is Cory Lyle.
It means caring for others.

Cory Lyle Parker, Grade 2
Keone'ula Elementary School, HI

Alligators

Alligator
Alligator
Chomping their teeth
Behind me
They are scary
Too too scary
They say they won't do anything wrong
But
Chomp Chomp

Samantha Mazeda, Grade 1
P H Greene Elementary School, TX

Spring

In the spring what do I see?
I see a bumblebee buzzing by me.
I love the rainbow so pretty and high.
Oh look there goes a butterfly.
Everywhere there's flowers growing.
Beautiful colors start showing
I love the spring, it makes me sing.

Gianna Sotere, Grade 1
Woodcrest School, CA

Transformers

Transformers protect the humans
They rescue them from danger
There are no more Decepticons
My favorite one is Optimus Prime
He is blue and red and shiny light blue
And behind the blue is gray.

Aiden Hernandez, Kindergarten
Legacy Christian Academy, NM

Ice Skating

I like ice skating.
It is fun.
Twisting,
Gliding,
Jumping high,
That is my hobby.

Cecilia Rodriguez, Grade 1
Longfellow Elementary School, TX

Grass

Grass, you have gone through
Ran over,
And stepped on.
But, you are still there.
You have brought fresh smell to us,
But, you still need water.

Isiah McClure, Grade 3
Three Rivers Elementary School, TX

Rain Boots

I'm a pair of rain boots.
I keep your feet dry and warm.
When I am made with rubber,
I can even help block out the electricity during a thunderstorm.
But remember to keep me away from dogs,
because they like to chew on me…Ouch!

Dallen Franchina, Grade 3
Providence Hall, UT

Tigers

Tigers are one of the biggest cats in the world.
It's impossible for a tiger to live without food.
Growls after catching it's pray
Eats other animals to survive
Runs like the swift wind
Stripes all over its body.

Mason Lahti, Grade 3
Providence Hall, UT

I Wish I Were Nature

I wish I were the birds singing on my head. I wish I were the forest with so many
wild animals. I wish I were the ocean with sea life like turtles and whales and
dolphins splashing in my body. I wish I was nature. I wish I was the park with
rocks to climb and kids to play, so families could have picnics and walk around
me. I wish I was the scooters and the balls that the kids play with. I wish I were
the kids that get to run and play! Hey, I am a kid! Yeah!

Coco Hawkins, Grade 2
Annunciation Orthodox School, TX

A Girl Named Erin

There once was a girl named Erin.
She met a best friend named Farren.
Their brothers were rebels and loved throwing pebbles.
How lucky that girl named Erin.

Erin Hall, Grade 3
Blackland Prairie Elementary School, TX

Bubble Gum

Bubble gum is so sweet
It's the greatest treat
It is so neat

Hammad Shami, Grade 2
Tracy Learning Center - Primary Charter School, CA

Blue

Blue is the sea, blue is the sky.
Blue is the blue jay flying by.
Blue is the lake, blue is the eye.
Blue is the tear of a baby's cry.

Blue is the waterfall, blue is the tide.
Blue is the jeans with mud on the side.
Blue is the bubble, blue is the flower.
Blue is the feeling that's rather sour.

Blue is a heron, blue is a tie.
Blue is the filling of blueberry pie.
Blue is a diamond, blue is a fish.
Blue is a blueberry served on a dish.

Blue is a puddle, blue is the rain.
Blue is a typical type of pain.
Blue is a robin egg, blue is tie-dye.
Blue is a bluebird flying way up high.

Blue is a bluebonnet, the tail of a whale.
Blue is a princess in a fairy tale.
So you know most things are blue.
It's a typical color, could even be you.
Brennan Keimig, Grade 3
Wilchester Elementary School, TX

Mouse Love

There was a mouse,
lived in my house.
He ran around
and touched the ground.

What a clever little mouse!

He climbs up me
and nibbles my ear.
I love that mouse,
he is so dear!

What a loving little mouse!
Raegan Jabor, Grade 1
St Mark's Elementary School, TX

My Sweet Beta Bessie

Bessie Beta swirls her tail,
Blue, purple, and blue — violet.

Making bubbles in the water,
Chasing little brine shrimp.

Eating only fresh food,
And breathing through her gills.

Rainbow in her circle tank
With red eyes open wide.

I can see sweet Bessie
Looking back at me.
Varun Bommaji, Kindergarten
Scholars Academy, CA

Poor Kitty

Kitty
hiding,
behind
the couch,
huddling
and shivering.
How cold
it is
outside.
Poor, poor kitty.
Then the kitty
comes out
as the sun rises
up in the sky.
Savannah Werelius, Grade 2
Robert L Stevens Elementary School, CA

Spring

I can see a chipmunk eating nuts.
I can hear blue jays singing.
I can smell my Aunt Chris making bacon.
I can taste mint chocolate chip ice cream.
I can feel the fresh air.
Elyssa Gilbertson, Grade 2
Woodcrest School, CA

Oh to Be

Oh to be a cat
Tip toeing no one can hear
Laying in the sun on a hot summer day
Walking around at night like a guard

Oh to be a fish
Swimming around waiting for food
Never blinking when in water
Fun to swim

Oh to be a pencil
Being used to write this poem
Touching the paper with my sharp tip

Nicole Summerfield, Grade 3
Coeur d'Alene Avenue Elementary School, CA

Here Comes Spring

Gardens, gardens here comes Spring.

Let's get ready for Spring.
Birds, birds, let's go sing.
Boys and girls, go on the swings.
Butterflies, butterflies, flap your wings.
Get ready, get ready, it's almost Spring.
Here it comes.
Spring is here.
Spring is there.

Spring is everywhere!
Welcome, welcome, welcome, Spring!

Hoda AbouEich, Grade 2
Islamic School of Muslim Educational Trust, OR

Green as Grass

Green as a grasshopper
Green as leaves
Green as a frog
Green as a leprechaun
Green as an army hat
Green as a green apple
Green as grass.

Braxton Whitney, Grade 3
Thomas Edison Charter School - North, UT

DARK MIDNIGHT

Sitting by a window at dark midnight
Crickets chirping all night long
Tiny fairies carrying big sacks of teeth
Fireflies lighting up the night sky with the sweet moon.

Santa Claus in a bright sleigh
Trees falling asleep with the wind
Unicorns running on concrete roads
I feel like I'm on a cloud in the sky.

I miss morning
Though I know the bright sun is always there
Owls singing their song till night's end
Bright birds come at day and leave at night
Waves crash against the shore.

Stars make me think of the sun's glowing children
Looking through the telescope seeing the planets
The rings of Saturn make me think of jewelry.

Peace is everywhere
You just have to find it
And find the one
That makes you happy.

Skye Davis, Grade 3
Coeur d'Alene Avenue Elementary School, CA

Zoo

The caring zookeepers opened the iron gates for the excited visitors.
The respectful owners of the silly zoo had the friendly visitors
pay to go in to see the excited powerful bears and friendly llamas.
In the middle of the day, the loving zookeepers happily fed the silly zebras
and the rest of the silly animals.
When the happy people got to see the silly flexible animals, the sad ones
were stuck behind gray bars, and the swinging monkeys felt free.
When the blissful visitors went to the next exhibit,
the joyful children were happily laughing at the wild elephants' tricks.
At the end of the silly performance, six friendly kids were able to
gingerly feed the lovable animals.
When the loud zookeeper said, "The silver gates will close soon,"
the pleased parents and kind kids set off for home as the iron gates closed.

Nyah Harrison, Grade 3
The Mirman School, CA

Great Green Mountain

I leap on top of a great green mountain
My shoes wait beside the weeds
The daisies dance between my feet
Clouds came to take a look
Drops of water slowly drizzle on my head
I hear them drip down on my ears
Hail comes
I slip on my shoes
At home I curl in my bed
Burrow in my covers
Good night Mom
Good night mountain
I slowly drift to sleep

Talia Kelly, Grade 3
Coeur d'Alene Avenue Elementary School, CA

What Is Pink?

Pink is a wild rose
Pink is a thumping heart
Pink is a pile of love
Pink is a fluffy cloud
Pink is a bright ladybug
Pink is a little twinkle in my eye
Pink is a box of some of my favorite things
Pink is a pretty flower
Pink is a wonderful word to say
Pink is a beautiful butterfly
Pink is a sweet sound
Pink is a pearl
Pink is…pink!

Grace Jenkins, Grade 3
Lolo Elementary School, MT

Nice to Mean

Nice
Helpful, shares
Loving, caring, sharing
Dogs, people, sharks, prisoners
Beating, lying, mocking
Brags, pushes
Mean

Gabriel Pacana, Grade 3
Tracy Learning Center - Primary Charter School, CA

Easter Morning

Today is the day I wake up and feel thrilled,
For today is the day we call Easter.
I scream and I yell because I want to find my Easter basket,
What a marvelous day.

My eggs must be waiting as I try
To find them all. Where did the Easter bunny
Hide them??? I hope he hid them good.
Easter is one of my favorite holidays,
We will celebrate my birthday today!!!
Easter is an awesome holiday!!!

Caroline Elliott, Grade 3
Wilchester Elementary School, TX

A Day at the Zoo

As the steel and rusty gates open...
The happy animals behind the gray fences quickly rush out of their shelters.
The free creatures happily roam across the exciting zoo while the
amazed humans watch the exploring natural beings.
They blissfully play with the shocked humans.
The cheerful children enjoy riding on the backs of the welcoming animals.
The glad children and joyful adults have a great time until it is time to leave.
As the gloomy visitors leave at the end of the day, the exhausted zookeepers
bring in all the weary animals into the gray cages and slowly close the metal cages.
And the sleepy animals tiredly go to sleep.

Chloe Kim, Grade 3
The Mirman School, CA

Nature

The snow showers on the ground.
The moon circles the Earth.
The rushing rivers yell.
The sky looks down.
Birds hop on their worms.
Monkeys yell as they eat.
Lions eat their prey.
Cows munch on grass.
Crocodiles sweep the water with their tails.
Chameleons stick their tongues out.

Akash Chinthamani, Grade 3
CLASS Academy, OR

Easter

When I was sleeping,
It was Easter.
My mom and dad were still up.
They saw the Easter bunny.
The Easter bunny saw them.

Cathy Carlson, Kindergarten
Notre Dame Academy Elementary School, CA

Dragon

Dragon
Fire breathing
Flying, huge reptile
Always makes me feel excited
Scaly

Jack Grant, Grade 2
Tracy Learning Center - Primary Charter School, CA

My Little Cousin

Lily.
Young, exciting.
Crying, playing, laughing.
She will torture me all the time.
Monkey.

Hena Osmani, Grade 3
Tracy Learning Center - Primary Charter School, CA

Pennies

Pennies
Smallest, brownest
Cheapest, puny, tiny
Happy feeling flipping money
Awesome

Matthew Ramirez, Grade 2
Tracy Learning Center - Primary Charter School, CA

Yellow

Yellow is the hot hot sun in the sky,
and the color of peace and happiness
Yellow is the color of bananas and smiles too,
it brings cheer to the world,
and it's a primary color too.

Hagen Bach, Grade 3
Wilchester Elementary School, TX

All About Rachel

I am generous as a starfish,
cheerful as a cherry tree,
sweet as the color apple red,
sad as a sphere,
loving as the number 100,
nice as a diamond,
and friendly as a crystal lake.
Rachel Loh, Grade 1
Baldwin Stocker Elementary School, CA

Great Jonathan

I am Energetic as a cheetah,
sloppy as a vine,
even-tempered as the color dark gray,
trusting as a cone,
honest as the number 100,000,
cool as a diamond,
and friendly as calm water.
Jonathan Hsieh, Grade 1
Baldwin Stocker Elementary School, CA

Tiger's Stripes

I am fast as a tiger,
powerful as a thorn,
happy as the color ocean blue,
fair as a cube,
nice as the number 125,
kind as a sapphire,
and friendly as a light wind.
Quoc Cao, Grade 1
Baldwin Stocker Elementary School, CA

Chandra Star

I am fast as a cheetah,
sharp as a thorn bush,
interesting as the color blue,
respectful as a rectangle,
confident as the number one hundred,
gentle as a diamond,
and strong as hurricane water.
Chandra Pedaballi, Grade 1
Baldwin Stocker Elementary School, CA

As Strong as I Am

I am proud as a lion,
Strong as an oak tree,
Calm as the color blue,
Open as a circle,
Straight as the number one,
Brilliant as the aquamarine,
And fiery as an inferno.
Brandon Wong, Grade 1
Baldwin Stocker Elementary School, CA

My Symbols About Me

I am brave as a pufferfish,
Awesome as a cactus,
Caring as the color green,
Round as a circle,
Ambitious as the number five,
Cool as an aquamarine,
And fast as water.
Andrew Green, Grade 1
Baldwin Stocker Elementary School, CA

All About Me

I am fast as a coyote,
Light as a sunflower,
Fiery as the color red,
Open and honest as a circle,
Independent as the number one,
Red as a ruby,
Fiery as a firelight.
Sean Huang, Grade 1
Baldwin Stocker Elementary School, CA

Vega Is a Star

I am energetic as an eel,
kind as a fern,
shy as the color gray,
proud as a square,
trusting as my mom's love,
funny as a topaz,
and cool as a palm tree.
Vega Pierce-English, Grade 1
Baldwin Stocker Elementary School, CA

Spring
Spring brings us wonderful things.
Like flowers, trees, and friendship.
So come in and join my tea party set for 3.
So come right in and sit right down and enjoy a drink,
Home made from me.
And some cookies for 3.

Samantha Borris, Grade 3
Edward Byrom Elementary School, OR

Family
Family, oh family is great to have around.
They bring joy when you are lonely and sad.
Family oh family I love so much.
My great-grandma and my great pa-pa.
Mom, Dad, sister and step-dad too.
Cousins are great and so are you.

Briana Hawley, Grade 3
Pleasant Valley Elementary School, TX

Gulf of Mexico
I hear crashing waves.
The air smells just like a minty breeze.
I see seagulls, white as snow flying above me.
When I swam, I tasted sandy, salty and gritty water in my mouth.
The water felt cool like lemonade on a hot day.
Where am I?

Jenna Matthews, Grade 3
Old Town Elementary School, TX

What I Love
I love God.
I love Jesus so so much.
I love my mom and dad too.
I love to play Monopoly.

Kyle Lee, Kindergarten
Notre Dame Academy Elementary School, CA

Dogs
Dogs are white
Some fight
Come and see them bark at night

Nicole Young, Grade 3
Tracy Learning Center - Primary Charter School, CA

I Made a Noise This Morning

I made a noise this morning that was very very loud
That made the teacher faint and also the crowd.
There must be something wrong with me
Can you please call the nurse to see if she could fix me?

Now I think it's getting worse
I just ate some pizza that was curse
And now I feel so bad and my stomach feels so sad.
I feel the vibration inside me! Oh! What a day I had.

Now please don't run!
Because I'm not having so much fun!
I just ate some pizza is that too much to ask!
And we have a test this morning; I better not fail on this task!

Well, now school is over no one is running away
But I still failed the test, Oh! What a day!
Oh no! Guess what happened last night?
No, it wasn't a pillow fight!

Cameron Rodriguez, Grade 3
West Avenue Elementary School, TX

Doctors

Night and day doctor stay at the hospital.
Help all their patients and think very fast.

They need to embrace and know what is going to happen.
That's what I want to be when I grow up, a doctor.

Doctors are like Moms they make the sickness go away,
Unpack their bags on another person.

Doctors give you medication
For your sickness,
And helps with broken bones
And
Everything else.

Doctors help with all the pain,
All the hurt, and all the
Sadness.

Ronan McDonnell, Grade 3
Wilchester Elementary School, TX

Horses

I like to ride horses
I like them when they trot
I like them when they lope.
I like to feed them too
I like to feed them hay.
I like to feed them grain too.
I LOVE HORSES.
Elizabeth Johnston, Grade 3
Three Rivers Elementary School, TX

Rabbits

Rabbits are fluffy
They are beautiful
Five white bunnies
They sleep during the day
And they sleep at night.
They eat rabbit food
Outside my grandma's house.
Alicia Salazar, Grade 3
Three Rivers Elementary School, TX

Make a Good Choice

If you want to rob a bank
Go ahead, because you're the one
That is going to be caught
By the police, and be stuck
In jail for months or maybe even years!
And I will be all free so know you
Got the point! So make a good choice.
Stefano Benedetto, Grade 3
Wesleyan Academe, TX

Soccer

S erious sport
O n a field
C ool
C ertainly a good sport
E veryone is a team
R eally hard sometimes
Rylan Uchita, Grade 3
St Aloysius Parochial School, CA

Favorites

I like puppies.
I think penguins are cute.
Dragons are neat.
Reading books is fun, too.
I like math and snakes,
But I like my class and teachers
a whole lot more!
Phoenix Belle Page, Grade 3
St James Episcopal School, TX

The Frog

I heard a little croak
in the dark
when I woke up
I really screamed
and ran to the door
I heard the croak
and it was a frog.
Erin Darling, Grade 3
Three Rivers Elementary School, TX

Candy

Candy is such a wonderful treat,
Because it is so delicious and sweet.
For example, when I eat the candy cane
I feel kind of insane.
Candy is kind of tricky
And also so sticky
On your happy teeth.
Sabrina Torres, Grade 3
St John's Episcopal Day School, TX

The Thunder

Hear the thunder
make a scary sound,
in the clouds.
It's loud in the city.
It creaks a building in the city.
Thunder makes the ground shake.
People run away.
Brady Charith, Grade 2
Robert L Stevens Elementary School, CA

The Rain and the Thunder
The rain and the thunder have their own rhythm.
The rain whispers to the thunder,
And the rain gets louder,
The whisper has disappeared.

The thunder frightens the earth.
The afternoon sky turns gray.
All the shadows are darker.
The earth is midnight black.

The air is moist,
The air hits my skin,
Air bounces off.
The rain makes me feel shallow.

The sky rumbles just like a rocket taking off.
The rain makes me cover my ears,
And I scream because of the rain!

Kamryn Folh, Grade 3
Wilchester Elementary School, TX

My Hero
My hero likes to bounce,
She's always on my mind.
My heart wouldn't be complete without her,
Nothing can wedge us apart.

We live right next door,
She's in her junior year of high school.
She's like an umbrella,
Protects me from danger.

We're the same I understand her she understands me.
I'm short she's tall I don't see a difference.
I want to be like her when I'm that age,
Because my hero will someday rescue me!

You're the best,
You can do it.
I call her Carrie Beckham!

Grace Mosby, Grade 3
Wilchester Elementary School, TX

Puppy
Small, energetic
Running, playing, jumping
Cute, tan, baby dog
Frosty
Leah Ho, Grade 3
Goethe International Charter School, CA

Penguins
furry, waddlers
wearing fancy tuxedos
cute, blubbery, little feet
plungers
Lanora Maldonado, Grade 3
Henry Haight Elementary School, CA

My Dogs
I have a dog who loves to play
Who likes to wrestle with my other dog
And my other dog
Likes to wrestle too
Jace Gutierrez, Grade 1
Legacy Christian Academy, NM

Desert
I live in the desert
Every time I go outside
There is a coyote
And on Saturday, he caught me
Antonio Biancaniello, Kindergarten
Legacy Christian Academy, NM

Moon Dancing
Nervous fish tapping
dark-feeling music for dogs.
Dogs, cats, rabbits dancing
on the half moon.
Aby Craft, Grade 2
Annunciation Orthodox School, TX

Lamp
Lamp —
Bright, electric, gold —
Lights
Often, quickly, outside
Thomas Cancio, Grade 3
St Mary School, CA

Killer Whale
Killer Whale —
Cool, big, can swim up to 30 mph —
Eats fish
It swims quickly, smoothly, carefully
Michael Merino, Grade 3
St Mary School, CA

Fish
Fish —
Scaly, slimy, three —
Swimming
Swiftly, underwater, every day
Amanda Soto, Grade 3
St Mary School, CA

Hyper
I ate to much sugar
Just watch me jump
Kick and run
Maybe I should stop!
Autumn Christman, Grade 3
St Raphael School, CA

Heart
Heart —
Light, real, red —
Pumps
Slowly, always, everywhere
Dominic Ragazzo, Grade 3
St Mary School, CA

Winter

Snow giggles when it falls onto the ground.
Rain falls on branches in many different countries.
Lightning runs from place to place.
January skips day to day.
Ice stays on the ground when it is cold.
Winter wakes in December and falls asleep in March.
December runs because it is snowing.
Newspapers stick to the ground when it is icy.
Rivers freeze when it is winter.

Jason Seiple, Grade 3
CLASS Academy, OR

Black Is

Black smells like the olives on my anchovy pizza,
Black sounds like the dark night in the shadow of a building,
Black tastes like your fresh homemade coffee,
Black looks like a dusty car in the garage,
Black is a dark hole in a volcano,
Black is the mane on a horse,
Black are the cards in a poker game,
The sound of black lightning is rare,
These are all black to me.

J.T. Luis, Grade 3
Marguerite Hahn Elementary School, CA

Swing

Once I was about 6 years old
I love swinging a lot with my brother
and sister. We loved to play on my favorite
tree where my swing was. My swing was a tire
swing, we loved to play with it and swing on it.

Rachel Cruces, Grade 3
Three Rivers Elementary School, TX

Rainbow

Oh, rainbow, how delightful
So adorable with 7 colors.
My favorite colors of the rainbow
Are orange and yellow.
And these are the colors of the rainbow
Red, orange, yellow, green, blue, indigo, and purple.

Jocelin Alesandra Ramirez Serna, Grade 3
Three Rivers Elementary School, TX

Homework

Homework is a dreaded, boring thing.
With some brain shrinking stuff here and there.
Got some sense killer too.
Troubling, deadly everywhere every kid's enemy!
We've gotta do it every night,
now we've gotta do some more.

Tuff Seamons, Grade 3
Thomas Edison Charter School - North, UT

Lunch

Lunch lunch
I like to munch
My Mom packs me a bunch
When I eat chips it makes a big crunch!
Lunch lunch it's filled with food
Lunch lunch it puts me in a good mood!

Zakaria ElGharabli, Grade 2
Islamic School of Muslim Educational Trust, OR

Summer

Summer summer I like to play
I like summer I want it to stay
Summer summer it's not cold,
and in summer the flowers are gold.
Summer summer the sun is bright.
Summer summer is always right.

Michael Jordan, Grade 2
Islamic School of Muslim Educational Trust, OR

Last Night's Dinner

Last night's dinner was gross.
I ate rotten eggs and a burned toast.
I also ate mac and cheese.
Instead of cheese it was peas!

Laura Rivera-Salgado, Grade 3
Thomas Edison Charter School - North, UT

Spring

In the spring what do I see? I see the bees buzzing at me!
The animals are sleeping underground! Animals are hiding all around!
The rainbows are up in the sky. With the sun and clouds so high.

Kyla Mowry, Grade 1
Woodcrest School, CA

Clouds and Thunder Rain

Clouds come
near your home,
make thunder and rain.
It is the dark clouds
that have nasty rain and thunder.
It will rain hard,
it will scare you,
you will want to run
to your mom's room,
hide under the bed,
cover your head,
and beg God to stop it.

Alexia Varela, Grade 2
Robert L Stevens Elementary School, CA

Minnesota

Cabins everywhere
Animals all over
My old family
is still there

My feelings
for this place
I feel like
I'm back home
Happiness
Joy
Faith

Madison Erickson, Grade 3
Old Town Elementary School, TX

My Family

My family is sweet,
kind, caring,
sharing, and loving.

They love everyone
Mom, Dad, Grandma, Grandpa
and lots of others too!

And they love me too!

Corina Torres, Grade 2
Camino Grove Elementary School, CA

Dancing

I hear music that flows
In my ear,
And when I hear my favorite song
The beat makes me move.
The music plays quickly
In my ear
The way I move is super!
I want to be a super star
When I grow up.
When I am a star
I will show my hip-hop moves.
I want to hear the audience
Shouting my name!

Adyson Fore, Grade 3
D P Morris Elementary School, TX

Mom Rules

Who's the one who
Makes your breakfast?
Mom is!
Who's the one who
Takes you to school?
Mom is!
Who's the one who
Buys you toys?
Mom is!
Mom is the one who
Loves you most,
Except for Dad!

Travis Ashley, Grade 3
Wilchester Elementary School, TX

Stinky

Why do I smell stinky?
They think I smell like trash.
Or fish,
or shoes when you take them off
at the end of the day.
I do not smell stinky.
I smell sweet,
like coconut soap.

Byrnn Vanhnachit, Grade 2
Robert L Stevens Elementary School, CA

My Two Black Cats: Porthos and Aramis

My two black cats,
Jump on me and nibble at my toes.

And when it's time to go to bed
They'll go crazy, ya know.
Knocking over the water glass
And spilling it all over me.

In the darkness,
I can barely see them at night.
Their eyes start to shine
When the light hits them,
And all I can see are those glowing
Green-gold eyes wandering all around.

And in the morning,
Don't even get me started!
They lie on my clothes
So I can't get dressed,
And when I brush my teeth
They'll crawl around my feet!

I love my black cats dearly,
But I'm warning you:
Porthos and Aramis are crazy, ya know.

Madison Elise Boudreaux, Grade 3
C W Cline Primary School, TX

What Is Lime Green?

A lime in a tree
A patch of grass where beetles live
A princess' crown with sapphires all around
A frog in a swamp sitting on a lily pad floating gracefully along
Other frogs nearby see dragonflies
A leaf with its shade of dark green is dark
I'm getting hungry to eat the lime-green grapes, zucchini, pear and
Pickles in my sack
I see a caterpillar whose mother should be here
Oh, there she is…wow, she's a pretty butterfly!
I'm itching!
Oh, I'm sitting in a poison ivy patch!

Kiahna Thorsell, Grade 3
Lolo Elementary School, MT

Opposites

Martha is a Maine-Coon
That looks a lot like a raccoon.
She has a tail like a feather duster,
And her mane looks as impressive as
That of a male Lion.
Oh! That Cat!

Smeogol is a Siamese
That looks a lot like a Chinese.
His eyes are shimmering blue like the sea.
And he is sleek, short-haired, and soft as
A cotton ball.
Oh! That Cat!

Playful and perky,
She sneaks up on the unsuspecting
Like a thief in the night.
Oh! That Cat!

Sweet and somber,
He always gets caught by the fury
Like an innocent sheep.
Oh! That Cat!

Wesley Gunther Brigner, Grade 3
Texas Tech University Independent School District, TX

Butterflies

Butterflies here, butterflies there, butterflies everywhere.

Colorful butterflies flying,
Sick butterflies laying on the ground,
Hungry butterflies eating,
Grown-up butterflies taking care of their babies.

Butterflies on the flowers nectar,
Butterflies on the sky,
Butterflies through the clouds,
Butterflies in their homes.

Butterflies here, butterflies there,
Butterflies! Butterflies! Butterflies!

Ashley Lee, Grade 1
Forest Park Elementary School, CA

Healthy Living

Healthy living is part of your life.
Healthy living keeps you in good shape.
You live healthy, you can get good health!
Not getting sick,
Eating healthy at home and at school,
When you eat healthy you grow healthy.

Shasha Yousuf, Grade 3
Islamic School of Muslim Educational Trust, OR

Best Friends

Best friends are sweet,
And very good to you,
They are people you can lean on,
They are always there and will never disappear
When you need a shoulder to cry on, go to them,
Everyone needs a best friend.

Annie Goss, Grade 3
Wilchester Elementary School, TX

Jennah Haven Is Wonderful

I know Jennah is wonderful because the Quran says so.
Jennah is the place I dream to be in.
There are rivers that flow so calm and peacefully.
There are fruits so sweet and healthy you can't go wrong.
What's on Earth is nothing compared to Jannah.
Jannah is better than anything you could imagine.

Sarah Hmoud, Grade 3
Islamic School of San Diego, CA

Hide and Seek

Kids
Running, counting, hiding
Trying to hide behind a tree
Game

Elyas Alamshahi, Grade 2
Tracy Learning Center - Primary Charter School, CA

Grass

Decorating Earth
We walk on it day by day
Green, outdoors, playing

Anthony Pike, Grade 3
Tracy Learning Center - Primary Charter School, CA

Figure Skating
A little different from other sports
Hard and fun at the same time
If you fail a competition you still feel happy that you tried hard
Makes yourself feel happy all the time
If you keep doing it you can stop
Everybody can do it even boys
It makes you feel beautiful as a flower
And that sport is
Figure Skating

Sarah Myung, Grade 3
Wilchester Elementary School, TX

Beautiful Sights
The Milky Way is as beautiful as
a huge splash of milk.
Earth's indigo ocean is a swirling,
snowy blanket of clouds.
Other planets say enviously,
"I wish I looked like that colorful marble."
Comets are as bright as the Sun and
as fast as an athlete jogging in an Olympic race.
Beautiful sights of a magnificent galaxy.

Jessie Wu, Grade 3
Saigling Elementary School, TX

Rainbows
Rainbows,
colorful, cool
swiftly, sweetly, moving
rainbows, treasure trove, discovery
awesome

Pooja Adapa, Grade 3
Tracy Learning Center - Primary Charter School, CA

Once I Was...
Once I was a scoop of ice cream now I am an ice cream cone. I used to be an apple but now I am a cake. Once I was a seed now I am a maple tree. I used to be paint but now I am a beautiful picture. I used to be sticks but now I am a bird's nest. I used to be a gray sky but now I am a blue sky. Once I was a baby now I am a grownup.
That's who I am.

Isabella Shin, Grade 3
Annunciation Orthodox School, TX

Winter

I like to go outside in the winter
Call my friends to go sledding with me.
Going faster and faster down the hill,
Snow hits my face as I rush down
Let's build a snowman round and fat,
With some sticks for its arms
A carrot for the nose,
And two coals for eyes,
Raisins for a mouth,
And maybe a scarf.
Now let's go inside and have some nice
Warm HOT CHOCOLATE.
Aspen Collett, Grade 3
Flaming Gorge School, UT

The Pink, Purple, and Yellow Monkey

The pink, purple, and yellow monkey
is as strange as can be.
He lives in the jungle
right next to a tree.
He eats lots of bananas
that's his favorite dish.
He's pink, purple and yellow
and sometimes finds fish.
He is very playful
and also very nice.
He catches lots of things
but most of the time, mice.
Melanie Bezinover, Grade 3
Woodcrest School, CA

Music

Fantastic
waves hitting the bay, softly

flowing along,

walking the shore happily
a fluffy pillow
good dark chocolate,
ice cream sundaes
Conner Adzgery, Grade 2
Annunciation Orthodox School, TX

Tiger

Tiger
Strong, stripes
Running, pouncing, hunting
Be careful they are dangerous
Predator
Kevin Ajcuc, Grade 1
Kentwood Elementary School, CA

Wisconsin

Wisconsin
Cold, icy
Snowing, raining, milking
Very, very, very milky
State
Christopher Hensel, Grade 3
Selwyn College Preparatory School, TX

Christmas Eve

Christmas Eve is here.
Wintery cold night.
Full moon shining
Snowflakes falling from the sky.
Christmas is finally here!
Billy Groth, Grade 2
Sierra Hills Elementary School, CA

Red

Spicy chili on corn chips.
Warm covers on my bed.
Singing birds in the garden.
Big boats sailing in the ocean.
Chewy gummy bears in my mouth.
Myles Brame, Grade 1
Kentwood Elementary School, CA

Monkeys

Monkeys
Strong, wild
Smart, playful, fast
Swings from vine to vine
Primates
Fardin Zaman, Grade 1
Kentwood Elementary School, CA

Dancing Dragonflies

Bouncing helicopters in the sunlight
Zooming around buildings
Racing over towns
Flying above mountains
Over streets and over people
Over school and creatures
Over clouds and fields
Dragonflies in flight
Adam Hettman, Grade 3
Lolo Elementary School, MT

A Bear

There was a bear
Her name was Bella Rose
She swam in the water
I went to see the bear
To make friends
With the bear
We went to the store
She was very good to the people
Emma Nichols, Kindergarten
Legacy Christian Academy, NM

Snow Bells

Snow bells are beautiful
The bells glisten in the sky
Snow glitters on the ground
Snow bells are in the light
Snow is a light.
Bells can sing
Snow bells can flutter
Snow bells can ring.
Sarah Baertsch, Grade 3
Lolo Elementary School, MT

The Sea

The waves at the sea
Come to the shore.
They splash on me.
I want some more.
I also want to swim.
Abhinav Balla, Kindergarten
Scholars Academy, CA

The Beach

You will have fun at the beach,
If you use time wisely!
You will have fun in the ocean,
As long as you don't drown
You could build sandcastles,
Hope no one steps on it!
Come back with your family and
Make sure no one drowns!
David Zhu, Grade 2
Camino Grove Elementary School, CA

Twinkling Snowflakes

Fluffy cotton balls glittering in the air
Melting sugar on my tongue
A mouse sneaking from a sleeping cat
My mom's gentle hand on my cheek
Stars falling from the sky
Floating flowers sailing through the night
Sparkling jewels falling
Candy in my mouth
Angela Hovdenes, Grade 3
Lolo Elementary School, MT

Brownies

B rownies are good
I love them in **R** ound bits
O r rectangular and big
W hen I take a bite
N othing comes
I n my mind that is bad
when I **E** at
brownie **S**
Mathilda Kloepping, Grade 3
Horn Academy, TX

Sunsets

Sunsets
In the evening
Pink, purple, blue we see
We like to see it set on the
Trampoline
Olivia Porter, Grade 3
Wasatch Elementary School, UT

Sunshine

The sunshine makes me very hot.
It's like a very big fire dot.

The sunshine makes flowers bloom.
It always goes in my room.

It melts my ice cream.
It makes jewels gleam.

In the sunshine I go out to play.
When it is very sunny in May.
Jennifer Pizarro, Grade 3
Hamlin Street Elementary School, CA

Snow Boomer

S now mover
N ot his
O nly
W ork

B oomer works in the summer to mow
O nly grass and weeds
O nly at work,
M aking progress
E very minute
R ain and snow don't stop him.
Conner Campbell, Grade 2
Cache Valley Learning Center, UT

Spring

During spring I have fun.
I always see the sun.

In early spring the flowers bloom.
I put the flowers in my room.

In the morning a bird sings.
I see it flapping its wings.

I saw a bird's nest in the tree.
Then they grew and they were free.
Sergio Zuniga, Grade 3
Hamlin Street Elementary School, CA

Tree

It is fun to sit under a tree.
Because there are many fruits to see.

The branches are big and strong.
It is also very long.

When I bounced a heavy ball.
All the leaves started to fall.

When I left the big tall tree behind.
I always think of it in my mind.
Michel Renomeron, Grade 3
Hamlin Street Elementary School, CA

Blue

Blue is three fourths of water
All over the world.
Blue is the sky
On a hot summer day.
Blue is the color of some eyes.
Blue is the blueberries on my table
Blue is your mom's warm smile
When she welcomes you home.
Blue is the tears
When you are sad.
Blue is blue.
Grant Harger, Grade 3
Wilchester Elementary School, TX

Score!

Score: nine-to-
six in the bottom of
the ninth inning.
Full count. Two
outs bases loaded. The pitcher
zooms it right
down the pike.
The batter swings and he
hits it and it's soaring. It's
gone! A grand slam!
They win 10-9!
Ben Ledig, Grade 3
Annunciation Orthodox School, TX

Lunch Time

First we order lunch, I order a soda.
Slurp, slurp, slurp!
After I drink all of my soda, my brother steps on it.
Pop!
My mom orders soup and stirs it.
Whoosh whoosh!
My brother orders a bowl of spaghetti
and he reaches to go grab a drink before he eats but,
Crash!
He knocks the bowl right off the table.

My dad orders a big sandwich and he makes the noises,
Munch, Crunch!
The side dish for my mom's soup is a hard roll.
She makes the noise,
Rip!

My brother drops his fork in his bowl,
Ding ding!
All of a sudden I hear lots of noises,
Slurp, ding, ping, crunch, whoosh, rip, munch, crash, pop!
It can be noisy during lunch time!

Mia Dominic, Grade 3
CLASS Academy, OR

Many Ways to Say Goodnight

Crickets say it hopping around
Peeping happily on the wet grass
Cars speeding on the dark street
Hitting the roads with a loud hum
Houses falling fast asleep blending into the dark blackness
Diggers say goodnight when they stop lifting heavy loads
The moon lifts higher and higher into the sky
Going into my dark living room and reading exciting stories
Until my mom calls to me come eat it's supper time
The smell of the warm food
I guess it was spaghetti
Hope I was wrong
It was brown rice
My mom says goodnight by kissing me and tucking me in
That is how I know it's night.

Deniz Uzun, Grade 3
Coeur d'Alene Avenue Elementary School, CA

The Ants Are Working*

Ants are working, ants are working
All day long, all day long.
Going to get food, going to get food.
Oh my! Oh my!
Ants are working, ants are working
All day long, all day long.
Laying eggs, laying eggs.
Oh my! Oh my!
Ants are working, ants are working
All day long, all day long.
They talk to each other, they talk to each other.
Oh my! Oh my!
Ants are working, ants are working
All day long, all day long.
They live in colonies, they live in colonies.
Oh my! Oh my!
Ants are working, ants are working
All day long, all day long.
The ants dig tunnels, for their home.
Oh my! Oh my!

Nicci Delk, Grade 1
P H Greene Elementary School, TX
*To the tune of Frére Jacques.

Wonderful Spring

W onders all around
O ut in the sun
N ever dreadful
D reams
E very day
R ead about the sun
F un in the sun
U nder an umbrella
L ovely skies

S potted butterflies
P erfect weather
R ather fine
I n the spring
N ever will it end
G rowing flowers there

Nelson Porter, Grade 3
Thomas Edison Charter School - North, UT

Sun and Moon

Sun
Hot, cool
Shining, fusing, warming
Gas, fire, rocks, dust
Brightly, shining, lighting
Cold, big
Moon

Kennedy Carmichael, Grade 2
St John's Episcopal School, TX

Day and Night

Day
Light, warm
Soothing, cooling, moving
Sun, space, world, craters
Moving, going, rotating
Cold, dark
Night

Sam Mehaffey, Grade 2
St. John's Episcopal School, TX

The Lion

The big old lion,
Prowling behind the trees,
For he has gotten hungry,
He has gone out hunting,
The mighty King of Animals.
Now that he has gotten and retrieved,
He has gotten his juicy meat.

Kai Moore, Grade 3
Goethe International Charter School, CA

Stars

Stars in the sky,
Shining so bright.
Just like a firefly,
Glowing up the night.
Try your best to catch one, if you can.
If you can catch one,
You can use it as a night light.

Riley Villard, Grade 2
Jackson Elementary School, CA

Outside

I smell the grass,
Nice and green
I hear the truck's motor
I hear quietness in the air
I feel the hot sun
I hear birds chirping
It feels like flying in the air.

Isaiah Vallejos, Grade 1
Mosaic Academy, NM

Ocean

The ocean is so cool and strong
It goes are far as I can see,
Mysterious as it can be.
The waves come and go.
Soothing my soul.
The perfect place just to be
Whatever I want to be!

Samantha Giusti, Grade 3
St John's Episcopal Day School, TX

Water

Water, water don't kill it
Because you have to survive.
It gives you health
It's the only thing you can survive with.
Don't put chemicals in it.
Water is great just great
Water, water don't kill it.

Maya Muckatira, Grade 2
St John's Episcopal School, TX

Penguins and Polar Bears

Penguins
Cute, cuddly
Swimming, diving, catching
Eat, check, care, sleep
Sleeping, fighting, traveling
Fluffy, smart
Polar Bears

Jack Phelan, Grade 2
St John's Episcopal School, TX

A Magical Fantasy

I dream of going to a magical place,
with unicorns,
leprechauns,
fairies,
and much more.
A magical fantasy,
is a beautiful place,
so green with beautiful flowers.
You could hear the water's rush,
from miles away.
The sound so soothing,
you feel like you are lost in paradise.
A magical fantasy,
is where I want to be.

Sarah Millan, Grade 3
Wilchester Elementary School, TX

The Sparkling Moon

The moon sparkles
Like a diamond
Beautiful stars
Around it
Wonderful light
Shines on me
the brightest light
I've ever seen
How it hits
The snowy meadow
Is wonderful
The sparkling moonlight
Is beautiful to me

Leah Workman, Grade 2
Sierra Hills Elementary School, CA

Kitty Cat

Like a vibrating phone by your ear.
Like a cotton ball in your arms,
Running down the twinkling sky.
A tiger in the beautiful air.
Jumping rabbits in the bursting air,
Like a cheetah across the open floor

Kaitlyn Croft, Grade 3
Lolo Elementary School, MT

Soft and Brown

It's soft and brown and
Melts in your mouth.

It is not dark but light.
It tastes creamy in your mouth.

It shouts out "Hey, eat me I'm delicious!"
It smells like a rose,
On a warm summer day.

It looks like
A candy bar.

When your mom says…
You can have it after lunch,

You get anxious,
And eat your lunch real fast.

When you finally get it,
You scream "MILK CHOCOLATE!!!"

Isabel Vierra, Grade 3
Wilchester Elementary School, TX

Music…

Music is like
happiness spreading through the world
Music sounds like
children singing right into your
ear. The flute
sounds beautiful and pretty and
makes me want
to do a smooth ballet
twirl. Sometimes music
can show sadness in a
heart that was
once full of joy. Music
can have such
a strong and a sad
feeling it makes
me want to cry quietly.

Reeti Mangal, Grade 2
Annunciation Orthodox School, TX

My New Puppy

My puppy is tame.
But sometimes she is wild!
When she barks
Her fur comes up in a spiky way!
I laugh!
She barks loud at me.
I love my new puppy.
It eats a lot!
I want another!
Kailey Huff, Grade 3
Three Rivers Elementary School, TX

Lily

A lily is a flower,
A springtime shower,
A sign of power

A lily's a beautiful thing
Like a diamond ring

A lily's a flower
A beautiful sign of power
Charlotte Benes, Grade 3
Wilchester Elementary School, TX

Scared Inside

At school,
I am scared inside.
People are close to me,
I barely can move,
I do not feel safe.
Ring, ring!
School is over!
I run to Cool School.
I am happy now.
Deshawnae Mauldin, Grade 2
Robert L Stevens Elementary School, CA

Katherine

K ittens are funny.
A chapstick to put on my lips.
T eeth are getting loose.
H as big brown eyes.
E ats spaghetti and meatballs for lunch.
R ed apple for a snack.
I have a hard time with homework.
N ice to my grandma
E than is my brother.
Katherine Herrera, Kindergarten
Woodcrest School, CA

Eagle

Big, soft
Flying, eating, jumping
Eyes, beak, claws, wings
Looking, flying, grabbing
Brown, white
Bird
Victor Lomholt, Grade 1
CLASS Academy, OR

The Oak Tree at Sunrise

I used to be
an acorn lying in
the pasture. But
now I'm an oak tree
in the misty sunrise.
Alexander Haney, Grade 3
Annunciation Orthodox School, TX

Dallas Cowboys

Dallas
Blue, silver
Entertaining, flashing, winning
The cowboys are awesome
Cowboys
Devin Pullin, Grade 3
Connally Elementary School, TX

Red

Roses in Papa's yard.
Dracula's satin cape.
Fire trucks rushing.
Apples on a tree.
Salsa, strawberries,
Chilies, and spaghetti.
Tyler Torstenson, Grade 1
Kentwood Elementary School, CA

The Cheetah's Sounds

Sniff, sniff.
Smelling some delicious food in the warm, misty air.

Tramp, thud, tramp.
Running through the tropical trees as gracefully as a bird.

Grr, grr.
Finding someone had already reached the food I had found.

Scratch, thump, chomp.
Fighting in the grassy terrain.

ROAR!
Roaring in triumph and pride as I beat the panther.

Thump, thump, thump.
Devouring the fleshy, tasty meat of the dead deer.

Swish, ripple.
Swimming quietly in the crystal clear creek.

Thump, thump, snore.
My heart beating as I peacefully fall asleep under the blinking bright stars.

Hannah Lee, Grade 3
Juliet Morris Elementary School, CA

Cheetah

I'm running on swift grass like a race car.
Swish!

Devouring tasty, delicious meaty deer with a yummy taste.
Chomp! Chomp!

Fighting with another ferocious, swift cheetah with razor sharp fangs.
Scratch! Bite! Roar!

Sleeping in my cool, warm den in grassland terrain.
Snore!

Fighting a ferocious lion that was a fighter for 20 years.
Scratch! Roar! Chomp!

Brian Park, Grade 3
Juliet Morris Elementary School, CA

Summer

Flying butterflies.
Butterflies are beautiful.
Butterflies are cool.
Madison Jacobs, Grade 3
Beitel Elementary School, WY

Leaves

Rake up the leaves now.
They will scatter everywhere.
Rake them back up. Jump.
Karsten Sorensen, Grade 3
Beitel Elementary School, WY

The Circus

The circus is fun,
I like seeing the clowns do tricks,
I love the circus!
Shaelin R. Abbatiello, Grade 3
Blackland Prairie Elementary School, TX

Iguana

Crawling up a tree
An iguana you can see
Going up smoothly
Kullen Whittaker, Grade 1
Boones Ferry Primary School, OR

Fireworks

Fireworks wow!
They light up the sky
Like fireflies do.
Demi Kouzounis, Grade 3
Annunciation Orthodox School, TX

A Lune Song

Soothing, soft, still,
Slow as an old turtle
Sad songs — music.
Moriah Feng, Grade 2
Annunciation Orthodox School, TX

Geo Sphere

Geo Sphere
hollow, round
breaks, rolls, does nothing
amazing, hard, and fun
Geo Sphere
Matthew Lutz, Grade 3
St Pius X School, TX

My Hideous Brother

My brother Denny he's like a germ.
He would look great if he had a perm.
He'd look like a girl what fun it would be.
Right now he looks like a monster to me.
Yes that is true he looks like a worm.
Abigail Beutler, Grade 3
Wasatch Elementary School, UT

Outside

I had a little turtle
And I put it outside
I brought my kite outside
So I could fly it
Caitlynn Oechsner, Kindergarten
Legacy Christian Academy, NM

Horses

Beautiful creatures
Racing, galloping, searching
White four legged flashes
Mustangs
Alexandra Sands, Grade 3
Carlthorp School, CA

Hook 'Em Horns

I am a huge Texas fan.
I love Texas.
I used to be a Baylor fan.
But they are not good.
Jase Ayala, Grade 3
Connally Elementary School, TX

Winter

I love winter it is fun.
Winter is exciting for everyone!
I love snow I love to run.
Winter is fun, fun, fun!
I love to make snowmen tall.
Winter makes me slip and fall!
I love winter it is fun!
Winter is exciting for everyone!

Kusai Abu Al-Rob, Grade 2
Islamic School of Muslim Educational Trust, OR

A Day on the Beach

I go to the beach on a sunny warm day,
I enjoy the breeze and go out to play,
I fly my favorite kite,
With it's color so bright!
I build a castle out of sand.
I surround it with a protective land.
After watching the sunset,
I say goodbye to the people I met.

Tarek Jabakhanji, Grade 3
Islamic School of Muslim Educational Trust, OR

I Am an Athlete

I am a basketball, soaring for the hoop.
I am a hockey stick brushing the puck.
I am a soccer ball going past the speed limit for the goal.
I am a football heading to the touchdown.
I am a lacrosse net diving for the puck.
I am a baseball heading high speed for the bat.
I am a water polo ball going for the goal.
I am a person who never gives up on sports.

Rohan Kumar, Grade 3
CLASS Academy, OR

Purple

I eat a juicy plum.
My warm cozy robe I wear before I go to sleep.
Butterflies, hippos, beetles, pansies,
Fluttering ribbons through the air.
I smell really ripe grapes.

Tiffany Sun, Grade 1
Kentwood Elementary School, CA

Zoe

Zoe
Nice, respectful, girl
Child of Dewayne and Chantee
Lover of God
Who feels happy
Who needs air
Who gives smiles
Who fears the dark
Who would like to see a dinosaur
Lindsey

Zoe Lindsey, Grade 1
Kentwood Elementary School, CA

White

A dove is as white as
    snow,
    sugar,
    salt,
    and clouds.
A dove is white like
    bunny rabbits,
    polar bears,
    and cotton balls.
A dove is WHITE!

Chinmayi Reddy, Grade 3
St Aloysius Parochial School, CA

Angry Feelings

Angry feelings
like a scribble on a page.
Angry feelings
like a cold hard stone.
But
when you think about it
it's nothing
but a tiny
grain of sand
from life

Lucy Reasons, Grade 3
Old Town Elementary School, TX

Heart

Black as night,
Your heart does not have light.

Hate is wrong,
Try to sing a song.

Have some love,
Reach for the above.

Be a leader,
Not a cheater.

Crying is OK,
But not to stay.

You are cool and nice,
But not a block of ice.

Lupine Cramer, Grade 3
Cache Valley Learning Center, UT

Black Holes

When giant stars die, I form.
I suck everything up with my mouth.
I am a panther — dangerous and black.
Even though I'm as small as a city,
I can devour the world.
Once you are inside me,
There is NO WAY OUT!
Even if you shout,
You cannot be freed.
So do not come close to me,
Or doom will come to YOU.
Remember, I am as dangerous as death.
My abyss never ends.
I am a black hole.
Beware of your fate in space.
Beware…OF ME!

Kasey Wu, Grade 3
Saigling Elementary School, TX

Blue

Flowers growing in the dirt
Cold ice to play hockey
A whale spouting
A baseball hat
Juicy blueberries
Jackson Steinberg, Grade 1
Kentwood Elementary School, CA

Rhyan

R uns lots of laps
H appy dogs are happy
Y um this is the best thing ever
A t the park I went to the jungle gym
N othing is like fresh air
Rhyan Thomas, Grade 1
Kentwood Elementary School, CA

Red

Red smells hot.
Red feels like fire.
Red is loud.
I see fire
It tastes nasty.
Kenneth White, Grade 1
Kentwood Elementary School, CA

Rhino

Rhino
Gray, thorns
Jumping, kicking, tapping
Can be found in desert
Female
Anthony Garcia, Grade 1
Kentwood Elementary School, CA

Airplane

Airplane, oh airplane
You go places and carry cases
You go over the ocean and drop potions
In the water and we go farther
When we get there, we are not in the air.
Brandon Melton, Grade 3
Three Rivers Elementary School, TX

No Name Calling

If you are not a bully,
Help me get the message out:
Bullying and name calling
Are awful, no doubt!

Name calling is bad,
As bad as can be.
It is so sad…
If only bullies could see!
Katherine R. Long, Grade 2
Trenton Elementary School, TX

The Fat Cat

I have a fat cat
Who's cute as a button.
She plays in the backyard
And she's scared of nothin'.

She's scared of some dogs.
She keeps on runnin'.
She always plays fetch
And she's scared of swimmin'.
Camryn Nagy, Grade 1
Spring Creek Elementary School, WY

Croak, Frog, Croak

Croak, frog, croak
What do you say?
I do not know,
Well,
I think you're saying,
that you want
to play leap frog with me.
Do you?
Flop, flop, pop, flop, flop.
Tonantzin Meza, Grade 2
Robert L Stevens Elementary School, CA

Noah

Noah caught a huge shark,
the animals didn't want it on the ark.
Ayden Smith, Grade 1
St Pius X School, TX

Strong Fish

I am curious as a fish,
Kind as a sunflower,
Cool as the color blue,
Funny as a star,
Creative as the number six,
Faithful as garnet,
And strong as fire.

Faith Landis, Grade 1
Baldwin Stocker Elementary School, CA

Friendly Flower

I am friendly as a brown dog,
Quiet as a sunflower,
Energetic as the color purple,
Smooth as a circle,
Orderly as the number three,
Loving as an emerald,
And smooth as water.

Mejan Khan, Grade 1
Baldwin Stocker Elementary School, CA

Braeden Loves Baseball

B raeden loves baseball.
R eading is fun for him.
A lways likes to play with his neighbors.
E veryone likes his trampoline.
D oing homework is fun!
E nergetic always!
N aps aren't for him.

Braeden Long, Grade 3
C W Cline Primary School, TX

Fire Scorpion

I am dangerous as a scorpion,
Tricky as a black hole plant,
Powerful as the color orange,
Strong as a triangle,
Mysterious as the number nine,
Protective as a ruby,
And scary as fire.

Maximillian Briggs, Grade 1
Baldwin Stocker Elementary School, CA

School

School, school, school!
Sometimes I like you.
I don't like behavior marks!
I like recess,
But, I don't like to work!
All school is WORK!
School days are my worst days ever!

Billie Holbert, Grade 3
C W Cline Primary School, TX

Happy

I am nice as a panda,
Pretty as a rose,
Peaceful as the color blue,
Calm as a circle,
Orderly as the number four,
Loving as an emerald,
And smooth as water.

Britney Chieng, Grade 1
Baldwin Stocker Elementary School, CA

Snowflakes

They float and glide,
They are so small.
Some people like to
Catch them on their tongue.
There are so many.
All snowflakes
Are different.

Jonathan Blecher, Grade 3
C W Cline Primary School, TX

Brave Lion

I am brave as a lion,
Calm as an orchid,
Energetic as the color red,
Hardworking as a triangle,
Ambitious as the number five,
Honest as a period,
And powerful as a tornado.

Richard Kim, Grade 1
Baldwin Stocker Elementary School, CA

Nature

As the wind blows,
Water flows.
We all share this earth together.
As people smoke,
Birds choke.
We all share this air together.
As the animals die,
People cry.
Their memories will be with us forever.
We all live the same life.
We're born, we live, we die.
As the wind blows,
Water flows.
We all share this earth together.

Ishani Cheshire, Grade 3
Stratford School - Deanza Park Campus, CA

The Wizz Bang Doodle

I looked outside my window, and what did I see?
A Wizz Bang Doodle flying at me!

1,500 legs, 3 eyes, and 5 wings,
'A Jolly Good Fellow' was the song he would sing.

The Wizz Bang Doodle pulled out his guitar.
And man-oh-man, it sounded great from afar!

He flew up high, he flew down low...
This Wizz Bang Doodle was on the go.

The last I saw him he was flying away,
But this time he sang, "This Is the Day."

Sloan Taylor, Grade 3
St James Episcopal School, TX

Is Like...

Snow is like a big white blanket.
Rain is like an outdoor shower.
A booger is like a green alien that lives in your nose.
Your hand is like a rock with five sticks that move.
Your hair is like long worms that stick to your hair.

Mariah Edwards Saechao, Grade 3
Elder Creek Elementary School, CA

Rain Forest
The rain forest,
is a place,
where a lot of animals live.
The place where
the birds chirp
loudly in the trees.
A hungry tiger,
looking for some food.
Monkeys climbing
all over the trees and
making their loud noises.
A sloth slowly making its way across the trees.
The rain forest,
a wonderful place.

Abby Molina, Grade 3
Wilchester Elementary School, TX

I Wish
I wish I had 1,000 dollars, so I can buy the whole set of tech decks
and I can fix a broken window for 100 dollars.

I wish I could be president.
I would give a good speech to over 1,000 people.
I'd make fair rules for all kinds of races.

I wish I would never get in trouble, so I could do whatever I wanted.
It is boring to follow people's rules. I wish I had my own rules.

I wish I was a police officer because I like to be running and catching people of crime.
I would get a promotion for catching a lot of criminals. I can't wait to be a sergeant.

Seven Eaves, Grade 3
Roosevelt Elementary School, CA

Once I Was
Once I was a pen but now I am a thought on a piece of paper. I used to be a
mixture of baking ingredients but now I am a birthday cake. I used to be lost in
the woods but now I am found. I used to be a waffle but now I am an ice cream
cone being topped with infinite ice cream flavors. I used to be writing but now I
am done!

Caroline Keller, Grade 3
Annunciation Orthodox School, TX

Snakes/Reptile
Snakes
big, black
rattling, slithering
Reptile
Paxton Hanna, Grade 2
St Pius X School, TX

Universal Studios
Orlando
fun, excited
walking, standing
Universal Studios
Nicholas Garza, Grade 2
St Pius X School, TX

Ranch/Snakes
Ranch
peaceful, flowers
shooting, roping
Snakes
Michael Speed, Grade 2
St Pius X School, TX

Clouds
Some clouds are blue,
Some clouds are black.
Some go away,
Some come back.
Dimitri DesJardins, Grade 3
Wesleyan Academe, TX

Hearts
Hearts —
Big, red, one —
Pump
Quietly, always, here
Madelyn Bacashihua, Grade 3
St Mary School, CA

Teacher
Teacher —
One, kind, smart —
Teaches
Nicely, here, today
Madison Azzolino, Grade 3
St Mary School, CA

Ice Cream
Ice Cream —
Brown, pink, big —
Melts
Every day, around, soft
Emily Ramirez, Grade 3
St Mary School, CA

Outside
I hear the wind blowing
I taste air
I hear a dog
I see cars
Augustus Guikema, Kindergarten
Mosaic Academy, NM

Softball/Girls' Sport
Softball
fun, challenging
running, throwing
Girls' sport
Rilley Arreola, Grade 2
St Pius X School, TX

My Red, Ripe Raspberry
Raspberry, raspberry in a dish —
How many pieces do you wish?
I could eat them all day long;
I want more but they're all gone!
Hallie Morgan, Grade 3
Providence Hall Charter School, UT

Day and Night
Day
Bright, sunny
Playing, waiting, running
Sun, kids, moon, owl
Sleeping, peeking, snoring
Dark, starry
Night

Megan Chambers, Grade 3
Tracy Learning Center - Primary Charter School, CA

Games and Computer
Games
Fun, nonstop
Playing, running, yelling
Facebook, computer, type, download
Opening, closing, spacing
Gray, cool
Computer

Taylor Gonser, Grade 2
Tracy Learning Center - Primary Charter School, CA

Sometimes
Sometimes I feel like meteors because somebody scared me.
Sometimes I feel like angels because I'm happy.
Sometimes I feel like a tornado fighting everything.
Sometimes I feel like a mummy, because I'm scared.
Sometimes I feel like running one thousand days.
Sometimes I feel like an astronaut flying in space.
But sometimes, I feel like a super star.

Alexandr Ermilov, Grade 2
Longfellow Elementary School, TX

Words
Words are helpful
Words are fun
Words are used by the ton
Words are used in lots of things
Like acrobats and cats on swings
Words can be a lot of fun
But wait! Words are done

Sabina Mintz, Grade 3
Wonderland Avenue Elementary School, CA

An Awesome Explorer

Magellan was very brave
He sailed above many tall waves
He explored faraway lands
Ones with rocks and others with sand
Anthony Rodriguez, Grade 3
Montessori Learning Institute, TX

Snow

S led
N orth Pole
O utside
W inter
Jacob Trickler, Grade 3
Cache Valley Learning Center, UT

Good Night

Good night, good night, it is midnight
So go to bed and sleep tight
Have good dreams and say good night
It's time to go to bed, it is midnight
Gideon Bagwell, Grade 3
Legacy Christian Academy, NM

Rain

R ain falling
A lways falling
I sn't stopping
N ever ending rain rain rain rain!
Aidan Childs, Grade 2
Cache Valley Learning Center, UT

The Leafless Tree

I see a leafless tree
that is not so free, it has no green.
I don't know why I have seen no green
in the not so free leafless tree!
Juztin Galvis, Grade 3
Faith Academy of Bellville, TX

Dogs

D ifferent from humans
O bedient
G obbles up food
S ometimes stinky
Ryan Cummings, Grade 3
Horn Academy, TX

Bike and Trike

I ride my bike
My brother rides his trike
We roll down the hill
Having quite a thrill
Jodi Kain, Grade 3
Flying Hawk School, CA

Macy

M y friend
A ttractive
C aring
Y es she is very nice
Mollie Boggs, Grade 3
Horn Academy, TX

Hector

Hector is an animal.
He is as large as a pig.
Hector likes to play soccer,
but he runs and trips on his feet
Marco Martinez, Grade 3
Foothill School, UT

Pizza

Cheesy, saucy
Baking, heating, warming
Tasty, flat, bumpy bread
Pie
Leslie Ochoa, Grade 2
Dixie Sun Elementary School, UT

Moose

Moose
Very large
Eating, walking, sleeping
Loves the cold weather
Alaska
Erika Bevelheimer, Grade 1
Kentwood Elementary School, CA

Gold Fish

Fish
Shiny, gold
Swimming, breathing, eating
Always swims round and round
Cold-blooded
Ella Sommer, Grade 1
Kentwood Elementary School, CA

Lion

Lion
Fast, angry
Running, roaring, attacking
The lion is very wild
Fierce
Kevin Sandoval-Lopez, Grade 1
Kentwood Elementary School, CA

Penguin

Ice bird
Fat, cute
Swimming, hatching, eating
They are in Alaska
Bird
Tyler Booker, Grade 2
Robinson Elementary School, TX

Karis

K arate kid
A rtistic
R adical
I ntelligent
S pectacular
Karis Cisneros, Grade 3
Horn Academy, TX

Penguins

Birds
Smelly, fat
Sliding, feeding, splashing
They live in the South Pole.
Penguins
Samantha Baty, Grade 2
Robinson Elementary School, TX

Family

My mom and dad
And my sisters
Are a part of my family.
I am the only
Brother in my family.
Juan Cruces, Grade 3
Three Rivers Elementary School, TX

Parrot

Parrot
Feathers, bites
Eating, flying, talking
Pretty colors with a beak
Bird
Denise Martinez, Grade 1
Kentwood Elementary School, CA

Seabird

Penguin
Smelly, playful
Dancing, swimming, eating
They huddle together.
Bird
Lyndsay Weatherby, Grade 2
Robinson Elementary School, TX

Snake

Scaly
Skinny, slithery
Long, deadly, venomous
Poisonous, fast, strong, scary
Cool
Andrew Yang, Grade 3
Horn Academy, TX

Flamey Giant

Flames spurting out of my gassy crust,
Just like ravens flying outside of the flock.
I am the giant security camera of the solar system.
I warm and give light to the planets.
Everyone sees me —
Absolutely everyone —
Venezuela, Nigeria, even Malaysia!
I am the sun.

Ella Goeckner-Wald, Grade 3
Saigling Elementary School, TX

Babies

Babies are cute and cuddly.
I love them and they love me
But when I smile I'm going to tickle the baby.
They laugh like a new little puppy
But they never let me touch them.
I saw one baby and got to hold it
And that was when it was my birthday.
Do you love babies?

Alyssa Ponce, Grade 3
Three Rivers Elementary School, TX

The Day We Played Football

My cousin passed the ball,
He threw it into the hall.

I ran and fell down on the street,
A gash, a rash, and broken feet.

My cousin ran and galloped to catch,
Jumped, tackled, blocked, and got a scratch.

Stephanie Huynh, Grade 3
Oak Park Elementary School, CA

Unicorns

Unicorns sound like hooves pounding
the ground. Unicorns look like horses with
horns. Unicorns smell like fresh roses. Unicorns
feel like a bear's warm fur. Unicorns taste like
chocolate cakes and pastries.

Persephone Fossi, Grade 2
Annunciation Orthodox School, TX

Technology

We pollute the air with technology.
But without technology…
we would
be S L O W.
Sick people
need technology
for x-rays and
ambulances.
Air used to be clean
until
technology came along.
Technology
has ups
and downs.
Benjamin Nederveld, Grade 3
Wilchester Elementary School, TX

By the Pond

The pond,
is like a big patch of
dark grass.
Lily pads,
floating around.
Rattlesnake,
hissing for his prey.
Frogs, jumping in happiness.
And the moonlight,
shining through the big, tall trees.
Owls, shooting
their eyes at everything.
The pond,
is very important.
Lauren Hall, Grade 3
Wilchester Elementary School, TX

Spring

Spring is finally here!
I can hear the bees buzzing in the air.
I can see bees flying in the air.
I can smell the sweet strawberries.
I can feel the hot air.
Christian Taylor, Grade 2
Woodcrest School, CA

Travel

Come with me,
Far over the sea,
To New York City!
It won't be a pity!

We might go to China,
Or South Carolina.
We will go to
The Grand Canyon!
We might become
Companions!

Come with me,
Far over the sea.
Where would you
Rather be?
Allie Hansen, Grade 3
C W Cline Primary School, TX

Snakes

Snakes
Slimy, scary
Slithering, hiding, sliding
Eyes, scales, tongue, tail
Looking, gliding, gulping
Spooky, sneaky
Reptiles
Anwesha Mukherjee, Grade 1
CLASS Academy, OR

Pets

Pets can be wet.
They can get messy.

Pets you have to love,
Like cats and dogs.

You can find them everywhere.
In the car and at your house.

They just need to be loved.
Elizabeth Farrell, Grade 3
C W Cline Primary School, TX

All About Alyssa

I am bouncy as a bunny,
Rich as an apple tree,
Pretty as the color red,
Sweet as a heart,
Free as the number seven,
Loving as a garnet,
And tall as a waterfall.
Alyssa Lin, Grade 1
Baldwin Stocker Elementary School, CA

The Loving Girl

I am small as a Chihuahua,
Colorful as a blueberry bush,
Fair as the color green,
Loving as a heart,
Together as the number two,
Lucky as an oval,
And kind as the desert.
Karena Pai, Grade 1
Baldwin Stocker Elementary School, CA

Loving Me

I am playful as a golden retriever,
Sweet as a rose,
Happy and joyful as the color yellow,
Loving as a heart,
Friendly as the number two,
Brilliant as a garnet,
And beautiful as a garden.
Jacqueline Shaw, Grade 1
Baldwin Stocker Elementary School, CA

As Fast as I Am

I am fast as a tiger,
Rich as a peach tree,
Strong as the color red,
Good as a diamond,
Lucky as the number four,
Brilliant as sapphire,
And tall as a tornado.
Justin Chen, Grade 1
Baldwin Stocker Elementary School, CA

Bike

Bike
Hard, blue
Racing, bouncing, riding
Wheels, seat, gears, pedals
Turning, jumping, skidding
Fun, fast
Two wheeler
Oscar Lombolt, Grade 1
CLASS Academy, OR

Water Dragons

Water dragons
Two heads, six legs
Swimming, walking, flying
Eyes, claws, teeth, tail
Looking, catching, biting
Blue, large
Monsters
Satvik Duvuru, Grade 2
CLASS Academy, OR

Tadpoles/Frogs

Tadpoles
microscopic, floppy
swarming, wiggling, eating
cattails, plankton, water striders, flies
living, hopping, creeping
athletic, poisonous
Frogs
Faith Howell, Grade 3
Ygnacio Valley Christian School, CA

Spring

Spring is finally here!
I can see fresh lemons
in my backyard.
I can hear birds singing.
I can smell the purple flowers.
I can taste the fresh apples.
I feel warm in the spring.
Cole Le'au, Grade 2
Woodcrest School, CA

Water Cycle
Small drops of water
When frozen, it is cold ice
And when heated, gas.
R.J. Shreeve, Grade 3
Reid School, UT

Bees
Bees fly in the air.
They like to eat good honey.
Bees are beautiful.
Zoey Seith, Grade 2
Robinson Elementary School, TX

Red
R ed as a fire hydrant.
E verybody loves red.
D ays as hot as a volcano.
Parker Johnson, Grade 3
Providence Hall Charter School, UT

Fall
Fall down to the ground,
They are red, yellow, and orange.
People can rake them.
Elaina Loiacano, Grade 2
Robinson Elementary School, TX

Living and Laughing
Living and laughing
Eating cake and playing games
Embrace happiness
Josef Labermeyer, Grade 3
Plum Creek Elementary School, TX

Leaves
They are colorful.
In the winter they are not.
They fall off sometimes.
Madison Justice, Grade 2
Robinson Elementary School, TX

Winter
Silent snowflakes fall
On freezing, icy fingers
Holes in my mittens
Alyssa Adams, Grade 3
Plum Creek Elementary School, TX

Vipers
They eat lots of bugs.
Make new skin and climb on trees.
They slide on the ground.
Isaiah Lerma, Grade 2
Robinson Elementary School, TX

Dogs
Dogs like to run fast
Playing outside in the sun
Rolling in the grass
Jessica Conkle, Grade 3
Plum Creek Elementary School, TX

The Venus Flytrap
On my windowsill
A bug flying by, and…snap!
The Venus Flytrap.
Abby Watkins, Grade 2
Rio Del Mar Elementary School, CA

Summer Breeze
As the sun beats down
We play in the summer breeze
Until darkness falls
Simon Strickland, Grade 3
Plum Creek Elementary School, TX

The Cat
The cat sat on a mat.
Why is the mat so flat?
The cat must be fat.
Sophia Andtbacka, Grade 1
Reid School, UT

The Funny Girl

I am happy as a rabbit,
Sunny as a sunflower,
Sweet as the color peach,
Funny as an oval,
Smart as the number five,
Shy as gold,
And kind as the ocean.
Nicole Kunzel, Grade 1
Baldwin Stocker Elementary School, CA

Nature

Flowers are beautiful
Flowers are red, yellow, purple
Soft green grass
The pollen smells like perfume
They feel smooth
There is peace everywhere
I am calm.
Stephanie Buitrago, Grade 2
Annunciation Orthodox School, TX

Smooth Water

I am friendly as a hummingbird,
Carefree as a dandelion,
Bubbly as the color pink,
Cheerful as a star,
Balanced as the number two,
Happy as a tourmaline,
And gentle as a smooth stream.
Nicole Teav, Grade 1
Baldwin Stocker Elementary School, CA

All About Renee

I am friendly as a cottontail bunny,
Strong as a maple tree,
Calm as the color blue,
Honest as a circle,
Independent as the number one,
Beautiful as a pearl,
And gentle as a breeze.
Renee Lotfy, Grade 1
Baldwin Stocker Elementary School, CA

Happy Josiah

I am kind as an eagle,
Warm as a sunflower,
Peaceful as the color blue,
Sunny as a circle,
Complicated as the number five,
Fiery as a ruby,
And strong as a tornado.
Josiah Wiggins, Grade 1
Baldwin Stocker Elementary School, CA

Bouncy and Calm

I am strong as an eagle,
Sharp as a cactus,
Happy as the color yellow,
Fair as a square,
Bouncy as the number eight,
Rich as a pearl,
And calm as a wave.
David Siegrist, Grade 1
Baldwin Stocker Elementary School, CA

Happy Me

I am strong as a puppy,
Nice as a rose,
Respectful as the color green,
Free as a heart,
Brave as the number one,
Shiny as garnet,
And fast as a waterfall.
Andrew Wu, Grade 1
Baldwin Stocker Elementary School, CA

Rich and Strong Kimberly

I am strong as a wild cat,
Shy as a jasmine,
Sensitive as a color purple,
Rich as crystal,
Creative as the number fourteen,
Loving as bloodstone,
And mysterious as mist.
Kimberly Yu, Grade 1
Baldwin Stocker Elementary School, CA

Monarch Butterflies

They start as eggs so proud and round,
Until they hatch and are able to get around.

The caterpillar then eats and eats
Until the chrysalis and caterpillar meet.

It snuggles tight into the chrysalis,
And inside it transforms into something you'll never miss

It sits and waits not yet ready to fly,
It has to wait for its wings to dry.

When it is ready to fly, it knows just what to do.
It waits until autumn to migrate to Mexico,
its home that is new.

They find a place with milkweed flowers to give food to their newly born young,
Then sadly their life is done.

Though their life is short, they are a beautiful sight.
I'm glad they live long enough to keep their life cycle going right.

Kimberly Lindquist, Grade 3
RD Martinez Elementary School, TX

The Crash

At a football game.
He was there,
But suddenly he heard a thunderous KA-BOOM!
The crash of helmets collided!
It made him mad
Because he remembered the frustration of his parents.
He didn't feel glad
Because he hates sadness.
Sometimes it brings madness!
A bowl of cereal he spilled — CRASH! A thunderous KA-BOOM!
He heard frequently.
It brought perplexed feelings.
Why is he hearing all these noises? He felt sad again.
Because all the time he spent with his parents were joyful,
But this moment wasn't. His parents were brave.
Thank you for creating me.

Bryan Ukeje, Grade 3
D P Morris Elementary School, TX

Things I Wish to Be

I wish to be a doctor.
I wish to be a lacrosse player.
I wish to be a soccer player.
I wish to be a football player.
Sports are so fun.
They are so great.
I watch them all the time,
Don't you?

Michael Hanson, Grade 2
Kingwood Montessori School, TX

Junior

My baby is the best ever!
Junior kicks me in the foot.
Junior can eat like animals.
Junior is going to preschool.
Junior has a pretty car.
Junior cannot sit properly in the chair.
Junior lives in my house.
And I like Junior.

Lydia Perez, Grade 1
Greenleaf Elementary School, CA

The Sun

My favorite color is yellow.
A sun is yellow
I could feel the sun but not smell it.
It is hot.
I can't hear the sun it is really quiet.
I can't taste it.
I like to draw the sun.
The sun is bright all the time.

Farhan Zaman, Grade 1
Kentwood Elementary School, CA

Home Is Peace

It is full of peace.
It is a place to be.
It is as peaceful as silent hummingbirds.
It is a special place to me.
It is my home, peace.

Sara Toumi, Grade 3
Islamic School of San Diego, CA

My Dog, Hunter!

Here comes Hunter!
Hunter,
Full of hair!
Mom is
Doing laundry.
Hunter runs away
With socks
And underwear!

Walter Mouttet II, Grade 3
C W Cline Primary School, TX

Blue

We all love blue 'cause it's
such a beautiful color.
Blue as the sky,
Blue on the flag,
Blue as our shirts,
Blue as the walls in our school,
Blue as the ocean.
Blue is such a good color.

Brody Pete Schiller, Grade 3
Faith Academy of Bellville, TX

Fire

The sound of a fire is
burn
sizzle
crackle
roar
sparkle
blasting
warming.

Wilburt Niem, Grade 3
Elder Creek Elementary School, CA

My New Kitty

My sweet, sweet kitty
With hair long and pretty
She is so mighty
My kitty is a beauty
I love my new kitty

Sudip Kanchi, Kindergarten
Scholars Academy, CA

I Love Camp Allen!
I liked sleeping in a cabin.
I slept in a bunk bed.
I slept with Divya,
Tomi, Ms. Heather, Kendra,
Sreeya, Joy, and Sarah.
I liked sleeping in the cabin.
But I only slept one hour and forty five minutes
I liked to see the trees moving from my window.
It was fun because we played lots of games.
We went hiking.
We went fishing.
I saw lots of flowers.
I even saw a small gray snake.
I saw blue birds, red birds, and yellow birds.
It was so much fun!

Natalia Garcia, Grade 2
Kingwood Montessori School, TX

Leaves Are All Around
When fall is here, there's a cool breeze in the air,
Leaves are scattered all around like as if the
Ground is chocolate.

Fall is the season of leaves,
From trees the leaves fly down and
Scatter all around a shower of leaves every day.

Fall is a mess of leaves that will soon blow
Away, so start having fun before
It's too late.

Fall is full of fun that
Will always come around
With lots of leaf piles.

Grace Gibler, Grade 3
Wilchester Elementary School, TX

Me and Vegetables
When I got home
I ate carrots so my eyesight could get good.
I ate lettuce, spinach and pears so my body could get healthy.

Nathan Moya, Grade 3
Three Rivers Elementary School, TX

Rain

When rain appears
Everyone sneers
All gets wet,
Even your pet
When it's done
There is no need to run.

P.T. Plew, Grade 3
Goethe International Charter School, CA

Me...

A pples are my favorite
L love is my strong feeling
I gloos are houses I'd like to live in
S un is the light that makes me sparkle
O n cold days I don't wear my hair down
N ow I always wear it up.

Alison Reynolds, Grade 3
Foothill School, UT

My Cousin Trey

One day I had to play
with my cousin Trey.
It was not a good day.
Because he came to play.
All we did was drink,
and sit around to think.

Cassidy Smith, Grade 3
Foothill School, UT

Spring Is Here!

Rabbits hopping swiftly
Daisies blooming on the ground
Spring is here!
Grass all around
Leaves sprouting on the trees
Spring is here!

Rosalind Anne Coats, Grade 2
Annunciation Orthodox School, TX

The Bee

The bee went out last night
He sang a storm
He has a family
A very happy family
A bee — A bee — A bee.
A bee

Jared Bergerson, Grade 3
Neskowin Valley School, OR

The Bird in My Garden

I have a garden with a rose
That is red as blood.
There's a bird in my garden
It can fly in the blue sky
It flaps its wings as it sings
There's a bird in my garden.

Meha Gaba, Kindergarten
Scholars Academy, CA

Park

P laying on the slides,
A dventure everywhere!
R econnecting your heart.
K nowledgeable about the park.

Austin Robison, Grade 3
Providence Hall, UT

Rose

Rose —
Pretty, light, small —
Grows
Slowly, now, cool

Brianna Sykes, Grade 3
St Mary School, CA

Anger

An island in a storm
Is anger from the Gods
And sadness from the Lord

Reagan Creese, Grade 3
Selwyn College Preparatory School, TX

Lions

Lions can eat deer
Lions can be big and fast
Lions can eat meat

Amir Hawash, Grade 2
Salam Academy, NM

Puppy Party

I have a little dog
Who doesn't like to play ball
He always licks me
And he plays with me
And we're having a puppy party
Today is his birthday.
Novelyn Samson, Kindergarten
Legacy Christian Academy, NM

Baseball

What is a baseball?
It is a ball that flies
across a stadium. Does the
pitcher throw the ball?
Does it fly across the sky
for a home run hit?
Drew Mytchak, Grade 3
Annunciation Orthodox School, TX

Easter Fun

Easter sounds like joy.
Easter feels like care.
Easter is very rare!
Easter tastes like candy.
Easter looks like happiness.
Easter is playfulness!
Brooke Peterson, Grade 3
Providence Hall Charter School, UT

Sun

Sun you are so bright.
You shine like gold.
You are very hot.
You are a circle.
Like a basketball.
Sun you shine on me.
Carolina Cruces, Grade 3
Three Rivers Elementary School, TX

Equal Rights

People will have equal rights,
No more boycotts and no more fights.
Preachers stand up with us all,
Together we can stand very tall.
In liberty and freedom too,
Kind, caring nations for me and you.
Sierra Stern, Grade 2
Laurence School, CA

I Had a Cat

I had a cat
named Boo Boo.
He was cream and tan
He liked to play
Every day
And he was really fun.
Brianna Western, Grade 3
Warren Elementary School, OR

Easter Cheer!

Easter is exciting and full of joy.
We have some fun get a toy.
We play some games and now it's time,
To stop this poem and end this rhyme!
Lillian Elliott, Grade 3
Providence Hall Charter School, UT

Bird

Bird —
Big, black, round —
Glides
Quickly, later, nearby
Bernice Solis, Grade 3
St Mary School, CA

Mountains

High pointy mountains
Challenging, climbing with friends
Peaceful scary tall
Spencer McCarty, Grade 2
St John's Episcopal School, TX

Heart

Heart —
Round, red, shiny —
Pumps
Alexis Molina, Grade 3
St Mary School, CA

Where I'm From
I am from running, jump roping, and walking.
I am from a deer running in the woods.
From a red bird flying around everywhere.
The daisies that are shining around a garden that is full.
I am from Grandma Lorenzano's homemade molé on a sparkly plate.
From Silvia and Coy to Jonita and to Pap Coy.
I am from brown eyes to my mother's family.
From "Don't forget to brush your teeth" and "Take a shower."
I am from the furry ferret that slips on the floor called Max.
I am from my grandma and grandpa.
I am from Silvia, Coy, Thiara, Alex, and Brandon, the one that makes me laugh.
I am from giving Dottie some milk when I was small.
I am from my grandma's song called 'Al La Nita.'

Yadeniza De La Rosa, Grade 3
Juliet Morris Elementary School, CA

Saule Baipsys

S unny, sparkly
A nd funny
U nder the blanket I hide.
L icks ice cream
E njoys puppies

B eautiful butterflies I see
A rts and crafts I love.
I lost my two front teeth!
P ink and purple I wear
S illy playing with my friends
Y ahoo, yahoo down the slide I go!
S ugar and spice and everything nice makes a girl like me.

Saule Baipsys, Grade 1
Kentwood Elementary School, CA

Percy Jackson*
A bad kid
Exploded a bus.
He has a sword,
That is really a pen.
He has a friend,
His name is Grover.

Isaac Finley, Grade 3
Thomas Edison Charter School - North, UT
*Inspired by the book "Percy Jackson"

Gabe

Gabriel
It means excited, lazy, and kind.
It is the number ten.
It is like fire.
It is going to Las Vegas and Disneyland.
It is the memory of my mom getting sprayed
While I was spray painting,
Who taught me to be a thinker and a risk taker
When she said to try new things.
My name is Gabriel.
It means to be the best.

Gabriel Soriano, Grade 2
Keone'ula Elementary School, HI

A Bird

A bird is soaring through the sky.
It flapped its wings and drifted high.

It landed on a tall and skinny tree.
So happy that it was finally free.

It hurried toward its babies' nest,
And not stopping a minute to rest.

They opened their tiny mouths to be fed.
They chirped a while and slowly went to bed.

Sophia Makarem, Grade 3
Hamlin Street Elementary School, CA

Popcorn

Pop, pop, pop
The popcorn is popping,
Mine has a caramel topping,
YUMMY!
Popcorn is very good too.
DING!
Oh! I think it's ready,
Wow! It even looks delicious,
CRUNCH, CRUNCH,
It tastes so good,
I love popcorn

Joy Kong, Grade 3
Wonderland Avenue Elementary School, CA

Reading

If you read,
You will feel a book is like a treasure
A book is like a magic carpet,
Because a book can take you wherever you want.

You can sit with the nights of the round table,
And fight with King Arthur.
You can dance with Beauty and the Beast,
And run through the woods with Robin Hood.
You can also fight Lord Voldemort,
With Harry Potter,
You can learn about his story.

You can cross,
The Delaware River with George Washington,
You can be in the civil war,
With Lincoln.

You can feel the scared feeling,
With Harriet Tubman.
You can live in a wagon,
On the Oregon Trail.

If you read,
You can go wherever you want.

Sophia Ebel, Grade 3
Wilchester Elementary School, TX

A New Fresh Day

It was a warm summer day but the rain was
dripping hard.
There were booms and crackles and booms all
over the dark gray sky.

There were little drops of rain dropping to the
ground landing gently on the pavement.

But as you gently go to sleep you'll see one thing
close your eyes and imagine a perfect dream.
When you wake up get out of bed and smell the
fresh air of a new fresh day.

Georgia Harper, Grade 3
Wilchester Elementary School, TX

Learning

Learning is fun
You might learn how to run.
You can learn math
You might learn it on a path.
If you have luck
You can learn how to train a duck.
You can be a zookeeper
You can learn how to use a car beeper.
If you are smart
You can learn how to throw a dart.
If you try
You might learn how to fly way up high.
You can learn how to play on any day
You might ask your friends and they will say no way.
You will keep on learning and learning.

Clare Arnold, Grade 3
St. Joseph Catholic School, CA

Sparkly Little Diamond

Sparkly little Diamond,
How you'd shine like the stars,
Up above so bright you'd be,
Like a Beauty that I'd smile.

Sparkly little Diamond,
How you'd light up my heart,
Up above over the sea,
Like a Rainbow you will fly.

Sparkly little Diamond,
How I wish for your kind,
Up above you will see,
Like Forever you'll be mine!

Jasmine Haji, Grade 1
Islamic School of Muslim Educational Trust, OR

School

School is fun, I love school
You can meet lots of kids
When you meet them and play with them
You get used to them and you can be friends forever

Talon Oechsner, Grade 2
Legacy Christian Academy, NM

Moon Light

Full moon light
Icy stream
Glistening in
The night,
As full moon
Whispered good
Night when glittering
Frost sat down,
Meadow diamonds glistened
In Full Moon light.

Elizabeth Cerna, Grade 2
Sierra Hills Elementary School, CA

Love!

Love is many things
like a recipe
with,
hope, peace, and happiness.
Love is not mean,
bad or rude.
Love is nice,
forgiving, and peaceful.
Love is like being in heaven.
Love is fantastic!

Peyton Nichols, Grade 3
Wilchester Elementary School, TX

Bright Night

Trees glittering
meadow white
I almost
thought it was paper
Moon still
bright, pond still
icy mountains
so bright
Snow flakes
I love snow

Emma Erickson, Grade 2
Sierra Hills Elementary School, CA

Pink

Pink is a rose.
Pink is a shirt.
Pink is pants.
Pink is socks.
Pink is a hat.
It is a flower.
It is paper and
an Easter egg.
Pink,
is a fantastic color.

Julia Meraji, Grade 3
Wilchester Elementary School, TX

My Pet Dogs

My pet dogs
are so cool.
They walk around
the pool.
They really need
to go to school.
But that's just not
the rule.

Not at my school!

Collin Cartwright, Grade 1
St Mark's Day School, TX

Camp Allen

C abin in the trees
A t the lake we canoe
M ake my sleeping bag cozy
P lates on the table

A nts
L eaves
L emonade
E ggs of a snake
N ature

Sarah Lehmann, Grade 3
Kingwood Montessori School, TX

Cats

Cats taste like fur,
Soft and cute.
Cats feel like velvet,
Smooth and warm.
Cats smell like shampoo,
Strawberry and cream.
Cats look like love,
Cuddly and adorable.
Cats sound like soft voices,
Quiet and lovely.
Sophia Fernandez, Grade 2
Round Rock Christian Academy, TX

My Favorite Part of Me!

My favorite part of me
My face!
Smooth face
Tan in summer
Smells like perfume
Teeth so white
Smiley person
So beautiful
My favorite part of me
My face!
Kimberly Rodriguez, Grade 3
Los Medanos Elementary School, CA

Cheetahs

Cheetahs smell like danger,
Powerful and ferocious.
Cheetahs taste like fur,
Soft and fluffy.
Cheetahs feel like velvet,
Plush and thick.
Cheetahs sound like tigers,
Loud and wild.
Cheetahs look like wild cats,
Prowling and fast.
Shahan Perera, Grade 2
Round Rock Christian Academy, TX

BFF

Hey, you wanna be best friends?
My mom has one
And it might be your mom.
I love my BFF.
They are good
We might be forever
And it might be for me
It might be for you, JP and me
We are best friends forever
You should try it too.
Quinton McIver, Grade 1
Legacy Christian Academy, NM

A Lonely Play Ground

An empty swing set
begging for someone,
to swing,
a slide going around and around
waiting for someone to go down,
A football sitting waiting
for boys to pick him up
and play,
A lonely playground.
Will you play?

Sophia Early, Grade 3
Wilchester Elementary School, TX

Apples

Apples look like a big cherry,
Red and sweet.
Apples feel like the moon,
Smooth and round.
Apples smell like food,
Fresh and crisp.
Apples taste like juice,
Nice and yummy.
Apples sound like fruit
Crunchy and ripe.
Mia Kemp, Grade 2
Round Rock Christian Academy, TX

Spring

Spring is here!
The flowers are beautiful,
blooming so bright.

The wind on the wavering
trees is so light.
Breezes cooing the water
in the rivers and lakes.

People camping and fishing
through spring break.
The warmth which makes the
birds come back and sing.

The warmth that makes the
plants grow in the sunlight.
The warmth that makes the
animals come back.

Children play in the parks.
Emily Zhang, Grade 3
Spring Creek Elementary School, WY

Spring

Spring is here the leaves are green and
The birds are chirping with each
Their own tune.
The grass is greener than
All the seasons.

When the day starts you see the sun rise
And when the day ends you see it set.
Flowers bloom right in front of you.
The water is as blue as the sky,
And you feel a warm breeze on your face.

All the rocks sparkle and the river flows,
It's not too hot or cold.

You know spring is here,
And you know it's perfect!
Sam Hanszen, Grade 3
Wilchester Elementary School, TX

I Wish Bullies Would Stop

I know I don't,
I know I won't.
Sometimes
They don't,
And something they
Won't.
I just wish
They would stop.
Sometimes
They stop,
Sometimes
They don't.
Some won't ever stop.
Some are bullies,
Some are not.
I just wish
They would stop!
But they never will…
Sometimes I hate it,
Sometimes I don't.
Joshua Kathrein, Grade 3
Warren Elementary School, OR

I am a Cheetah!

Roar! Crash! Thump!
I am fighting my enemy.

Shhh… Wham! Crunch!
I am hunting a deer.

Chomp! Chomp! Yum-yum!
I am devouring my food.

Grrr… Hew… Belch!
I am sleeping under the tree.

Prrr! Prrr! Prrr!
I am playing with my friends.

Swish! Swish! Swish!
I am running through the grass.
Suzie Choi, Grade 3
Juliet Morris Elementary School, CA

The Ocean

Oh the ocean,
the calm, soothing ocean,
the waves crash,
then slither up the beach,
like a snake creeping up on its prey.

The ocean, oh the ocean,
the white crest of waves
looks like ice, for a snow cone.
The ocean can rock you to sleep
like the best lullaby there ever is.
Far out in the distance
the gulls circle around a shrimp boat.
The waves, the gulls and the wind through the palm trees
is the perfect place to be
(at least to me!!!)

The ocean, oh the ocean,
my special ocean
(also known as the Pacific!!!)

Alexandra Lorentzatos, Grade 3
Wilchester Elementary School, TX

Sun Souls

The nature above us is the sun souls
We know the sun soul is very good for us
The plants are good and nature sings about the sun souls
Angels sing to the sun soul within us
In the place of harmony the sun is true with nature
Within our hearts we know when we can pray to the sun to go to another land
Here comes the night
We dream waiting for the sun souls
We know we can be so good when we see the sun
The sun we know is very good
The sun souls know so many things
We pray to sun souls because we know things are known to sun souls
Sun, sun, please don't go where we can't see you
Please stay here and let us feel you
Please stay when it is night, stay when it is day
Stay all night and stay all day
When you are not there stay, stay in my heart

Emma Wallenfels, Grade 2
Dixie Sun Elementary School, UT

War

It's loud with bombs bursting in the air,
Guns firing at the enemy,
Explosions from the weapons,
And then America wins!
Caleb Litz, Grade 3
Old Town Elementary School, TX

Shark

Shark —
Big, strong, scary —
Swimming
Closely, quickly, yesterday
Ronaldo Flores, Grade 3
St Mary School, CA

Macaroni

Macaroni
Pink feet, white belly
Catching, swimming, fishing
Males take care of the baby.
Trinity Simons, Grade 2
Robinson Elementary School, TX

Love

Love is when everybody hugs.
Love is when my dad plays with me.
Love is when my mom reads to me.
Love is the best!
Amelie Sato-Veillon, Grade 1
Woodcrest School, CA

Rainy Day

At school it was rainy.
Everybody got wet.
When we went to lunch,
We ran the whole way.
Joseph Flores, Grade 3
Three Rivers Elementary School, TX

Golden Retrievers

Golden Retrievers are my favorite pet.
They fetch the ball whenever you throw it.
They bring the ball back.
Golden Retrievers are really fun.
Dylan Farnsworth, Grade 1
Troy Elementary School, OR

Rain

Rain is so wet
That you get soaked
We like to play
In the rain.
Marcus Bryant, Grade 3
Three Rivers Elementary School, TX

Spring

The water sparkles
In the river
On this spring day
Rainbows in the sky
Mila Sayers, Grade 2
Whale Gulch Elementary School, CA

Crow

Crow —
Black, flies, lands —
Eats
Lives here
Jonathan Lopez, Grade 3
St Mary School, CA

Rose

Rose —
Pretty, lovely, lavender —
Blooming
Often, slowly, everywhere
Inna Tagarino, Grade 3
St Mary School, CA

Waves

Many ocean waves
Crystal clear and powerful
Crash against the shore

Eli Heyman, Grade 3
Wonderland Avenue Elementary School, CA

Worms

Slimy and squishy
Are inches long and dig deep
Very gross and weird

Damian Rangel, Grade 3
Lorenzo De Zavala Elementary School, TX

Books

I like books they are so cool.
You learn about animals
There is different kinds of books you can learn about people.

Liwa Kurtzman, Grade 2
John Cabrillo Elementary School, CA

Video Games

Win, play, and have fun
That's what it's all about
A really good time

Justice Hudson, Grade 3
Lorenzo De Zavala Elementary School, TX

Flag

Need to give respect
Not to throw away in trash
Fold a certain way

Cody Lowell, Grade 3
Lorenzo De Zavala Elementary School, TX

George Washington

The first president
A very good commander
Intelligent man

Robert Penafiel, Grade 3
Lorenzo De Zavala Elementary School, TX

Charge!

I am energetic as a tiger,
bold as a thorn bush,
tough as the color fire red,
calm as a sphere,
cheerful as the number 10,000,
kind as platinum,
and honest as tiny flames.
Jeffrey Eng, Grade 1
Baldwin Stocker Elementary School, CA

Honest Tyler

I am friendly as a happy monkey,
funny as a cherry tree,
happy as the color fire red,
honest as a ice cream cone,
proud as the number one,
sloppy as a blue diamond,
and trusting as green grass.
Tyler Shang, Grade 1
Baldwin Stocker Elementary School, CA

Christine the Expert

I am fast as a tiger,
sweet as a pink rose,
entertaining as the color rose pink,
honest as a rectangle,
friendly as the number five,
interesting as a diamond,
and gentle as air.
Christine Law, Grade 1
Baldwin Stocker Elementary School, CA

Erik Is Cool

I am brave as a bear,
friendly as a vine,
funny as the color blue,
patient as a hexagon,
tough as the number 200,
curious as a garnet,
and shy as flat land.
Erik Lopez, Grade 1
Baldwin Stocker Elementary School, CA

Benny

My dog Benny is a Bichon Frise.
His fur is as white as snow,
Eyes as black as the midnight sky,
With a real heart of gold.

My dog Benny is very loyal,
He follows me everywhere.
Egypt, France, Brazil, England,
Wales, and even Africa, too!

My dog Benny is very sweet,
He'd never hurt a fly.
Eats only dog food,
With treats, too!

My dog Benny is a very good dog.
He loves my family very much.
Every day he gives me kisses,
With lots and lots of love.
Rachel Harsley, Grade 3
Wilchester Elementary School, TX

New School

Big school,
I don't know this school.
It's a science school.
I think I am in
a college
I am scared.
I have never been
to a college before.
Never
in my life.
I don't know what to do.
My body
is trembling
like an earthquake
Phew!
It was just
a dream!
Leslie Gomez, Grade 2
Robert L Stevens Elementary School, CA

Spring

Spring is finally here!
I can see my pets are happy!
I can hear chipmunks squeaking.
I can smell horses all around me.
I can taste a cake.
I feel happy.

Kristina Bagdasaryan, Grade 2
Woodcrest School, CA

Bo

I have a fish named Bo.
He lives in a bowl.
When I see him wiggle
It makes me giggle.
He's the best pet
A girl could ever get!

Presley Looney, Grade 3
St James Episcopal School, TX

The Dog

Gladly,
Happily,
Honestly,
The dog
Chased the cat.
— Cool!

Christopher Boyd, Grade 1
Fir Grove Elementary School, OR

Sun

Sun —
Sunny, shiny, hot —
Floats
Air, Milky Way, Often

Kaci Peeler, Grade 3
St Mary School, CA

I Love Soccer

I hate tennis balls
I hate baseballs too and bats
I like soccer balls

Shoaib Ishaq, Grade 3
Salam Academy, NM

The Cowgirl

Gladly,
Gracefully,
Happily,
The cowgirl kissed
Her husband.
— Gross!

Jayellen Slone, Grade 1
Fir Grove Elementary School, OR

Spring

S pring
P eople
R evel in
I t
N ature gives us
G rass

Logan Spencer, Grade 2
Cache Valley Learning Center, UT

Sports

S ports rock
P eople play a lot of sports
O n holidays sports are on TV
R evenge is pretty fun in sports
T ell people to watch sports
S ports can help you

Peter Gonzalez, Grade 3
St Aloysius Parochial School, CA

The Star

I saw a star
from my car
late at night
so shiny and bright!

Devin Martinez, Grade 1
St Mark's Day School, TX

Dolphins

Dolphins jump in air.
Dolphins live in water.
I like them a lot.

Promise Noble, Grade 2
Robinson Elementary School, TX

Rain and Storms
Rain comes
People get scared
They get their mom
Wind comes, sunlight,
When you go to bed
It is midnight.
Jessica Rodriguez, Grade 3
Three Rivers Elementary School, TX

Princess
I like to be a princess.
I like to be cute.
Dancing,
Shopping,
Dressing up.
That's my hobby.
Julian Forte, Grade 1
Longfellow Elementary School, TX

Blue
Blue is the color of the sky.
Blue is the color of the sea.
Blue is the color of a ball.
Blue is the color of shoes.
Blue is the color of a Jolly Rancher.
Blue.
Natalya Alvera, Grade 1
Heritage Elementary School, UT

God's Things
I love trees,
Especially in the fall with leaves,
And these are God's Things.
I love leaves in the summer,
When the sun shines through.
I love God's things.
Caleb Matthews, Grade 2
Home School, OR

White Winter Days
Snowflakes fall in the winter mist.
All is calm, all is bliss.
Winter pastries
Go here and there,
Winter white,
Love is in the air.
Sophia Tiche, Grade 3
Marguerite Hahn Elementary School, CA

Kaiden
Kaiden is my little brother
He laughs
He likes people
My little brother is cute
He likes me and he plays with me
He is my little brother
Madison Welch, Kindergarten
Legacy Christian Academy, NM

Building
Building —
Brown, big, wide —
Stuck
Here, still, every day
Jesse Katz, Grade 3
St Mary School, CA

Star
Star —
Big, pointy, shiny —
Shines
Up, at night, brightly
Laraba Pizano, Grade 3
St Mary School, CA

Robots
Robots can serve you
Robots must be very smart
Robots can protect you
Jack Giddings, Grade 3
Ygnacio Valley Christian School, CA

see the plants
see as the plants grow
it is an amazing thing
it's magnificent
Seth Richardson, Grade 3
Wasatch Elementary School, UT

A Man's Best Friend

There is a friend so marvelous
He's a man's best friend
He gives me kisses and pushes me to
The ground

There is a friend so sweet
I can't bare to leave
But I might have to leave him
When I'm 19

I go hunting and fishing with him
He goes for the Doves
He jumps into the lake for the
Fish

He used to nip and bite
But not anymore
I trained him well and swell

He protects me from robbers
Bites him so hard
He calls the pound
Do not take him he was protecting me
A man's best friend is bigger than a house
And at school he's my inspiration.
Madison Dunbar, Grade 3
Wilchester Elementary School, TX

Spiders

Spiders,
I like spiders.
They are like
leaves falling
to the ground.
Hairy spiders,
Creepy spiders,
Shiny, black spiders,
I like them all.
They are like
leaves falling
to the ground.
Alex Ramirez, Grade 2
Robert L Stevens Elementary School, CA

Jake

Once a long time ago
in a place where they get snow,
I had a bird named Jake
a lot of noise he'd make.

Across the cage he would hop
then all of a sudden he'd stop.
In front of his mirror to see
and looked at himself with glee.

Sometimes Jake would get angry and bite
but not with all of his might.
This meant he was on edge
so he'd move away to his ledge.

When he felt safe in his home
he sat still and looked like a gnome.
He still does this nowadays
but in many different ways.
Caroline Bizarro, Grade 3
C W Cline Elementary School, TX

Noise

Hi
Bang!
Zoom!
Crash!
WOW!
Zeem!
Cool!
Beep!
Pin!
Pong!
Thhhh!
Ahhhh!
Ka-Boom!
Click!
Pang!
Pop!
Kling-Klang-cch!
That is Noise!
A. Brooks, Grade 3
Connally Elementary School, TX

Fake Information

I built a fake computer
Dad said that it would work

I tried to type a file
It didn't seem to work

I saved the file and I confess
I tried out all the rest
Life is a test

Is this friend or foe?
I'm mad from head to toe!

I open it up —
Where's the info?
Elizabeth Wyatt, Grade 3
Aveson Charter School, CA

Angel

My daddy is an angel
Watching over me
My daddy is an angel
Cute and cuddly
I miss him so much
That's why I'm singing this song
My daddy is an angel
Forever all along
My daddy is an angel
Can't you see that he's not gone
He's here in my heart
He's here in my mind
He's right behind me all of the time
I know this is true because I have faith
In *you*
Matthew Roth, Grade 3
Warren Elementary School, OR

Growing Crops

First you dig a hole put the seeds
in the hole then water it.
They grow.
Mark Gentry, Grade 3
Three Rivers Elementary School, TX

Mittens

My first cat —
Mittens.

You were as cute as a button,
Mittens.

You were soft and cuddly,
Mittens.

Sorry I lost you —
Still love you,
Mittens.

I got another cat
But you are my favorite,
Mittens.

You'll always be
My favorite cat,
Mittens.

You'll always be #1,
Mittens.
Claire Clauson, Grade 3
C W Cline Elementary School, TX

In the Jungle

The sun is fun
The sky is blue
The jungle is green
And beautiful too.

It rains in the jungle
And animals run
When they get all wet
They have real fun!

When the sun goes down,
The animals go
To find their beds because
They are slow.
Celestina Craft, Grade 3
Goethe International Charter School, CA

Spring

Spring, spring, spring is here,
It brings a lot of happy cheer.
I love the spring the way it shimmers,
I love the spring the way it glimmers.
I love the spring 'cause as they say,
The bumble bees come out to play.
From their nests and from their hives,
They all come when the day arrives.
I love the spring, I love the sun,
I love the trees when the day is done.
As the sun dies down through the trees far away,
I think to myself what a wonderful day.

Emma Matthews, Grade 3
Home School, OR

We Were Walking in the Fields

Once upon a time
there were a mallard, a widgeon, a chukar, a hun, and one gecko.
All five of them
were walking in the field.
They wanted to go
to the mallard's nest.
They had fun
playing there.
They spent the night
at the mallard's nest.
Then they all
went to their homes.

Julian Rich, Kindergarten
Troy Elementary School, OR

Beautiful Land

I walk with the soft grass beneath my feet
I look around to see a pond that shimmers in the sun
I feel the soft breeze against my face and the field around me
The trees rustle in the wind
A flock of birds pass by
I listen to their wings as they flutter
I see clouds wandering in the sky and the sun so bright yellow
I see the fawns eating grass minding their own business
I think of the animals that live here and the beautiful land

Isabelle Brown, Grade 3
Coeur d'Alene Avenue Elementary School, CA

Apple on the Tree

Apple, apple on the tree
How happy can our life be?
Apple, apple on the tree
How happy can you be?
Apple, apple on the tree
Me and you are best friends
Happy birthday little tree
Happy birthday apple tree
Madison Opp, Grade 2
Legacy Christian Academy, NM

My Favorite Part of Me!

My favorite part of me
My index finger!
Bright yellow polish
Wrinkly in water
Points at people
Writes a poem
My favorite part of me
My index finger!
Suman Singh, Grade 3
Los Medanos Elementary School, CA

Dreaming of Penguins

When I dream of penguins
I think of their beautiful eyes
Also, their funny fat wings and stomach
To glide on icy ice!
Little orange flippers
Help them flop around!
I think penguins are so cute
How about you?
Uzoulu Obijiofor, Grade 3
Mission Bend Christian Academy, TX

Lizard

I know my lizard
Scratching his cage at night,
Digging in the sand at night,
His tail hitting the cage
I know my lizard
Jumping
Tan bumpy skin
I know my lizard
Austin Howard, Grade 3
Horn Academy, TX

Ode to Flowers

Dear Flowers,
I like it how you're here and there
now and then
I wish you would stay forever
and ever
and even in wintertime
high in the sky.
Your Friend
Danielle Archuleta, Grade 3
Henry Haight Elementary School, CA

Christmas

D ecember is my favorite month.
E verything I buy is nice.
C hristmas is in December.
E lves come in December.
M y birthday is on December 19.
B eing good is better.
E ating food at peoples' houses is fun.
R unning in the snow is fun.
Ghalib Abdulla, Grade 3
Midland Elementary School, CA

My Brother

I love my brother.
He has a band in school.
He likes to play football.
I wish I was like him,
Someone to be admired.
Abishek Iyengar, Kindergarten
Scholars Academy, CA

The Lion

The lion, it is fast, strong, and dangerous.
It is used to killing, running, and eating.
It is a mammal that roars.
It is a carnivore.
And is a great animal.
Sanjit Shirol, Kindergarten
Scholars Academy, CA

Volleyball

She furiously tosses the ball to me,
I jump for the ball and miss
For the fifteenth time.
I groan with frustration —
I think, I may as well stop now.
I hear the other team
Cheering with enthusiasm —
They found their weakness: me!
She throws the ball.
"I got it!" I howl.
Someone shoves me out of the way,
And makes me land flat on the floor.
I feel like I am in the middle of a bull ring —
Hurt, embarrassed, and perplexed.
I run and sit down,
Crystals sliding down my cheek.
I'm not crying because it hurts,
I'm crying because I am useless
Just like a cockroach.
I can't quit the team because…
I want to make history in volleyball.

Lexi Facundo, Grade 3
D P Morris Elementary School, TX

Brave as a Lion

Bold as an eagle
A symbol of peace
Martin Luther King Jr.
One of the symbols of the Civil Rights Movement

Strong as a rhino
Rosa Parks was a woman who fought for equality
The most famous symbol of the Montgomery Bus Boycott

Brave as a lion
Ruby Bridges, an African American,
Who went to an all white school

Knowing of these three African Americans
And their courage and bravery
We appreciate what is on the inside, not out.

Alexander Stern, Grade 2
Laurence School, CA

Books

Books are good for your mind.
They're fun to read too!
I love to read, how about you?
It's fun to read, you learn
At your beginning. It's fun
Being read to, along with solo read.

All books have subjects, or
Main ideas.
Fiction is fun, oh, yes.
Nonfiction can be dull
Biographies are exciting,
Poems too!

Reading is part of language arts.
You do it at school, you do it at home.
You do it...

EVERYWHERE!!! "YAY!" you shout.
You read another book. "NOOO!" the book
Cries as you SLAM it shut.
WHAM! It sounds like a door.
"Mom! My book sounds like a door!"
BOOKS are amazing things.

Benjamin Burnham, Grade 3
Wilchester Elementary School, TX

Ursa Major

I am big and brown, but clear
looking down out of the sky.
My two nicknames are "Spoon" and "Bear."
Call me either one.
I roar from the black abyss of the sky.
Do not worry.
I can't leave my spot, even if I want to.
I protect my cub, Ursa Minor.
I am an enormous compass in the sky.
Look for a spoon in the heavens
before you go to bed.
That is me...
Ursa Major

Genevieve Paugh, Grade 3
Saigling Elementary School, TX

NAOMI

N ever get enough to eat.
A lways do my best!
O nly I want to be a teacher.
M aybe I can do better!
I love you so much!

If I
used only
two words
on each
line to
describe me,
here's what
those words
would be:
Sings songs,
Reads books,
Eats treats,
Loves mama,
Hugs daddy —
That's me!
Naomi Fox, Kindergarten
Woodcrest School, CA

Being Healthy

I had a friend who drank coke.
I saw him smoke.
This is bad, so please
do what I say.

Please, don't do what my friend did
and you'll have a good day.
Especially if you're a kid

Parents watch what you do,
or it's coming to boo hoo!

Please be healthy
and not wealthy!
Don't go the wrong way,
then you'll have a great day!
Haven McKay, Grade 3
Foothill School, UT

The War

Don't go near!
I'm telling you
It's not a lie.
We fight for our freedom

We fight for our lives!
Some of us die,
Some of us survive.
We fight for our country,
And for our families
And our loved ones.
We fight for our state
And everyone.
We scare our opponents away.

No more fighting —
No more, no way
We have our freedom,
We should stop and be friends.
We should all get along.
We're on the same planet.
Let's all get along.
Addison Carter, Grade 3
D P Morris Elementary School, TX

Little Sister, Little Sister

Little sister,
Little sister,
Crying all night!
Waking
Me up at
Two o'clock!
Saying that her
Stomach hurts,
Making me
Mad!
All night
Long
She
Says
"Mommy!"
Haley Hubbard, Grade 3
C W Cline Primary School, TX

Butterflies

Butterflies are colorful
They blend with colors
They land on flowers
They soar through the air
Butterflies have wings
That,
Flies like birds
What a view to see
Christine Chacko, Grade 1
P H Greene Elementary School, TX

Baseball

My favorite sport is baseball,
Because it's lots of fun!
The Astros are my team
And we score lots of runs.
I hit the ball, and run real fast!
Around the bases I soar!
They didn't tag me out, and so
We win 'cause we scored more.
Nolan Beck, Grade 3
Providence Hall Charter School, UT

Spring

It's spring. It's spring.
And what do we see?
We see rainbow ponies
As pretty as can be.
It's spring. It's spring.
And what do we see?
We see yellow fish
Swimming by me.
Nour Elzarou, Grade 1
Woodcrest School, CA

Barbies

I love my Barbies
You can dress them
You can take them everywhere.
They are pretty!
You can buy them a house
I love them very much.
They are very fun
Why does my cousin dislike them?
Dini Villagordoa, Grade 3
St John's Episcopal Day School, TX

Spring Time

Butterflies in the air,
lizards in the trees.
Birds chirping and flying around,
squirrels jumping tree to tree.
People away on spring vacation
having a lot of fun.
Spring time is really fun,
a spring time is a fun time.
Brandon Hancock, Grade 3
Wilchester Elementary School, TX

A Snowy Night

Meadow is white
Branches are white
White grounds
Frozen ponds
Moon shining its light
Stars are twinkling bright
Smokes rises from chimneys
Mountains are frosty.
Katie Neal, Grade 2
Sierra Hills Elementary School, CA

Spring

Spring is warm.
Spring is flowers.
Spring is bugs.
Spring is blue sky.
Spring is happy.
Benjamin Meibos, Grade 1
Cache Valley Learning Center, UT

Spring

Spring is flowers.
Spring is grass.
Spring is warm.
Spring is rain.
Spring is swimming.
Frankie Hinkle, Grade 1
Cache Valley Learning Center, UT

If I Were an Animal...

If I were an animal
A dog I would be.
I'd be so sweet and gentle,
Everybody would love me.

Every day I'd go for walks.
I would always jump and play.
I would live in a long apartment,
And I'd run around all day.
Eden-Rose Baker, Grade 2
Woodcrest School, CA

Christmas

C hristmas is my favorite holiday.
H appy families celebrate.
R eindeer are magical.
I t's a perfect present.
S anta gives you lots of toys.
T he elves
M ake the toys.
A t Christmas you enjoy family.
S inging is fun at Christmas
Brianne Schott, Grade 3
St Aloysius Parochial School, CA

Sweet, Sweet, Sweet

Oh, I love candy!
From lollipops to ringpops
Gummy worms to gummy bears –
they're both animals you see!
Candy's made for you and me.
Joe Simon, Grade 3
Annunciation Orthodox School, TX

Nachos

N on gross
A wesome
C heesy
H ot
O fficial
S uper good things
Parker Davidson, Grade 3
Horn Academy, TX

Hawaii*

Ocean waves crashing
against rocks.
Birds chirp everywhere.
Kids giggle
and play.
This place
brings joy
to everyone.
Jacob Lambert, Grade 3
Old Town Elementary School, TX
*Dedicated to my sister Ella Grace

Hyper Dogs

Hyper dogs
sleep on mats.
Hyper dogs
chase all cats.

Hyper dogs
like to whine.
Hyper dogs
they are mine!
Jayden Johnson, Grade 1
St Mark's Day School, TX

Lonely

I
quietly sleep
in the
sandy Egyptian country
alone
Walter Hlavinka, Grade 2
Annunciation Orthodox School, TX

Sun

Sun
So shiny and
Bright
So nice
The absolute
Best
Max Lee, Grade 1
P H Greene Elementary School, TX

Cheetahs

Devouring my food.
Chomp, chomp!

Running by cats and dogs.
Zoom!

Attack with a mean panther!
Thud, scratch, roar, chomp!

Running across the world!
Foosh!

Now my cubs are near me.
Purr, purr!
Zachary Riggins, Grade 3
Juliet Morris Elementary School, CA

Responsibility

R is for reading books
E is for eating your lunch
S is for saying please
P is for playing nicely
O is for obeying
N is for nice work
S is for super
I is for I like being nice
B is for being happy
I is for improvising
L is for learning
I is for intelligent
T is for trying new things
Y is for Yes!!
Alessandro Fisslinger, Grade 3
Goethe International Charter School, CA

Spring

Spring
Beautiful, wonderful
Planting, caring, growing
I love bright flowers
Easter
Madi Christian, Grade 3
Ygnacio Valley Christian School, CA

Pinkland

I heard of Pinkland far away
And couldn't wait to see
What would it be like
And what would there be?

Pink ice cream flowing everywhere.
There are pink trees and plants,
The sky and the birds and people
And rosy little ants.

There are eleven pink hippos
And I am almost finished
Strawberries, hair, and grass
And don't forget the spinach!
Allison Wheeler, Grade 1
Home School, ID

Roar!

I sleep under the trees.
Snore! Snore!

I eat my prey.
Chomp! Chomp!

I run away from my predator.
Swish! Swish!

I have a fight with a lion.
Scratch! Roar! Thud!

I hear wind howling.
Ooh! Ooh!
Laasya Kadiyala, Grade 3
Juliet Morris Elementary School, CA

Football

Football
Fun, entertaining
Running, sweating, tackling
Football is very awesome
Sport
Sam Kamp, Grade 3
Ygnacio Valley Christian School, CA

Balls of Rock

I am a bold and rocky sight to see
Even though I have an orbit,
    I am still very destructive
A belt between Mars and Jupiter is where I live
One of my friends plunged down to Earth and
    supposedly killed the dinosaurs
People believe I am parts of planets that did not make it
I get fancied up in rock and metal every day
You can't see me from Earth because I dance in an
    orbit a planet away from yours
I lumber through space like a sleepy hippo
An asteroid — a rocky asteroid — is what I am!

Mackenzie Alpert, Grade 3
Saigling Elementary School, TX

Yellow Is My Cup of Tea

Yellow is a balloon, and it's the sight of puss in a tomb,
I am hungry,
Please, pass the sunflower seeds,
Hey guys! Let's look at the sun,
Come on people, let's have some fun!
Yellow is the color of SpongeBob,
And also the bread on a corndog,
Yellow is the color of marshmallow Peeps,
And those make you get yellow teeth,
Yellow is the color of a highlighter,
That will set your mind on fire,
And that is yellow to me!

Evan Crow, Grade 3
Marguerite Hahn Elementary School, CA

Morning

Clock screams as its alarm goes off.
Sun jumps as he comes up in the morning.
Sky looks as Sun comes up.
Clothes laugh as you put them on.
Pancakes squirm as you put them in your mouth.
Coffee yells as you gulp it.
Trucks grumble as you drive in them.
Stop lights swing as you come to a stop.
Work smiles as you go through the door.

Ezra Sargent, Grade 3
CLASS Academy, OR

Hopping Grasshopper
The grasshopper hops
on the big, big green tree leaf
stopping to see me!

His eyes look at me,
and he is wondering now,
who are you nice girl?

After a short while,
I say my name is Regan,
and I am in first.

Then, he seems to smile,
and hops closer to my hand
and this makes me jump!

We have become friends
this very sunny Friday
and we go hopping along!
Regan Hoblet, Grade 1
False Pass School, AK

Dogs and Cats
Dogs and cats chase and run
Grrr, meow, grrrr, meow!
Dogs and cats make a big mess,
Smash, crackle, boom!
Dogs and cats eat all day,
Crunch, munch, crunch!
Dogs and cats sleep the day away,
Zzzz, zzzz, zzzz!
Dogs and cats run all the time,
Whoosh, whoosh, whoosh!
Dogs and cats leap and jump,
Plop, hop, plop!
Dogs and cats race inside the house,
Prrr, grrr, prrr, grrr!
Dogs and cats scrape on the tile,
Scratch, scratch, scratch!
Dogs and cats time for bed,
Snore, zzzz, snore!
Matthew Sheppard, Grade 3
Round Rock Christian Academy, TX

The Monkish
The skinny brown monkish
is as weird as can be.
It looks like a monkey
but lives in the sea.
The monkish has stripes
and it is very cool.
It likes to play
around in the pool.
The monkish are
very cool and rare.
They don't like
their predators, the bear.
Oriel Nottea, Grade 3
Woodcrest School, CA

The Purple-Winged Ocelot
The purple-winged ocelot,
is a strange little creature.
It's actually so cool,
that is it's best feature!
The purple-winged ocelot,
feeds on its prey.
It sleeps through the winter,
then comes out to play.
It's so very happy,
like a happy little cloud.
Its mommy and daddy,
are so very proud.
Katrina Hornsby, Grade 3
Woodcrest School, CA

Butterfly
B utterflies are pretty
U nderneath the sky
T hey like to soar high
T hey are impossible to catch
E very butterfly is different
R avens eat them
F lying south like the birds
L oving flowers for their nectar
Y earning for freedom
Emily Lang, Grade 3
Dixie Sun Elementary School, UT

Polar Bear
fluffy
powerful, playful
killing, hunting, eating
huge, fighting, licking, strong
Bear
Hakeem Alsamma, Grade 3
Henry Haight Elementary School, CA

Olga
Friend
black hair
giving, playing, loving
I like her.
Olga.
Charlotta Truscott, Grade 1
Heritage Elementary School, UT

Waves
The sound of waves crashing
against the beautiful rocks.
The smell is fresh coral.
The taste is salty sea water.
The texture is smooth sleek water.
Bailey Schimerowski, Grade 3
Meadow Lark Elementary School, MT

Whale
W ith a big tail, it makes big waves.
H uge with an amazing sight.
A huge spout.
L ong whale that is amazing.
E lephant's size but bigger.
Conor Barres, Grade 3
Keone'ula Elementary School, HI

The Strange Pen
One day I saw a pen.
It said, "Hello there, Jen."
I asked "Who are you?"
He said "My name's Lou."
I never walked that way again.
Abbey Walker, Grade 3
Providence Hall, UT

Tylan
Friend
small, boy
laughing, playing, smiling
He is funny
Tylan
Kade Terry, Grade 1
Heritage Elementary School, UT

Ammon Olsen
A very curious kid
M aking trouble everywhere
M aking his sister miserable
O n her nerves every day
N ot liking his little sister
Ammon Olsen, Grade 3
Foothill School, UT

Baby
Baby
little, kind
funny, cute, playing
She is copying me.
Sadee.
Tylan Thompson, Grade 1
Heritage Elementary School, UT

Seal
Pup
White, nice
Playing, swimming, fishing
It is cute!
Seal
Sive Thompson, Grade 1
Heritage Elementary School, UT

Dog
Dog
black, white
playful, thirsty, happy
fun to be around
Cooge
Molly Bercutt, Grade 3
Goethe International Charter School, CA

A Butterfly

At first she's an egg and next a caterpillar;
then a chrysalis.
She turns into a monarch butterfly.
The monarch likes to fly high.
She goes to my house,
and sees a flower.

Jordan Harvey, Kindergarten
Notre Dame Academy Elementary School, CA

Fire and Ice

Fire
Big, orange
Moving, burning, smelling
Flames, light, ice cubes, freezer
Shiny, blue
Ice

Logan Mckee, Grade 2
Tracy Learning Center - Primary Charter School, CA

On Christmas

Santa was putting presents under the Christmas tree.
To get them, I needed to really bend my knee.
When it was opened there was a toy.
I was really, truly, full of joy.
On Christmas Day, when I woke up I heard Santa's sleigh bell
I couldn't believe that he gave me presents. I nearly fell.

Leon Bui, Grade 3
Oak Park Elementary School, CA

Homes for All

People should not cut down trees.
People should give food and homes to the homeless.
Give adequate homes to people who do not have homes.
We all need a good home.

Tosa Odiase, Kindergarten
Notre Dame Academy Elementary School, CA

Trees

Trees are big and green
Home to many animals
Bloom in only spring

Mariah Hu, Grade 3
Tracy Learning Center - Primary Charter School, CA

Water

Water tastes like nothing,
Plain and hydrating!
Water looks like waves,
Fizzy and vizzy!
Water smells very, very original,
Stainless and odorless!
Water feels like drip — drop — plop,
Soft and wet!
Water sounds like liquid crashing,
Swish, swesh, sweep, swash!

Alexander Chaiken, Grade 2
Round Rock Christian Academy, TX

Gallon to Gallon

Walking and walking,
with heavy gallons as heavy as the world.
Drinking and drinking,
dirty water.
Getting sicker
and facing death.
Coming together
to build a well.
Feel the happiness
from all the children.

Addison Cook, Grade 3
Wilchester Elementary School, TX

Friend

My friend
left me.
My body
is not smiling.
My head
can't stop
thinking of
my friend.
I feel
like I'm dreaming.

Israel Camacho, Grade 2
Robert L Stevens Elementary School, CA

Zachary

Zachary
It means smart, funny and creative.
It is the number 10.
It is the color of the ocean.
It is watching movies and eating popcorn.
It is the memory of dad
Who taught me to respect and help others
When he helped fix someone's car.
My name is Zachary.
It means to be creative and helpful.

Zachary Smartt, Grade 2
Keone'ula Elementary School, HI

Caterpillar

You have bright
Green balls
When you're done
Eating
You'll turn into a
Butterfly
How nice you are
With all of those
Bright
Colors

Hira Tariq, Grade 1
P H Greene Elementary School, TX

Cuddly Bunnies

The sound and stillness of night
Twitching like a snake
The swiftness of a river
Dancing angels
A puffy pillow sitting on a mattress
A bow running across a violin
A snowflake cascading through the sky
A warm pizza in the oven
Gentle as a sunrise
Naughty as a child

McKenzie Mazur, Grade 3
Lolo Elementary School, MT

Bella

Her eyes are as black as the midnight sky.
Her black and white fur,
Is as fluffy as a cloud.

Her paws are soft and clean,
And the color of brown, as in brand new wood.

She is as pretty as a brand new blossom,
That just opened on a spring day.

She is gentle to everyone and everything.
It is like her heart is made of gold.
Bella is mine and will always be mine!

Carley Overbergen, Grade 3
Wilchester Elementary School, TX

Black and Blue Dancing

A bird singing merrily
A river meeting the sea
A pirate song
An Indian singing
A wolf howling
A silent scream
A lullaby
A blue and black snake dancing
I wish I was a blue and black snake dancing
I would rattle my tail like maracas
If anything bothered me I would hiss
I would roll in the wet mud
I wish I was a blue and black snake dancing

Camden Collings, Grade 2
Annunciation Orthodox School, TX

The Zoo

When I was at the zoo
I watched my two favorite animals,
A lion and tiger.
A storm came.
The lion roared.
The tiger roared.
The tiger and lion grrrr at the clouds.

Earnest Greene, Kindergarten
Notre Dame Academy Elementary School, CA

Mist of Love

Mist fills the air and sky.
Mist of love, mist of love.
Come see the mist of love.

In my bed I wait for mist to come my way.
Mist of love, mist of love.

I wait under the starry sky.
Stars twinkle from above.
Share the mist of love.

Maya Mackey, Grade 1
Wetmore Elementary School, TX

Awesome

I'm in the championship
There're 5 seconds left
It's tied up 2-2
Ronaldo passes to me
I get the ball
I shoot…Whoosh…
It's a goal!!!
The crowd is going wild
Yeaaaaahh
"Winston wake up!"…said my teacher Mr. Earl

Winston Rothermich, Grade 3
Wonderland Avenue Elementary School, CA

All About Me

David
It means funny, silly, and kind.
It is the number 16.
It is like broccoli.
It is a movie in the house.
It is the memory of my grandpa telling me a joke,
Who taught me to be funny and kind
When he used to tell me a funny joke.
My name is David
It means forgiveness

David Pavlicek, Grade 2
Keone'ula Elementary School, HI

Crystal

Crystal is clearer than you can see,
His eyes are shining down on me,

He was on earth,
Here with me,

But then he had to leave the one and only,
Family that loved him most.
Cullen Hannigan, Grade 3
Wilchester Elementary School, TX

A Very Happy Girl

I am a very happy girl,
I love my mom and dad.
I hate to be away from them,
Because it makes me sad.
But when they are away from me,
I know they're coming back,
To snuggle, cuddle, hug me and
My brothers Jake and Jack.
Ellie Powell, Grade 1
Reid School, UT

Spring

It's spring. It's spring.
And what do we see?
We see white puppies
Happy as can be.
It's spring. It's spring.
And what do we see?
We see blue birds
In a big tree.
Alexa Sotere, Grade 1
Woodcrest School, CA

Flute Music's Song

sunshine
love movie, trees swinging
underwater, seaweed
opera, heaven, decrease motion
bird singing
Audrey Moffet, Grade 2
Annunciation Orthodox School, TX

Silent Night

I could see the moon
It was a
　　Silent night.
I saw a
　　Full moon.
The snow was
　　Glittering
The snow
　　As white as sugar
Pine trees and mountains
are white.
Winter will
　　End soon.
Madeline Cramer, Grade 2
Sierra Hills Elementary School, CA

April

April is like the summer, and it
is cold and warm.
It sometimes snows in April, but
not much now today.
April is a month out of the twelve,
and it is one of the hot ones.
It is starting to get warm, so
we can go swimming.
It is warm outside in April, we
can wear shorts.
April is a good month and
it only lasts one time a year.
Aprils is very warm and I like April.
David Zhang, Grade 3
Spring Creek Elementary School, WY

Rain

Rain, rain
Never go away!
I won't be happy
If you go away!
If you flood the school
I will be so happy
We won't have to do a thing
Matthew Wieding, Grade 3
Three Rivers Elementary School, TX

The Incredible Hulk
Indestructible
Mean, green muscular machine
Super strong and huge

Deus Cormier, Grade 3
Lorenzo De Zavala Elementary School, TX

Daredevils
Indestructible
No one can stop them
Really cool and fun

Jorge Torres, Grade 3
Lorenzo De Zavala Elementary School, TX

Principal
The head of a school
Says announcements in morning
Cares about the kids

Tiffany Cardiel, Grade 3
Lorenzo De Zavala Elementary School, TX

I Am...
I am a boy and a student
I wonder about swimming and soccer
I hear splashing outside
I see mummies banging at my door
I want a DSI
I am a boy and a student

I pretend I am a sheriff
I feel hot mocha in my hand
I touch a turtle in the pond
I worry the judges won't pick me
I cry when I can't have Legos
I am a boy and a student

I understand how to read
I say ghosts are real
I dream about driving a Lamborghini
I try to read chapter books
I hope to be a race car driver
I am a boy and a student

Carlos Harrison, Grade 3
Buena Vista Elementary School, CA

I Am a Homeless Cat
I am poor and lonely.
I wonder if I will ever get a home.
I hear a car.
I see a person.
I want shelter.
I am poor and lonely.

I pretend I have a house and food.
I feel rain.
I touch a tree.
I worry I may never be happy.
I cry when people come to me, then leave.
I am poor and lonely.

I understand my kittens' meows.
I say that life is hard.
I dream about having a human family.
I try to make people love and care for me.
I hope I will get an owner.
I am poor...and lonely.

Caitlyn Toutloff, Grade 3
Diane Winborn Elementary School, TX

Banana

Hey! Why eat me? Why not eat
my friend apple? The answer is, I
am so yummy! On no — here come
my enemies — human. No offense
human but you are cruel, you
got to admit. Nooo — give me
back my skin — no. I want
my head — no — no. Ugg, why didn't
I die? Well, at least I am
not a banana cream pie and
not eaten by monkeys. Wait!
This is the garbage, wait no,
I am still in the store —
whew! The only bad thing
is — I want my skin!
Qingfeng Li, Grade 3
Spring Creek Elementary School, WY

Olivia

O lives are good
L oves animals
I 'm seven
V ans are cool
I 'm almost eight
A round people

W illiams is my last name
I 'm nice
L oves people
L oves parents
I 'm cute
A nimals are good
M y favorite color is pink
S ix is my favorite number
Olivia Williams, Grade 1
Kentwood Elementary School, CA

First Day of Spring

The sun shines so bright
Little kids come out to play
There is no more snow
Lilla Crawford, Grade 3
The Mirman School, CA

Coast

Siesta time
after smelling dead fish
after waves crashing
reels casting
this is my place
on my boat
Will Davenport, Grade 3
Old Town Elementary School, TX

Spring

In spring, what do I see?
I see the sun shining at me.
The rainbow is colorful in the sky.
I see a flower gently swaying by.
Everywhere I see the green grass grow.
And I feel the wind softly blow.
Chloe Silver, Grade 1
Woodcrest School, CA

A Red Bird Flies

The snow sparkles
In the meadow by a pond
Sparkling in the moonlight
The soft snow was on the branches
A red bird flies in the moonlight
The bird is beautiful
Max Dwyer, Grade 2
Sierra Hills Elementary School, CA

Where Are the Birds

Birds, birds up so high,
see the cool night blue sky.
Birds, birds see my hair,
let it grow everywhere.
Kyle Francis, Grade 3
Wesleyan Academe, TX

Tigers

Tigers have sharp teeth.
Tigers have heads shaped like cats.
And they have loud roars.
Brock Welsh, Grade 2
Robinson Elementary School, TX

Josh

Joshua
It means funny, cool, and hungry.
It is the number of 10.
It is like a frog that hops in the bush.
It is when we went on a ride together.
It is the memory of my mom
Who taught me to be honest and caring
When she helped me by calming me down
When I am mad at my brother.
My name is Joshua
It means to always be smart.

Joshua Oshiro, Grade 2
Keone'ula Elementary School, HI

Music

I love music,
Music makes my foot go tap-tap-tap.
It makes me feel glorious about myself
In many different ways.
I can express myself.
It helps me learn music,
Makes me excited sometimes,
But sometimes it makes me down, too.
It has so many different sounds.
It's so glorious!
Music makes me feel so many different ways.

Parker Schweninger, Grade 3
D P Morris Elementary School, TX

California and Friends

California has a friend named Oregon.
She loves going to the beach.
Her favorite foods are olives, citrus fruit, and salmon.
She likes warm days, but she LOVES hot days.
In a long, long time, she will meet another friend
To enjoy the weather with her.
Her least favorite friend is Nevada,
Because he keeps sitting on her.
When Idaho tries to get through,
California can count on Oregon to protect her.
All of her forty-nine friends want each other together, forever.

Paige Lemire, Grade 3
CLASS Academy, OR

Summer All the Time

S ummer in Hawaii is HOT!
U sually in the afternoon it's hot.
M ittens are not what you're going to wear.
M aybe in spring there's lot of rain.
E very day you can have a cold drink.
R ed is what you will be if you don't have sun tan lotion.

A day to go to the beach.
L otion is what you need.
L ast hot time…NO WAY!

T he sun gives us lots of heat!
H ot is what we're known for!
E very day I want to go to the beach.

T imes are hot in Hawaii!
I t's almost always summer in Hawaii!
M ore sun for Hawaii.
E xcellent weather is in Hawaii.

Maya Woo, Grade 3
Keone'ula Elementary School, HI

Rides

Rides are fascinating,
Some are slow,
Some are fast,
Some immediately
Go.

Some are roller coasters,
That
Fly, like an eagle soaring
Through the sky!

Some are relaxing
Like sitting in a chair,
Enjoying yourself, while you haven't a care.

Some are scary, like a hairy monster
Meeting a devil,
Or fighting a dragon.

Kevin Rochelle, Grade 3
Wilchester Elementary School, TX

My Happy Classroom

My class is nice I like it so
The children scatter to and fro
The teacher asks a question
The children answer yes or no
It is a happy classroom we all like it it's so cool
It's good we don't have a teacher that's a ghoul
I like my teacher very much
Her name is Ms. Clutch
We have a happy classroom we like it very much!

Stephanie Miller, Grade 3
Goethe International Charter School, CA

Happiness and Sadness

When I am happy life seems like a slice of joy from the happiness cake.
I smile and say, "Oh it's so beautiful today."
I look at the flowers, the mountains, the treetops, and refuse to think bad of the world today.
But life isn't always this way.
When I am sad life is a drag, which keeps dragging me down.
I scowl and say, "Oh everything is so ugly today."
I look at the dark clouds, the rain, and refuse to think good of the world today.
And that's what I think of happiness and sadness.

Jaya Sandhu, Grade 3
Goethe International Charter School, CA

Snowstorm

Snowstorm
Frosty, snowy
Shoveling, snowball fight
Excited, gives me the shivers
Blizzard

Seth Parras, Grade 3
Tracy Learning Center - Primary Charter School, CA

Love You Mom

Mom, I love you a lot and always will
And you are the best mom in the world even when we fight.

I will always love you forever and ever
So Mom let me make one thing clear
I love you Mama!

Joshua Kleinhaus, Grade 2
St John's Episcopal School, TX

Animals

White is white
Black is black
White + Black = Zebra

Yellow is yellow
Black is black
Yellow + Black = Bee

Orange is orange
Black is black
Orange + Black = Jaguar

Yellow is yellow
Black is black
Yellow + Black = Yellow Jacket

Yellow is yellow
Gold is gold
Yellow + Gold = Camel

Yellow is yellow
Gold is gold
Yellow + Gold = Lion
Ahmoray Arana, Grade 3
Aveson Charter School, CA

My Dogs

I have three dogs,
Two big, one small.
They bark all day,
At night when
I am sleeping
They sleep too!

Bella bites me in my sleep
And it really hurts!
I start crying because her teeth
Sink into my arm.
Sometimes if I leave her alone
She'll be calm.

Basically she's just a bad dog!
But, we love her anyway!

My big dogs dig
Holes in my backyard.
My dad gets mad
Because they tear up his yard.
I like to play
In the big holes.
Hannah Stone, Grade 3
C W Cline Primary School, TX

River

A boat floats in the river.
And people see fish sliver.

A river is nice and wet.
It looks pink when it's sunset.

A big river can flow all around.
It also makes a beautiful sound.

When you walk by a river you might slip.
You can also swim there and do a flip.

In a river you can always fish.
And make it into a yummy dish.
A'shani Jasper, Grade 3
Hamlin Street Elementary School, CA

Cheetah Life

Yawn.
Wakening up from my slumber.

Scratch, chomp, roar, slam!
Fighting my worst enemy!

Zip!
Running after my prey!

Chomp!
Sinking my fangs into my prey.

Snore.
Resting under a shady tree.
Danny Brunet, Grade 3
Juliet Morris Elementary School, CA

The Zoo

The humongous gates open slowly with a crowd waiting
Mini school buses enter the huge parking lot slowly
At the large and full zoo tasty popcorn pops like filled balloons
Small children giggle softly at the funny monkeys
Kind tour guides give tours happily to families
Happy zookeepers feed the animals responsibly to keep the animals happy
Little gift shops attract customers quickly with exciting toys
Long snakes hiss softly with joy in their exhibit
Dark scary caves have gross bugs in them
A tall vendor sells cold ice cream happily with pride
Large hippos sun bathe in the hot sun
The humongous gates close slowly after the large zoo is empty

Joshua Levine, Grade 3
The Mirman School, CA

Australia

A borigines are the first people of Australia

U luru is a sacred rock to the aborigines. It is also known as Ayres Rock.

S outhern is what Australia means in Latin.

T asmania is Australia's biggest island. It is separated by the Bass Straight from Australia.

R oos are marsupials, animals that have pouches.

A ustralia is a country, a continent and an island.

L ake Eyre is the largest lake in Australia and fills with water twice every hundred years.

I t is all desert in the Outback of Australia

A nimals are very fun and fascinating in Australia. There are a lot of indigenous animals in Oz.

Himani Sood, Grade 3
CLASS Academy, OR

Dashing Snowflakes

Mice dashing through the floor
X's sitting on the ground
Cotton balls floating from the heavens above
Water tickling down my throat
Glass twinkling in the sunlight
Strings blowing in the wind
Dropping leaves from the tops of trees
Butterfly wings fluttering from high above
Rocks falling from the sky

Brendan Redd, Grade 3
Lolo Elementary School, MT

Tree

In the fall, the trees get too cold
and some of the leaves can't stay alive.
Their arms sway back and forth
as the trees dance with the wind.
It's not a protective shield anymore.
The wind was being mean and pushing on her,
the big oak tree.

It is winter, and the tree is now bare.
No animals can she protect,
maybe in the summer she can nurse little animals.

It is now spring, and the big oak tree is happy,
she is feeling the breeze, and
exercising with the wind.
Now animals that she can nurse are coming down to her.
She is in paradise.

Now it is summer, very hot,
but her leaves have grown back,
and she has a shield that gives her shade.

Now the cycle starts over.

Gwyneth Boyden, Grade 3
Blanton Elementary School, TX

Valentine's Day

V alentine's Day cards
A s sweet as a sucker
L et the holiday of love sweep you off your feet
E very February it comes
N ever ever stops
T rade cards
p **I** nk, red, and white are the colors thought of
N ever let hate or anger get out on Valentine's
sm **E** lls like sweets all in the air
S uper secret surprises are coming your way

D elicious purple, red, and violet vanilla cupcakes
p **A** rties all over the block
Y um! That tastes wonderful!

Courtney Keith, Grade 3
Lorenzo De Zavala Elementary School, TX

Glimmering Snowflakes

Twinkling Christmas lights shimmering in the night
Angels dancing down from the heavens
Shining glass shapes falling down to earth
Fairies swirling through the air
A melting marshmallow in hot cocoa
Or the soft delicate wings of a butterfly
As quiet as a flower petal
A yummy piece of cotton candy melting in my mouth

Kaylee Smith, Grade 3
Lolo Elementary School, MT

Dashing Dragonflies

Flashing lightning bolts all over in the sky
Landing on lily pads, frozen there
Sparkling in the moonlight
Hovering over a flower
Landing so slowly on the edge of the pond
Resting gracefully until it next takes off
Eating dry fruit while glistening like diamonds
Flying over the mountains before the sun rests

Elias DeWaters, Grade 3
Lolo Elementary School, MT

Black Is

Black is God giving us sin,
It might be a black knight at dawn,
Black smells like blackberry pie with a cherry on top,
It could be a crow at night nesting on a tree,
A black castle on a cliff is black,
Black looks like a black cat on a bed with its toy,
That is what black is to me.

Vincent Hackman, Grade 3
Marguerite Hahn Elementary School, CA

Math, My Favorite Subject

My favorite subject is math because it has division, multiplication and fractions.
At school math is exciting because it has interesting concepts such as geometry.
Third grade math chapters include probability, measurements, and of course money.
How I wish I could forever do addition and subtraction while regrouping with
three digit numbers.

Mihir Godbole, Grade 2
Scholars Academy, CA

Remember Happiness

In my heart
Friendship and dreams are really important.
I think love
Is a blue cloud of cotton candy in the sky.
There are beautiful places
I wish to be.
When I think of love
I believe in happiness.
I think love changes me
And everyone around me.
Love remembers a little of yesterday
And remembers a lot of today.

Bonnie Nguyen, Grade 3
Oak Park Elementary School, CA

Sports

I love to snowboard
I love to go fast
I never get bored,
And I always have a blast
Snowboarding is great,
But I also love to skate
Skating is fun,
And I love to run
I run in basketball,
And I run in baseball
I like to play badminton
Playing sports is fun!

Andrew Kim, Grade 3
Wonderland Avenue Elementary School, CA

Art

Plain paper on the table,
Crayons in the box,
I wonder what I should draw?
A flower, a person, a car?
I take a sharpened pencil from the jar,
I'm filled with ideas that I would love to try.
I think that I should draw a butterfly!
As I watch that piece of paper,
Turn into a work of art.

Brianna Moritz, Grade 3
Horn Academy, TX

Loud Baby

Baby at daycare,
loud and annoying,
Waaaaaaa!
Waaaaaaa!
Make the baby be quiet.
Give it a bottle,
a binky,
give it something
to make it be quiet.
It is silent in the room.
Waaaaa!
It starts all over again.
Amara Hummer, Grade 2
Robert L Stevens Elementary School, CA

Mark's Smart

Mark
It means smart, active, and caring.
It is the number 12.
It is like the deep sea waves.
It is going to Disneyland.
It is the memory of my mom
Helping me with my homework.
Who taught me to be caring and smart.
When she taught me lots of math
And picking up other people's spirits
My name is Mark
It means going for the best.
Mark Liu, Grade 2
Keone'ula Elementary School, HI

Christmas Is in the Air

You can smell it in the cookies
baking in the oven.
You can taste it in the peppermint
candy canes.
You can hear it in the twinkling
jingle bells
You can see it in the white,
fluffy snow
You can feel it in the joyful hearts
Alexandra Gil, Grade 3
A E Arnold Elementary School, CA

My Protector

My dog Shooter
Is fluffy and white.

He uses his big ears
To listen
And protect us all night.

He loves to hunt,
Fetch,
And wiggle.

Sometimes he smiles
And that makes me giggle.

He loves to do tricks.
Maybe he'll fetch sticks.

He's my best friend!
The end!
Madison Jenkins, Grade 3
C W Cline Primary School, TX

Rain, Wind, and Sun

Rain is the pitter patter of water splashing
Down on the hard concrete.
It's like a shower,
But don't get too wet or you'll get a cold.

Sun is the hot breeze,
That warms us during the summer.
It heats up the pool so we can swim.

The wind, the cool breeze
That brushes against your numb skin
You at least have to be wearing a jacket
Or coat so you don't get cold.
It brushes your hair
Backwards and forwards.

And speaking of wind,
Did I mention snow?
Allison Delgado, Grade 3
Wilchester Elementary School, TX

Spring
The ice is melting.
Many flowers will pop up.
Spring is here to stay.
Connor Kenefick, Grade 3
Carlthorp School, CA

Spring
The Spring flowers bloom,
Shames the winter wonderland,
Everything awakens.
Tyler Wong, Grade 3
Carlthorp School, CA

Oceans
Oceans are awesome
They are very, very blue
They are refreshing
Jakob Amster, Grade 3
Carlthorp School, CA

Easter
The Easter eggs hide,
Calling the children down stairs,
To join the delight.
Chase Branigan, Grade 3
Carlthorp School, CA

Pandas
White and black on them
White and black all over them
Bamboo munching bear
Hunter B. Pressley, Grade 3
Connally Elementary School, TX

Ballerina Moon
Beautiful dancer,
Gracefully spins around us,
Ballerina moon.
Mackenzee Brough, Grade 3
Dixie Sun Elementary School, UT

Spring
Spring is fun.
Spring is warm.
Spring is grass.
Cooper Sellers, Kindergarten
Cache Valley Learning Center, UT

Spring
Spring is swimming.
Spring is bees.
Spring is bugs.
Aidan Sowder-Sinor, Kindergarten
Cache Valley Learning Center, UT

Spring
Spring is fun.
Spring is rain.
Spring is warm.
Katie Meibos, Kindergarten
Cache Valley Learning Center, UT

Spring
Spring is flowers.
Spring is grass hills.
Spring is blue sky.
Hudson Spencer, Kindergarten
Cache Valley Learning Center, UT

Spring
Spring has quickly come.
Everywhere around me now.
Totally turns green.
Yu-Kai Ni, Grade 3
Carlthorp School, CA

Snow
Snow is freezing cold.
It is graceful when it falls.
Snow is fun to throw.
Kenneth Lee, Grade 3
Carlthorp School, CA

Home

Place to relax at
To play video games too
And my mother cooks

Trevon Mitchell, Grade 3
Lorenzo De Zavala Elementary School, TX

Dragons

Are very awesome
Beasts can breathe really hot fire
Scaly reptilians

Fabian Rangel, Grade 3
Lorenzo De Zavala Elementary School, TX

Friends

Always care for you
Help you when you need it most
Always tell the truth

Katelan Marcial, Grade 3
Lorenzo De Zavala Elementary School, TX

Springtime

Flying butterflies
The sweet, fresh-smelling blossoms
Some trees start blooming

Madilyn Lawrence, Grade 3
Lorenzo De Zavala Elementary School, TX

Days!

Rainy days, sunny days, cloudy days. All kinds of days. Each day is special to each of us! It might be mixed with other weather. And plus we can play together! And there might be a storm in our way. But that's ok. That's weather.

Allison Borris, Grade 3
Edward Byrom Elementary School, OR

Art

Art art let's make some art yay yay!
Let's make some clay, oh let's paint the clay
Yay yay! Let's sculpt some clay every day!

Yusuf Tune, Grade 2
Islamic School of Muslim Educational Trust, OR

Sydney's Magic Miracles
Sydney
It means funny, smart, and strong.
It is the number 18.
It is like a cloudless sky.
It is going to Disneyland.
It is the memory of my dogs
Who taught me to be responsible
When I have to refill their dish with water and food.
My name is Sydney.
It means to always try.

Sydney Gaskin, Grade 2
Keone'ula Elementary School, HI

Caring About My Family
Cassandra
It means clean, organized and relaxing.
It is the number 8.
It's like violets.
It's like going to Round Island with my family.
It is the memory of my dad falling down at the church
Who taught me to be a thinker
When he makes me think about my sisters and care for my mom.
My name is Cassandra.
It means to care for others and remember no one is perfect.

Cassandra Mo, Grade 2
Keone'ula Elementary School, HI

My Brother
Zoe
It means lazy and caring, and helpful.
It is the number 7.
It is like a Chinese lantern.
It is going on a trip for spring break.
It is the memory of when my brother lost more than 1 game
Who taught me to be caring
When he makes me apologize for being mean.
My name is Zoe.
It means to be caring.

Zoe Sialana, Grade 2
Keone'ula Elementary School, HI

Cave

Dark, black, dangerous
Scary bats, horrible walls
Water, tunnels, worms

Hannah Dominguez, Grade 3
Tracy Learning Center - Primary Charter School, CA

Stars

Hot, steamy, explode
Different colors, awesome
Small, medium

Affan Nauman, Grade 2
Tracy Learning Center - Primary Charter School, CA

Flowers

They have pink petals
They bloom in different seasons
They grow in the soil

Marzen Abala, Grade 3
Tracy Learning Center - Primary Charter School, CA

Summer

Playing when it's fun
Swimming in the pool for fun
In the nice, warm sun

Tyler Atkinson, Grade 3
Tracy Learning Center - Primary Charter School, CA

Birds

Nice, drinking, smelling
Hearing, looking, eating food
They are very cute

Jonathan Martinuic, Grade 3
Tracy Learning Center - Primary Charter School, CA

Money

Green, president, fun
Quarter, nickel, penny, dime
Half dollar, shopping

Samantha Chavez, Grade 3
Tracy Learning Center - Primary Charter School, CA

Pink

Roses in a vase.
A soft pillow from my grandma.
A running stream.
Pink looks like cotton candy.
It tastes like bubble gum.
Alexis Shelton, Grade 1
Kentwood Elementary School, CA

Bored

B ored
C an't find a thing to do
D own I go
E veryone is gone…and my
F riend too.
Flor Bustos, Grade 3
St Raphael School, CA

Legos

L egos are my hobby.
E ach piece is a brick.
G ot to have them all.
O h, I can't get away from them.
S o cool!
Jack Johnson, Grade 3
St Aloysius Parochial School, CA

Jaide

There once was a boy named Jaide
He was a very bad maid
So he went off to play
His boss sent him away
That is the sad story of Jaide.
Isabella Reichard, Grade 3
St Raphael School, CA

Dolphin

Dolphin
Big, long
Eating, splashing, swimming
They like to swim
Blue
Alitzel Gonzalez-Cortes, Grade 1
Kentwood Elementary School, CA

Worried

Worried
X-tremely scared
Yaks are chasing me...
Zebras are too!
Oh no!
Kenny Alvarez, Grade 3
St Raphael School, CA

Baton

B est sport ever
A nd you can
T wirl a stick.
O nly you have to practice.
N one of the judges miss it.
Jessica Gourley, Grade 3
St Aloysius Parochial School, CA

Pat

There once was a boy named Pat
Who had a big, long mat
He slipped on it
His head he hit
And that is the story of Pat
Kalissa Flint, Grade 3
St Raphael School, CA

Ice

Ice
Is frozen
Ice is water
Ice is
Nice
Jacob Berenzweig, Grade 1
P H Greene Elementary School, TX

Jack

There once was a boy named Jack
who had a big pack
wore it all day
but he had to play
and that was the story of Jack.
Chris Mesipam, Grade 3
St Raphael School, CA

Ailuj
Julia
It means fun, loving, and cool.
It is the number 8.
It is like a vampire's teeth with blood.
It is fun at the beach with your family and friends.
It is the memory of me, my mom and dad having fun at the beach
Who taught me to be a good sport and to have fun.
When they let me have fun and not do work sometimes.
My name is Julia
It means freedom, happiness, and always getting up when you fall.
Julia Gallagher, Grade 2
Keone'ula Elementary School, HI

Josie
Josie
It means clean, smart, and scared.
It is the number 15.
It is like a heart from us.
It is when I went to fun factory.
It is the memory of my cousin who went to the marines
Who taught me to be a risk taker and balanced.
When he was leaving to the marines I was sad.
My name is Josie.
It means to love the people you care about.
Josie DeCambra, Grade 2
Keone'ula Elementary School, HI

Tihane Loves Her Papa
Tihane
It means silly, funny and lazy.
It is the number 25.
It is like the color purple or blue.
It is when my friend says funny things.
It is the memory of my dog falling down a hill
Who taught me to be balanced and open-minded
When he made me laugh and not to be bad all the time.
My name is Tihane
It means always trying to do good.
Tihane Devera, Grade 2
Keone'ula Elementary School, HI

Forest
Forest
Gooey, icky,
Crying, scaring, searching.
It makes me want to run away.
Jungle

Brandon Metzger, Grade 3
Tracy Learning Center - Primary Charter School, CA

Racecars
They race on the track
And when they are done they leave
And Jeff Gordon wins first and Mark Martin wins second
He was going so fast but Jeff Gordon was faster

Kyle Stewart, Kindergarten
Legacy Christian Academy, NM

Colors
Pink is for raspberries, green is like a lime
Black is for blackberries, yellow is like a lemon
Blue is for blueberries, orange is like a clementine
Red is for strawberries, brown is like a nut

Saige Broadwell, Grade 3
Horn Academy, TX

NASCAR
NASCAR is fun to watch.
In NASCAR, cars have to do 100 laps.
It makes my eyes go around,
SO FAST!

Maarij Quadri, Grade 3
Islamic School of Muslim Educational Trust, OR

My Grandma's Flowers
Beauty is watching the flowers grow that I planted with my Grandma.
Beauty is watching the bees get nectar from the flowers I planted.
Beauty is making a home for bugs to live in the dirt under the flowers.
Beauty is seeing the flowers all around me.

Natasha Shaw, Grade 2
Eagle Valley Elementary School, UT

Crack

There once was a girl I knew well.
She was up high and she fell.
There was a smack and a crack,
As she fell on her back.
And the rest is not pretty to tell.
Sarah Chamberlain, Grade 3
Wasatch Elementary School, UT

May

There once was a girl named may
She liked to eat clay
She went to school day by day
She did not like to play
The girl named May
Marynicole Ramirez, Grade 3
St Raphael School, CA

Kalissa

There once was a girl named Kalissa
Who had a friend named Melissa
They went out to play
But stayed out all day
That is the story of Kalissa
Siena Rago, Grade 3
St Raphael School, CA

Kid with a Spear

There was a young kid with a spear
who accidentally cut off his ear
he did not die
but he cried
that's the kid with a spear.
Jack Horton, Grade 3
St Raphael School, CA

Geo Spheres

Geo Spheres
colorful, smooth
fitting, loosening, thinking
helps learn about shapes
Geo Spheres
Toby Johnson, Grade 3
St Pius X School, TX

Things I Like

I like
    learning things at school.
I like
    swimming at a pool.
I like
    Woodcrest because it's fun.
I like
    humming when I run.
I like
    skating because it's fun.
I like
    to watch the setting sun.
Nicole Rozenblat, Grade 2
Woodcrest School, CA

The Snaasorus

The long-necked Snaasorus
    is as long as can be.
I've never seen one
    because he lives in the sea.
The Snaasorus lives
    on sea and on land.
This strange creature does not
    play in a band.
The big green Snaasorus
    likes a lot of sand.
The baby Snaasoruses
    are normally found on land.
Chloe Austerfield, Grade 2
Woodcrest School, CA

Fantastic Football

I used to be a pig on a ranch in Texas.
But now I am being carried across
the Superdome in New Orleans, LA.
I used to be a lonely football on the
Colts logo but now I am being
carried into the end zone. I used
to be a ball being held to the
ground by Jordan Shipley but now
I am soaring through the goal posts.
Matthew Allen, Grade 3
Annunciation Orthodox School, TX

Nature in Spring

Nature in the Spring is wonderful.
I love when the flowers bloom.
Animal eggs hatch in Spring.
Spring is a very beautiful time.
Spring is the time when kids play outside.
In Spring farmers plant their crops.
Near the flowers I see colorful butterflies.
Spring is my favorite season.
Rina Kaura, Grade 2
Scholars Academy, CA

Red Flower

I went outside to play
When I saw a red flower
I was coming its way
I picked it up
I said, "What a pretty little flower"
I went home
I showed my mom and dad
I put a smile on their faces
Melissa Valverde, Grade 3
Three Rivers Elementary School, TX

Ocean

I went
Swimming
In the
Ocean
and the sea was
Silent
Silent
as a mouse
Kenedi Miller, Grade 1
P H Greene Elementary School, TX

Spring

It's spring. It's spring.
And what do we see?
We see pink flowers
As pretty as can be.
It's spring. It's spring.
And what do we see?
We see black kittens
Looking at me.
Leila Mirfakhrai, Grade 1
Woodcrest School, CA

Cars

Cars are machines
They have wheels under.
They move people around.
People can breathe inside.
They have steering wheels.
They have doors.
Cars can run fast.
They have seats.
Arhan Jain, Kindergarten
Scholars Academy, CA

Spring

It's spring. It's spring.
And what do we see?
We see brown puppies
Smiling at me.
It's spring. It's spring.
And what do we see?
We see blue birds
Flying by me.
Deven Yahraus, Grade 1
Woodcrest School, CA

Cotton Candy

My favorite food is
fluffy pink cotton candy!
It melts in your mouth!
It comes in sky-blue colors!
Cotton candy is the best!
Laynie Cafcalas, Grade 3
Annunciation Orthodox School, TX

Vacation Sounds

Chirping,
Seagulls singing,
The calm beach,
Seashells that make music,
Waves.
Trey Hewell, Grade 2
Annunciation Orthodox School, TX

Where I'm From
I am from basketball, handball, and tennis.
I am from the lions in the wild waiting to be petted.
From the grass is just waiting to have a haircut in my backyard.
I am from my mom's best mom-made shakes made with peaches, blueberries,
bananas, and fresh-picked strawberries in a shiny cup.
I am from my dad, my mom, my grandpa, and my grandma.
I am from an unzippered and talkative family.
I am from the "Study Land" in my house.
I am from my teddy bear with short legs, Teddy.
I am from my handsome John and my lovely Amy and also my pretty sister, Michelle.
I am from the time that I lost one of my jaw.
I am from my mom's room spilling water on my mom's clothes.

Kevin Song, Grade 3
Juliet Morris Elementary School, CA

Tigers
Tigers have sharp teeth and claws
Their orange-brown coats have stripes
Tigers are fierce predators with strong legs
They eat wild boars, antelopes, buffaloes and deers
Tigers love to swim and sleep
They sleep for hours in the daytime
At night, they are awake to hunt
Tigers are endangered species
People keep on hunting them
If we don't protect them
they will soon be extinct
Tigers can be found in Siberia, Asia
and other places too

Shyanne Zeng, Grade 2
Camino Grove Elementary School, CA

Spring Time
In spring time
butterflies come out.
They are blue.
They fly in the sky.
In spring time
flowers grow.
The wind will blow.

Morgan Sinnock, Kindergarten
Notre Dame Academy Elementary School, CA

The Moonlight

The moonlight
Bright this snowy night
The trees are
snowy tonight
The dark
snowy night
the moonlight
is bright

Zach Bliss, Grade 2
Sierra Hills Elementary School, CA

The River

A river flowing
Clear cold water going on and on
As it turns into a steady flow
And then into a rush
As it drifts on
Forever washing through
Like thin cloth —
cloth — cloth — cloth.

Lael Case, Grade 3
Neskowin Valley School, OR

Spring

Spring is finally here!
I can see beautiful poppies.
I can hear the birds
tweeting on a branch.
I can smell the roses growing
in the garden.
I can taste the yummy apple pie.
I feel happy when spring is here!

Kaelen Cook, Grade 2
Woodcrest School, CA

Dance

I love to dance.
I want to go to France.
My costume is my favorite;
It is a unique piece of art!
All the lace and frills
Bring me smiles and thrills.
Dancing sets me free;
It's when I can be me!

Gabriella Martinez, Grade 3
St John's Episcopal Day School, TX

My Teacher's Son Is Cool

My teacher's son is cool
I met him in school,
His name is Will
But my teacher says her son is a pill!
He plays football
But isn't very tall,
His eyes and hair are brown
You can tell he is mad by his frown!

George Ramirez, Grade 3
St John's Episcopal Day School, TX

Gods

Gods are rulers.
When they get mad,
things can go wrong.
Tsunamis, Tornadoes
Hurricanes, Earthquakes
and many more.
A lot of people
think the Gods are cool.

Diego Gutierrez, Grade 3
Wilchester Elementary School, TX

Horses

Horses
Gorgeous, friendly
Trotting, prancing, galloping
Leap like the wind
Mustangs

Audrey Godfrey, Grade 2
Dixie Sun Elementary School, UT

Pitbulls

Pitbulls
Strong, bulky
Digging, obeying, loving
Sniff hands and food
Dogs

Sofia Cuara, Grade 2
Dixie Sun Elementary School, UT

Reptiles

reptiles
old animals
walking, swimming, watching
live, scaly cruel, scary
monsters

Jaron Pape, Grade 3
Lorenzo De Zavala Elementary School, TX

Puppies

puppies
small babies
barking, clawing, crawling
furry, smelly, jumpy, playful
pets

Miracle Garcia, Grade 3
Lorenzo De Zavala Elementary School, TX

Penguin

Penguin
Black claws, yellow feathers
Hopping, swimming, sliding
Are up to 22 inches tall and weigh about 6 pounds
Rockhopper

David Williams III, Grade 2
Robinson Elementary School, TX

Clock

clock
electric object
ticking, moving, cranking
useful, mechanical, heavy, metal
timekeeper

Skyler Kibbe, Grade 3
Lorenzo De Zavala Elementary School, TX

Jesus

Jesus died on the cross
for our sins.
He rose from the dead.
I can be more like Jesus
by walking like Him.

Daniel Chang, Kindergarten
Notre Dame Academy Elementary School, CA

Creep

Creep at night
in the house.
Creep in the day.
Creep and
tiptoe in the house.
Hear a whisper
behind
my back,
I turn around,
Nobody is there.

Kate Primo, Grade 2
Robert L Stevens Elementary School, CA

Horses

Horses are in a bunch
Grass is their favorite lunch,
They run in the wind
And their fun never ends.
Their tails flick
And they are rarely sick,
The flies get in their face
Horses love to race,
They have horse shoes
But never get the blues!

Laura Cavazos, Grade 3
St John's Episcopal Day School, TX

Mule

There once was a mule
her sister was a donkey
and
her brother was a horse.
Her mom
was a donkey
and
her dad was
a horse.
Why couldn't she be a beautiful horse?

Ashleigh Loe, Grade 1
P H Greene Elementary School, TX

The Wind

Wind,
the leaves are
falling down,
Whooooooooh!
The wind blows,
Whooooooooh!
One leaf all alone
on the tree,
it is hoping it can fall down
and be with the others.

Belen Torres, Grade 2
Robert L Stevens Elementary School, CA

Poetry

Poetry is something
that I feel that I can
express myself
and I can let my feelings
and imagination have fun
I feel like I am in
a magical world
poetry is something new
that I discovered
and I love it!

Alyssa Clanton, Grade 3
Wilchester Elementary School, TX

Sweets

I eat lollipops with squirrels,
and donuts with kangaroos,
I had chocolate with bears
and Cub Scouts too.
I eat Skittles with raccoons
and sooo much too.
I eat meat with 200 walruses,
some honey with bees,
I had so much to eat,
you should try this too!

Azameet Gebremariam, Grade 3
Henry Haight Elementary School, CA

Sunshine

Sunshine's like a laser beam
shining on my face.
Sunshine's a flashlight
lighting my path.
Sunshine's a golden giraffe
giving birth to a baby calf.
Sunshine.

Hudson Brown, Grade 3
Wilchester Elementary School, TX

Swings

Do you like swinging?
Swinging up swinging down,
There are swings everywhere
Swinging is fun
When you have a contest
Or when you are trying to see over things,
Swinging is fun everywhere.

Derek Hinojosa, Grade 3
Three Rivers Elementary School, TX

Saw a Deer

When I went
I saw a deer on the side of the road.
Coyotes bite it.
We tried to help it.
But it went away.
The mom ran away.
And found its baby.

Noah Stewart, Grade 3
Three Rivers Elementary School, TX

Being a Butterfly

Flapping my wings,
Flying high,
Tall as the trees,
Touching the rainbow,
Visiting my sister in the clouds,
Nectar of flowers,
Sweet moments of a butterfly.

Apoorva Panidapu, Kindergarten
Scholars Academy, CA

What Is Green?

A ball is green in the playground grass
An apple is green on a desk
A poster is green in the sparkling sky
A water bottle is green in the glimmering water
A picture is green in the beauty of the flowers

Kali Lawson, Grade 3
Lolo Elementary School, MT

The Snowflakes

In the night it was snowing.
In the day it was snowing.
It was raining all day and all night.
The snow turned into ice.
It was Christmas and it was snowing.
The weather was cold and mean.
In summer the snow was gone.

Cory Austin, Grade 3
Lolo Elementary School, MT

Sleeping

I like to sleep in a big, cozy, bed.
Rolling,
dreaming,
snoring
with my teddy bear.
The moon is shining through my window.
I love sleeping.

Naiya Childs, Grade 1
Longfellow Elementary School, TX

Cat and Dog

Cat
Calm, graceful
Quiet, loving, friendly
Neat, nice, loud, cute
Trained, amazing, snores
Man's friend
Dog

Emma Barton, Grade 3
Horn Academy, TX

I Know My School

I know my school
The taste of the sandwiches
The taste of the juice and milk
The taste of pudding
I know my school
The smooth paper
The rough walls
The smooth pencils
I know my school
The brown roof
The white wooden walls
The orange bricks
I know my school
The sound of the bells
The sound of the teachers' voices
The sound of cars in carpool
I know my school
The smell of the cafeteria
The smell of the paper
The smell of the pizza
I know my school

Mason Pokorny, Grade 3
Horn Academy, TX

I Know KFC

I know KFC
The taste of pepper
The taste of macaroni
The taste of the crunchy outside
I know KFC
The smell of chicken
The smell of biscuits
The rotten smell of green beans
I know KFC
The ching ching of the cash register
The crunch of people eating
The beep of the oven
I know KFC
I feel the coldness of the floor
I feel the grease of my chicken
I feel the squeezy booth
I know KFC
I see a line for food
I see the parking lot full
I see my brother getting ready to poke me
I know KFC

Justin Owens, Grade 3
Horn Academy, TX

My Pikachu

I love my
Pikachu,

Even though
he's stuffed!

Oh shoot!
I just forgot!

Why
did
I
want
him
so
much!?

Jonathan Hager, Grade 3
C W Cline Primary School, TX

I Know Mexico

I know Mexico
The burrito burning
The cash register beeping
I know Mexico
The cold swimming pool
The ocean water on my feet
The sand on my hands
I know Mexico
The icy smoothie
The tostados crunching
The salt water
I know Mexico
The pretty flowers
The bathing suits
The people diving
I know Mexico

Juliet Gillis, Grade 3
Horn Academy, TX

Easter Fun

The sun is shining,
Kids playing outside with their friends.
Opening gifts from the Easter bunny,
Having fun with your family.
Going on an egg hunt,
Finding a lot of eggs,
Eating candy from the eggs,
Having dinner with your friends and family.
Easter is really fun,
And spring is finally here!

Jack Brady, Grade 3
Wilchester Elementary School, TX

Where I'm From

I am from wooden cars, a baby blanket, and bouncy balls.
I am from the scaly fish that is really swift.
I am from Mexican grilled tacos.
And from Happy Meals.
From Grandmas and Grandpas, to Fabi and Walter.
I'm from a blubbering family and chocolate eaters.
From "Brush your teeth" and "Go to bed."
I'm from Walter, Fabi, Danny, and Tony.
I am from a dog biting my aunt.
I'm from the time we went to Disneyland.

Fabian Munoz, Grade 3
Juliet Morris Elementary School, CA

Where I'm From

I am from soccer and homework.
I am from the cute little hamster in my heart,
I am from my mom's baked cake in the oven.
I am from my grandmother.
I am from my good mother.
I am from my bed waiting for me.
I am from my pet.
I am from my family.
I am from the spider that almost killed me.
I am from my good family.

Katherine Alonso, Grade 3
Juliet Morris Elementary School, CA

The Wave

There once was a big wave and it came CRASHING down.
All the surfers came crashing onto the shore.
People on the beach ran out of their seats.
Boats were crashing into big rocks.
But somebody stayed there.
It was a terrible sight to see.
But then he ran out of sight.
Nobody saw him for the next year.
That was the story of the big wave.

Jordyn Tetone, Grade 3
Sellers Elementary School, CA

Girl Scouts

Daisies, Brownies, Juniors, and Cadets
Innumerable badges
Manners
Colorful sashes and vests
Joyful friends
Uniforms
Thinking
But best of all for customers
Cookies!!

Emily Speth, Grade 3
Thomas Edison Charter School - North, UT

Orange

Orange is the color of yummy oranges
Orange covers pretty flowers
Orange covers people's hair
It also might cover a bear
Orange is the color of ducks feet and beaks
Sometimes your skin can be orangey
Orange covers pencils too
And if your shirt isn't orange boohoo

Sidnee Hoopes, Grade 3
Thomas Edison Charter School - North, UT

Hats on My Cats

When it comes to hats on my baby brother,
he puts them on my cats
and I say "Oh Brother!"

Christopher Rhea, Grade 1
Settlement Canyon Elementary School, UT

Acacia

Acacia
It means joy and fun also love
It's the number 22
It is like a wet summer spring
It is riding a crazy funky ride and enjoying
It is like the Memory of my sister
Who taught me to be polite
When I was treating my nephew mean
My name is Acacia
It means love

Acacia Higa, Grade 2
Keone'ula Elementary School, HI

Be Yourself

Karmenn
It means brave, caring and artistic.
It is the number 10.
It is like China's favorite color.
It is like going swimming in the salty sea.
It is the memory of my giant but sweet dog Clovis
Who taught me to be a thinker and patient
When he makes me happy and responsible.
My name is Karmenn.
It means always tell the truth.

Karmenn Branch, Grade 2
Keone'ula Elementary School, HI

Rock and Roll

Elijah
It means funny fun caring
It is 13
It is flaming hot fire
It is when I went to my uncle's house
It is the memory of my grandpa playing with me
Who taught me how to be respectful
When made me funny
My name is Elijah
It means strong and a fast runner

Elijah Felix-Vierra, Grade 2
Keone'ula Elementary School, HI

Candle
Candle —
Bright, warm, colorful —
Flickering
Lightly, now, today
Annika Matulac, Grade 3
St Mary School, CA

Bee
Bee —
Smooth, stripes, noisy —
Flies
Soon, tomorrow, nearly
Grace Calderon, Grade 3
St Mary School, CA

Dollar
Dollar —
Money, earned, used —
Used
Quickly, today, nicely
Sam Myers, Grade 3
St Mary School, CA

Bubble
Bubble —
Clear, shiny, fun —
Floats
Quietly, away, soon
Ashley Rodriguez, Grade 3
St Mary School, CA

My Dog
I chase my dog
and run in the sun,
my dog and I
have a lot of fun.
Hannah Cazalas, Grade 1
St Pius X Catholic School, TX

My Cat
My cat is furry and cute
Sometimes my dog bites my cat
My cat is tricky and cozy
But likes to eat, eat, eat, and eat
Matthew Lopez, Grade 3
Three Rivers Elementary School, TX

Dollar
Dollar —
Cool, green, and awesome —
Buys you stuff
Hard work, any time, anywhere
Elijah Cruz, Grade 3
St Mary School, CA

Heart
Heart —
Red, small, clean —
Pumps
Every day, quickly, far
Veronica Goalder, Grade 3
St Mary School, CA

Snail
Snail —
Slow snail, colorful snail —
Helps
Crazy snail, awesome snail
Thomas Rivera, Grade 3
St Mary School, CA

Green Vine Listens
Green vine sprays water
above the sky as it listens
summer to winter
beneath its life cycle.
Talyah Pierce, Kindergarten
Travis Elementary School, TX

Bats

Bats are black,
Flying in the night,
Spooky bats,
Black bats,
Tiny bats,
Fruit bats, too.
Flying fast as a cheetah,
Where are you going?

America Canchola, Grade 2
Robert L Stevens Elementary School, CA

Worms

Worms Worms
Worms are the
Best
They wiggle around
and slither the
Best!
They are like your
Shoelace

Ira Marshall, Grade 1
P H Greene Elementary School, TX

Spring

I can see a sunny day.
I can hear the kids play.

I can see a bird on the ground.
I can see a ball that's very round.

I can see the leaves on trees.
I can see the buzzing bees.

Naomi Talamantes, Grade 2
Woodcrest School, CA

Cooking

There sits a little tasty can,
Waiting to be on the pan.

I look in a book,
It said *To Cook*.

I look at the recipe to bake
To make a small pretty birthday cake.

Kristina Tong, Grade 3
Oak Park Elementary School, CA

Spring

It's spring. It's spring.
And what do we see?
We see green rocket ships
Flying by me.
It's spring. It's spring.
And what do we see?
We see a blue fish
Swimming by me.

Jalen Short, Grade 1
Woodcrest School, CA

The Art of Tennis

The tennis ball, green and smooth,
You should hit it in a quick move.

Hit it over the net and score,
Hit it over again and get more.

All the players run on the court,
That is part of the tennis sport.

Olivia Simon, Grade 3
Oak Park Elementary School, CA

New York

New York City
People everywhere
Zooming, running, driving
Roaring screeching traffic
Busy

Anita Anand, Grade 3
Carlthorp School, CA

Lemurs

Lemurs
Arboreal, nocturnal
Hibernating, climbing, purring
Long tongues suck nectar
Primates

Zayda Selemenev, Grade 2
Dixie Sun Elementary School, UT

Beautiful Blue

Blue is a cool color, pretty, pretty, yes
Blue is used on clothing, such as a dress.

Blue is the color the sky is at day.
Blue is the color of the beautiful bay.

Neptune has gasses that look like blue jello,
Sometimes the gas could even be mellow.

Some violets are blue too with their big and bright petals,
and sometimes there are even blue medals.

There are also blue eyes and blueberry pies.
Blue can be rain, or strong, strong pain.

There are blue bottles and even blue models.
That is my poem about blue.

Camryn Owens, Grade 3
Marguerite Hahn Elementary School, CA

Being Different

I am different, but that's OK
I still like to run and jump and play.
I wear crazy bright shirts and fun plaid socks,
But I also listen to music that rocks.
Being different is always OK
If you follow your dreams; I like it that way.
Not lacing my shoes, that's different, right?
And sleeping with a book on your head all night?
When I look in the mirror here's what I see,
A silly, fun girl looking back at me.
In my mind I'm pink with funky blue dots
And the earth is striped with white polka dots.
In my world aliens have antennas on their head
That make phone calls to family while they're lying in bed.
My drawings are fun and might not make sense
To someone who is boring and sleeps in a tent.
But I know I'm special and loved 'cause you see,
My mom and dad love me because I am me.

Taylor Duke, Grade 3
St James Episcopal School, TX

What Is a State?

What is a state? Is it a land with
large and small cities strewn across the area?
Is it a place made so people can call a certain
place home? What is a state?

Brian Ross, Grade 3
Annunciation Orthodox School, TX

Love

Love is when my dog licks me.
Love is when Mom puts me in this wonderful class.
Love is when my grandma knits me a sweater.
Love is when she picks me up!

Richard Batchley, Grade 1
Woodcrest School, CA

Friends

Friendly, funny
Laughing, running, playing
They sometimes are very silly
Girls

Marissa Magana, Grade 3
Tracy Learning Center - Primary Charter School, CA

The Green

Green feels like the very sharp blades of a field of pointy grass.
Green sounds like someone breaking a big, fresh, tasty piece of celery.
Green taste like yummy, smooth, barely been cut fresh apple.
Green looks like a big, beautiful, blossoming tree in the Spring.

Brittney Richins, Grade 3
Providence Hall, UT

Mr. Hall

Tall, nice
thinking, helping, caring
He is the best
teacher

John Choe, Grade 3
Wonderland Avenue Elementary School, CA

Lost

Have you ever
Had a pet,
A pet so special
As special as a mom
Or a dad?

I did!
My dog, George
Was great!

But one day,
He got out
And I
Lost him,
Forever.
Alex Elguezabal, Grade 3
C W Cline Primary School, TX

Cleo

Scratch, meow
Cleo
She's running fast
Cleo
Adventurous
Cleo
ROARING
Cleo

Clawing
Cleo
Nice
Cleo
Purring
Cleo
Abigail Colbert, Grade 3
C W Cline Primary School, TX

Winter

White snow softly falls,
Cold air dances around the sky,
Winds blow down the street.
Mindy Truong, Grade 3
Oak Park Elementary School, CA

My Key

My key is
Golden
And
Locks with
A
Kiss
My key
Is special
One of a kind
My key
Is given easily
My key...
Alexandra Perkins, Grade 3
Old Town Elementary School, TX

The True Magic of Love!

I think love
Is midnight heaven.
Love always wears
Beautiful angels.
There are places
I truly love.
In my heart
I understand how you feel.
When I think of love
I understand love's magic.
In the country of love
I will always understand you.
Huda Ahmed, Grade 3
Oak Park Elementary School, CA

My Family

M e and my sister are playful
Y es I am not selfish

F riendly
A wesome
M ad at no one
I s awesome
L oves apples
Y es we love each other.
Nicholas Shyu, Grade 2
Camino Grove Elementary School, CA

Soccer Game

A soccer game
I'm two points down — run
score, score, score!
I'm undefeated now
I've really got to win
to stay alive
William Symmans, Grade 3
Annunciation Orthodox School, TX

Mom and Dad

T oo nice to be my mom or dad
H elps me when I need help
A sweet person who loves me
N icer than anybody I ever met
K isses me like crazy
S ays they love me every day
Auzshia Clevenger, Grade 3
Elder Creek Elementary School, CA

1, 2, 3

One, two, three
I see a tree.
One, two, three
do you see me?
One, two, three
I want some tea!
Raygan Snyder, Grade 3
Faith Academy of Bellville, TX

Flowers

Flowers may be little
but when they sprout and
come out they mean more
then drops of rain more
then when the river flows
they mean the world
Kylie Witherbee, Grade 3
Edward Byrom Elementary School, OR

A Soccer Ball's Life with Players

The ball is shiny, rolling on the field
A player used his body for a shield
The goalie shirt is blue
The shorts are brand new
Soccer ball is shiny and small
The player is very smart and tall
Sammy Campos, Grade 3
Oak Park Elementary School, CA

Sydney

S miles when we get treats.
Y esterday, Mom made vegetable trays.
D one doing my work.
N ow I can read my new book!
E ats daddy's dinners.
Y es, Parker is my big brother.
Sydney, Kindergarten
Woodcrest School, CA

Rain

Drip drop
The lightning strikes
Then the thunder comes
Everybody screams!!
McCrae Crawford, Grade 3
Three Rivers Elementary School, TX

Beach House

I had a beach house
made of sand.
The waves came in
that house needs land!
Evan Bennett, Grade 1
St Mark's Day School, TX

Dogs

Dogs are so cuddly.
They like to play fetch a lot.
They are cute and nice.
Carson Myers, Grade 2
Robinson Elementary School, TX

Snakes

Snakes are cool, cool, cool.
At night snakes like to slither.
Their skin comes off now.
Harold 'Jay' Myers, Grade 2
Robinson Elementary School, TX

My First Love
I loved it at first sight
I got on it
I felt safe
with the sun shining
on its chestnut coat

I ride through the breeze
a sneeze, a wheeze
I'm riding my first love
that captured my heart
at first sight
Corinne Dundas, Grade 3
Old Town Elementary School, TX

Something in My Heart
Playing
Laughing
Giggling
Excitement
Fireworks
This reminds me
of something.
This something
is
called
JOY!
Tyler Sharp, Grade 3
Old Town Elementary School, TX

Red
A strawberry is as red as
a cherry,
an apple,
a rose,
and nail polish.
A strawberry is red like
punch,
an American flag,
a pen,
and a heart.
A strawberry is RED!
Madelynn Perez, Grade 3
St Aloysius Parochial School, CA

Lights
The lights
are so
shiny
like the sun
and stars.
Because the lights
twinkle like
stars.
And are bright
as the
sun.
Michala Lee, Grade 3
Old Town Elementary School, TX

Catapult o Catapult
Catapult o catapult
Shoot it high
Up all the way to the sky!

Catapult o catapult
Shoot one more!

Shoot it
All the
Way
To the front door!
Alexander Olsen, Grade 3
C W Cline Primary School, TX

A Black 'n' White Penguin
A black 'n' white penguin
Staring at me
With blue beautiful sparkling eyes
An orange scarf
The best smile
A beautiful silky coating
Perfect fur and
Perfect slim fins
Perfect belly
For sliding on ice
I named him Neko!
Ema Eshiet, Grade 3
Mission Bend Christian Academy, TX

Digging

I like to play outside.
I like to dig.
Digging,
Playing,
Making holes.
That is my thing.
Dominik Gaines, Grade 1
Longfellow Elementary School, TX

Sun

Sun
The sun
Looks like
A big
Ball of Orange Juice
Because it gets Dark
Tristen Garner, Grade 1
P H Greene Elementary School, TX

Basketball

I like basketball.
I make a hoop.
Spinning,
Shooting,
And, best of all, dunking.
That's my sport!
Mason McBride, Grade 1
Longfellow Elementary School, TX

Brown Dog

I had a little dog that was brown
And he barked at me
I put him in the garage
And I gave him some candy
Avani Koganti, Kindergarten
Legacy Christian Academy, NM

Fall

Leaves are coming down
kids eat in the sun and play
kids play all day long
Samantha Mendoza, Grade 3
St Raphael School, CA

Chocolate

C hewy
H ard
O ld fashioned
C andy.
O h so good
L oved by a lot of people
A lways yummy
T asty
E specially good
Adam Santana, Grade 3
St Aloysius Parochial School, CA

A Mouse

A mouse is in my house!
Ahhhhh!
He's eating all my food.
He's eating all my cheese.
He's making a mess with all my food,
And changing my mood.
Ahhhhh!
A mouse is in my house!
Lexi Little, Grade 1
P H Greene Elementary School, TX

Winter Fun

Snow day for playing
Kids throwing snowballs at friends
People running fast

Wind blows, people laugh
Birds flying south, kids wear jackets
Cold air, heater on
Danny Truong, Grade 3
Oak Park Elementary School, CA

Spring

Spring is flowers.
Spring is rain,
Spring is bugs.
Spring is snakes.
Maddisyn Lucas, Grade 1
Cache Valley Learning Center, UT

It's Spring

It's spring it's spring
  I'm having lots of fun.
Now it's time
  to play and run.
Flowers are here
  and all around.
I'm looking at beautiful
  grass on the ground.
Birds are chirping
  in the trees.
I see some
  buzzing bees.
        Josh Kelman, Grade 3
       Woodcrest School, CA

Feathered or Furry

What is an owl?
Is it an animal that
is nocturnal and sleeps
  in the light? Is it
hooting at night or an
animal with beautiful eyes?
Is it feathered or furry?
  Is it hard to see
  like a pin in a
  haystack? Is it
  scary or sweet?
What is an owl?
    Megan Niermeyer, Grade 3
Annunciation Orthodox School, TX

Christmas Is in the Air

You can smell it in the baked
  turkey right out of the oven.
You can taste it in the delicious eggnog.
You can hear it in the crunchy
cookies that the children are eating.
You can see it in the beautiful
  tree in the living room.
You can feel it in my
  soft little bed.
      Jordan Drake, Grade 3
A E Arnold Elementary School, CA

Disney World

One time I went to
Disney World.
I rode every ride that
Was possible.
I mostly liked
Down Town Disney,
'Cause you got to
Play free games.
I really liked
Epcot because
You can go
Round and round.
I really had a great time!
      Ryan Tostado, Grade 3
  C W Cline Primary School, TX

Art

What is art?

Is it only for the ones who find
the sound of paint being splattered
on the canvas or the slight sound
of pencil lead scratching on paper,
just waiting to become a masterpiece?

Is it a way to calm yourself down
when you are angry
or upset?

What is art?
      Natalie Peterson, Grade 3
Annunciation Orthodox School, TX

Alligators

Alligators can
Bite
Bite
Bite
Watch out
You may get bit
Ouch! Ouch!
    Donnie Colburn, Grade 1
P H Greene Elementary School, TX

Cookie
Cookie
crunchy, chewy
warming, relaxing, good
hungry, starving, sleepy, tired
tastes good

Sarah Howard, Grade 2
Tracy Learning Center - Primary Charter School, CA

Rainbow
Rainbow
colorful, fun
sliding down to the grass
makes me wonderful inside
colors

Sana Shokoor, Grade 2
Tracy Learning Center - Primary Charter School, CA

Cheerios
Crunch! Snap! Crunch! Snap!
Ravenous kids chomping loudly,
as crunchy as tromping on frosted grass.
Crummy circular cheerios crackling continuously.
Cracking!

Sydney Beck, Grade 3
Rae C Stedman Elementary School, AK

Lions
Lions
Furry and vicious
Running, jumping, scaring
Lions are kings of the jungle
Giants

Joshua Marlin, Grade 2
Tracy Learning Center - Primary Charter School, CA

Waterfall
You are pretty
You have blue fresh water
And you are on the mountains
Yosemite Falls
Many people visit you

Chae Hyun Kim, Grade 3
Wonderland Avenue Elementary School, CA

Bald Eagle
bald eagle
fast predator
flying, fishing, landing
smart, vicious, special, harmful
bird

Celeste Monasterio, Grade 3
Lorenzo De Zavala Elementary School, TX

Gold
Gold tastes like ripe lemons, juicy and sour.
Gold sounds like a bright yellow coin dropping to a marble floor.
Gold smells like sweet golden raisins.
Gold looks like leaves falling from a tree in Autumn.
Gold feels like paint slowly trickling onto your hand.

Liam Lounsbury, Grade 3
Providence Hall Charter School, UT

Spring Is Finally Here!
Spring is finally here, and all the snow has melted from the cold winter days.
Now that the ice is gone, we can go outside and ride our bikes and scooters.
It will rain instead of snow that is why everyone loves spring.
Also, all the plants and flowers have started to grow.
When it's winter again, we will go ice-skating and skiing.

Abby Kynaston, Grade 3
Providence Hall Charter School, UT

Kate
There once was a clover named Kate.
Who sat on the edge of a plate
The fancy fold dined,
On foods of a kind
Then, tossed her at quarter past eight.

Kyuhyuk Lim, Grade 3
Wonderland Avenue Elementary School, CA

My Dog Daisy
I have a young puppy named Daisy
And I really do think that she's crazy
Some think she's pug
But I know she's a chug
She's adorable, furry, and lazy

Rachel Rosner, Grade 3
Wonderland Avenue Elementary School, CA

Things of December

Families caroling,
People laughing,
Children playing,
These are the sounds of December.

Gingerbread baking,
Moms cooking,
Apple cider simmering,
These are the smells of December.

Trees are shining,
Paper tearing,
Everyone's playing,
These are the sights of December.
Elysia Nolan, Grade 3
Fort Worth Country Day School, TX

Amazing Goat

An amazing goat named Rockstead,
He can do a lot!
He eats anything!
He does anything we can do.
The goat can do anything we can do!
Rockstead can be crazy
But fun and lovable, too.
He's like a human.
Sometimes he tries to talk!
But all that comes out of his mouth is,
"Meeh!"
Sometimes I think
He's smarter than
Me!
Tia Armstrong, Grade 3
C W Cline Elementary School, TX

Tornadoes

Tornadoes
Destructive, windy
Twisting, destroying, chasing
A very powerful thing
Twister
Derrek Gardner, Grade 3
Ygnacio Valley Christian School, CA

Pretty Pink

Pink is a rose,
Pretty and prickly.
Pink is a pig,
Squealing in the morning.
Pink is a ribbon,
Shining bright as the sun.
Pink is a shrimp,
Very yummy like a treat.
Pink is a heart,
Pretty and sweet.
Pink is lipstick,
On your lips.
Katelyn Sheppard, Grade 1
Round Rock Christian Academy, TX

Owl

Owl, Owl how you hoot at night!
Owl, Owl
How high you fly in the dark sky!
Owl, Owl
How soft you are!
Owl, Owl
How you like the night.
Owl, Owl
Good night!
The sun is rising.
Owl, Owl
Go to bed!
Will Gregory, Grade 3
Three Rivers Elementary School, TX

Dog

Dog,
Dog,
You are fun
To play with,
But
Sometimes
You drive
Me
Crazy!
Colyn Buoy, Grade 3
C W Cline Primary School, TX

Writing
I see myself reading poetry
And I see Andrew playing around with Isaiah
I see a leaf falling from a tree
I feel breeze
I feel air
I feel grass
I see an airplane and a bird
It is fun writing

Drake Reed, Grade 2
Mosaic Academy, NM

Aaron
Loving, nice, playful.
Sibling of Andrew and Tyler.
Lover of playing outside.
Who feels happy about cats.
Who needs help with math.
Who gives to his brothers and friends.
Who fears the police.
Who would like to put all kittens in good homes.

Aaron Russon, Grade 3
Foothill School, UT

A Swift Fox
A flash in a field at night during a storm
A mountain lion chasing a rabbit in dark wet woods
Heat from a fiery furnace shooting at a carpet
A kangaroo hopping around in a zoo on a warm evening
A cat chasing its toy by a steaming hot fireplace
A piece of rough bark on a douglas fir tree
As slow as mice digging a deep and cold tunnel
A red kayak floating in a quick stream

Bella Christensen, Grade 3
Lolo Elementary School, MT

Tiger
Tiger
Fierce, powerful
Prowling, racing quickly
Feels like being invincible
Beastly

Tariq Gaba, Grade 3
Tracy Learning Center - Primary Charter School, CA

My Dog and the Car

Oh no!
Oh no!
How can this be?
My dog got hit
By a car!

Is she okay?
I don't know…

Oh, she's fine!
It's just a cut!
But we have to
Watch her
Just in case
It is more
Than a cut.
                Ross Lincecum, Grade 3
C W Cline Primary School, TX

Horseback Riding

Horseback riding
Exciting, enjoyable
Galloping, racing, kicking
Reins, saddle, blankets, hooves
Controlling, sitting, clopping
Awesome, easy
Riding
        Nellie Wilcox, Grade 1
            CLASS Academy, OR

My Dog Peanut

My dog Peanut
So nutty as can be!
I can't stand
His licking
Every day of the week.

If there was a contest
For the most licking dog
My dog would shine
And win every time!
            Robert Chuoke, Grade 3
C W Cline Elementary School, TX

I Know the Movies

I know the movies.
The sight of people meeting up together.
The people ordering popcorn and drinks.
The people parking their cars.
I know the movies.
The smell of buttery popcorn.
The smell of the seats filling the theater.
The smell of candy filling the theater.
I know the movies.
The soft seats I sit in.
The hard ground in the movie
The cold drink in my hand
I know the movies.
The sound of the people talking
The popcorn pop, pop popping
The starting of the movie
I know the movies.
The taste of buttery popcorn in my mouth
The Coke taste in my mouth
The chocolatey taste in my mouth
I know the movies.
            Olivia Lavorini, Grade 3
                Horn Academy, TX

Earth Is My Home

Earth is a land,
of cool water,
and green grass.
It's a part of,
nature,
like a sweet bird,
calling for me.
Earth is our,
perfect sphere,
like tasty,
round,
cookie dough.
Earth,
is a home,
for you,
and me.
        Jasmine Sigworth, Grade 3
Wilchester Elementary School, TX

Space

A place, **B** ack in space
C ars crashing into rocks, **D** ust all over the place
E very day with crashing cars
F reaky giants all over the place
G oing to different galaxies
H opping on Jupiter, **I** gnoring an alien
J umping all over the place
K icking a rock for a soccer ball
L aughing with friends
M aking other stuff, **N** ever fighting with an alien
O utside in space
P eople trying to get to Earth
Q uick people that are running in space
R unning in space, **S** hhhh I'm sleeping
T asting plants
U sing a rock to sleep on
V enus is a planet
W hy do astronauts come to my home?
X -ray in different places
Y ou can live in space
Z apping aliens with my rifle

Shams Awwad, Grade 3
Salam Academy, NM

My Schedule

Wake up!
It's morning!
Don't put the covers over your head
Get out of bed
Get dressed and go
No TV
Eat breakfast and get ready
Off we go
I'm tired so tired
I wish I could sleep
But no, I can't
I can barely talk
…zzz Ah, sorry
I wake up a…zzz
Sorry I wake up at 6:00 a.m.
Good night…zzzzzz

Harry Libowsky, Grade 3
Wonderland Avenue Elementary School, CA

The Soccer Game

The crowds are going wild,
Whoooo, whoooo, whoooo!

The girl ran yelling,
Pass it, Pass it!

She makes the first kick,
Crash!

The ball hit a tree,
Oh no!

I made a goal,
Score, score!

My team won,
Yay, yay, yay!

That was a ton of fun!
Elisan Wagner, Grade 3
Round Rock Christian Academy, TX

My Life

When I grow up
I'll learn to turn a car into a robot
I'll learn to become a scientist
I'll find dinosaur bones
To form them into a dinosaur

When I grow up
I'll help my Dad
To fix Mom's car
And fix the light.

When my sister needs help
I will tell her how to fix her belt.

I love you Mom
I love you Dad
And you are the best.
Andrew Tran, Grade 2
Scholars Academy, CA

Armadillo

Armadillo
Small, shell
Digging, rolling, crawling
Ball, claw, green, bumpy
Snapping, swimming, hiding
Big, small
Turtle
Javier Cruz, Grade 3
Creekside Park Elementary School, AK

Spring

Spring is warm.
Spring is grass.
Spring is fun.
Spring is baby animals.
Spring is flowers.
Spring is happy.
Spring is gardens.
Zac Dunker, Kindergarten
Cache Valley Learning Center, UT

Lizards

L ittle
I love lizards
Z ips after crickets
A gile
R un a lot
D efinitely adorable
S its in the sun
Nelson Kitsuse, Grade 2
Camino Grove Elementary School, CA

Wolf

Wolf
Mean, scary
Running, jumping, sneaking
Eyes, ears, teeth, claws
Looking, listening, biting
Fast, furry
Animal
Aseem Agarwal, Grade 1
CLASS Academy, OR

The Teacher

Mrs. Martin is sweet and kind
And when she reads she opens her mind
When we ask a big, big favor
She not only does it but adds flavor
Beginning of day comes rolling along
First comes flag and then a nice song
Spanish, Math, and Number Board
For Science we learn of a man with a sword
Recess, Reading, Language Arts
Lunch, Recess, and a pile of hearts
SSR or Silent Sustained Reading
Next Read Aloud and then Writing
Social Studies, PE, Health
A day done fine, better than wealth
But there's more, Show and Tell, Art
Then Mrs. Martin to the library cart
Then my teacher works far into the night
How can she work without sleep tight?
But she does it, she does it, and just fine
And that's a responsibility I wish were mine
And that is my teacher!

Olivia Farnsworth, Grade 3
Troy Elementary School, OR

Gravity

Yesterday I learned about gravity, what an amazing thing!
If you go up, then you'll come down, how exquisitely interesting!
But just this morning I was wondering if it works the other way
If you go down, will you go up? But then wouldn't we see people flying every day?
So today I decided to try it, to do a science experiment on my bike
You might doubt this method, but I won't throw it out the window, that would just
    be childlike
So I rode my bright cherry red bike to the steepest hill in our neighborhood
But as I looked down my life flashed before my eyes, just the beginning of my
    childhood
I jumped on my bike, and flew down the hill with my eyes shut tight
But suddenly my trusty bicycle hit a rock, my bike slid out from under me and way
    out of sight
I fell right on the asphalt street as my bicycle's wheels popped off!
This "science experiment" gave me a broken arm, while everyone called me a
    show off!

Mary Kate DuFour, Grade 3
Wagon Wheel Elementary School, CA

Butterfly

The butterfly is very tiny.
It has wings that are very shiny.

It flies away very fast.
When the big danger has passed.

When it flies it spreads its wings.
It looks beautiful when it swings.

It's so pretty like a high kite.
It glows beautifully at night.

Talia Menchio, Grade 3
Hamlin Street Elementary School, CA

Video Game

V iolence on the screen
I nteresting games
D onkey Kong
E xciting
O ccupy time

G ames
A wesome
M any games
E lectric

Jaden Wardwell, Grade 2
CLASS Academy, OR

Ivy

I love me
V ery much.
Y ou go girl.

G iggling is my favorite
R eading is fun
A pples are good
E njoy school
T reats are super
Z ebras are great

Ivy Graetz, Grade 3
Foothill School, UT

Fish

Two fish in a tank
Swimming around together
In fresh cool water

Shelby Grant, Grade 3
Plum Creek Elementary School, TX

Springtime

Trees in an orchard
Flowers bloom in the spring time
Juicy red apples

Meghan Murphy, Grade 3
Plum Creek Elementary School, TX

Music

Rhythm makes people
Move and dance to the beat
Music is awesome

Trenton Lorett, Grade 3
Plum Creek Elementary School, TX

Lightning

Lightning flashes fast.
From gray clouds in the dark sky.
Lightning scares people.

Emiliano Piña, Grade 2
Our Lady of the Rosary School, CA

The Rain

The rain makes puddles.
After rain comes a rainbow.
The rain comes from clouds.

Joseph Huerta, Grade 2
Our Lady of the Rosary School, CA

Rainbows

Rainbows are lovely.
Rainbows shine in the blue sky.
Colorful rainbows.

Katherine Quintero, Grade 2
Our Lady of the Rosary School, CA

The Meadow

The meadow is a perfect place
To feel the wind blow on your face

There, friends and I have so much fun
We all get warmed by the hot sun

We take a basket full of food
It puts us in a happy mood

We hear birds, and the swishing of trees
And we see plants, flowers, grass, and bees
Tiffany Curiel, Grade 3
Hamlin Street Elementary School, CA

Pink

A pig is as pink as
    a heart,
    Hubba Bubba Gum,
    an eraser,
    and paint.
A pig is pink like
    roses,
    my glasses case,
    lips,
    and babies noses.
A pig is PINK!
Madison Cotta, Grade 3
St Aloysius Parochial School, CA

Spring

Spring is when flowers bloom.
And the birds like to zoom.

When the birds tweet tweet tweet.
It sounds so very sweet.

Spring is when the birds fly.
Way high in the blue sky.

I really like the spring.
It makes me want to sing.
Matthew Taylor, Grade 3
Hamlin Street Elementary School, CA

Poppies

Flowers in red bloom
waving in the rushing wind
poppies in springtime
spreading all around
popping up in every park
poppies on the ground.
Lauren Jensen, Grade 3
Wasatch Elementary School, UT

Recess

R unning time
E xercise we get
C ease working — start playing
E nergy is needed
S cents are on the playground
S lides are there to go down
Hailey Wright, Grade 2
Lakeport Elementary School, CA

Sunlight at Last

In Texas the
sun is roaring up to
the sky. I
dash outside towards
the blue sky, yellow sun
prepared for today.
Ryan Shultis, Grade 2
Annunciation Orthodox School, TX

Snake

Snake —
Purple, mean, poisonous —
Bites
Hard, often, around
Dylan Ramos, Grade 3
St Mary School, CA

Angels

Angels are not seen
You always have an angel
They are not strangers
Marcelo Cavazos, Grade 3
St John's Episcopal Day School, TX

Dreams

The only place where dreams
are impossible is in your own mind
Well, to achieve a dream is
hard. A dream is something
waiting to happen that you want
to happen. A dream is sad as a
rainy day or happy as sunshine!

Lauren St. Paul, Grade 3
Annunciation Orthodox School, TX

All About Audrey Alatorre

I am wild as a horse,
Sweet as an apple tree,
Fiery as the color red,
Open as a circle,
Funny as the number three,
Beautiful as an emerald,
And gentle as a raindrop.

Audrey Alatorre, Grade 1
Baldwin Stocker Elementary School, CA

Kaylee the Great

I am cute as a bunny,
Loving and precious as a rose,
Sweet and fabulous as the color pink,
Brilliant as a heart,
Independent as the number one,
Beautiful and passionate as a tourmaline,
And gentle as a breeze.

Kaylee Cheung, Grade 1
Baldwin Stocker Elementary School, CA

All About Me!

I am gentle as a cotton tail bunny,
Cute as a rose,
Peaceful as the color blue,
Loving as a heart,
Friendly as the number two,
Fiery as a bloodstone,
And sharp as a mountain.

Catherine Rivera, Grade 1
Baldwin Stocker Elementary School, CA

Happy

I am smart as a tiger,
Sweet as a rose,
Responsible as the color red,
Open as a circle,
Fair as the number eight,
Strong as steel,
And warm as firelight.

Trevor Hwee, Grade 1
Baldwin Stocker Elementary School, CA

As Tall as a Cactus

I am strong as a tiger,
Tall as cactus,
Peaceful as the color blue,
Round as a circle,
Lucky as the number seven,
Clean as a sapphire,
And burning hot as an inferno.

Jefferson He, Grade 1
Baldwin Stocker Elementary School, CA

My Mandala

I am sleepy as a dog,
Happy as a dandelion,
Nurturing as the color green,
Calm as a circle,
Creative as the number six,
Courageous as a diamond,
And sweet as the wind.

Howard Chang, Grade 1
Baldwin Stocker Elementary School, CA

Strong Water

I am tricky as a blue bird,
Happy as a sunflower,
Peaceful as the color blue,
Interesting as a quare,
Creative as the number six,
Courageous as a diamond,
And strong as water.

Kyle Li, Grade 1
Baldwin Stocker Elementary School, CA

Gum
Smells like apple pie coming from the sky
Tastes like it came from heaven, or maybe from the
Moon
I don't care where it came from
I just want more and more
I tastes so good I think it doesn't exist
It might even be made in China
What is this?
It tastes and smells like strawberry and apple
I think I'm going to die from the "yumminess!"
Mmmm, good!!!

Laine Nyberg, Grade 3
Lolo Elementary School, MT

I Know My Chocolate
I know my chocolate
The creamy yummy smell
The nutty taste
I know my chocolate
The creamy taste
With nuts inside
Crunchy chocolate inside
I know my chocolate
A brown, white, light brown, dark chocolate
I know my chocolate
The sticky melty soft chocolate of mine

Andrew Tran, Grade 3
Horn Academy, TX

A Day at the Zoo
Very cheerful, kind people roughly rush into the giant zoo
The kind, happy zookeeper is quietly feeding the flamingos on the hard, dirt floor
A large, gray hippo is sleeping heavily on the sandy bank of the small pond
A furry, brown bear is lazily walking near a green tree
The small, orange fish are quickly swimming in the large lake
A short, skinny monkey is swinging fast on the long vines
The long, tough cheetah is swiftly running on the rocky ground
An old, olive green turtle is slowly walked on the warm sand
A fluffy, black fox is silently roaming the wet grass of the zoo
When the appealing, amazing zoo gates gradually close, the children
Are gloomy, not wanting to go home

Isadora Kleiman, Grade 3
The Mirman School, CA

I Know My Brother Colton

I know my brother Colton
I feel the slobber from his mouth on my arm
I feel the smoothness from his arm on my face
I feel the roughness of his diaper
I know my brother Colton
I smell the stinkness from his diaper
I smell the drool from his mouth
I know my brother Colton
I taste the pancakes from his plate
I taste his little feet
I taste the treats from his treat bag
I know my brother Colton
I hear his crying in the night
I hear his laughter in the day
I hear the yelling from his mouth
I know my brother Colton
I see his teeth in his mouth
I see the smile on his face
I see his hair all curly and short
I know my brother Colton

Conner Kornmayer, Grade 3
Horn Academy, TX

My Life on a Ranch

I live on a ranch in the hills and trees,
Where the Monarchs fly and my neighbors are bees.
A river winds through cool and clear
Giving animals a drink like birds and deer.

In the fields the blue bonnets bloom.
So sometimes they need a little elbow room.
My dad raises goats, cows, and sheep.
Every baby lamb I see, I just want to keep.
My horse is named Popcorn, and he brings in the stock.
He carries me through the canyons, over cactus, and rock.
Once each year we shear and mark.
It is hard work, and it goes until dark.
I love my ranch life; it's where I want to be.
It's the perfect place for my family and me!

Parker Alsup, Grade 3
St James Episcopal School, TX

Pizza

The pizza was really round.
The pizza weighed a pound.
I dropped mine on the ground!

Benjamin Albornoz, Grade 2
Tracy Learning Center - Primary Charter School, CA

Fire

Hot, burning, big, small
Bright, colorful, smoke, heat, red
Fire truck, water, spark

Jose Cortez, Grade 2
Tracy Learning Center - Primary Charter School, CA

Money

It can be dirty
Sometimes it can be smelly
But you can spend it

D'Asia Gonzalez, Grade 3
Tracy Learning Center - Primary Charter School, CA

Dolphins

Jumping in the air
Swimming through the blue water
Gray and beautiful

Vanessa Salas, Grade 3
Tracy Learning Center - Primary Charter School, CA

Sunset

Beautiful sunset.
Orange and red streaks in the sky.
It ends very quick.

Angelica Gudmunson, Grade 3
Thomas Edison Charter School - North, UT

Summer

I love the hot sun
Summer is so beautiful
The grass is so green

Bailey Ann Bodrero, Grade 3
Thomas Edison Charter School - North, UT

The Dragon

A smooth fire,
A giant boom
on the floor.
I don't know what it is.
It's loud,
Big BOOM!
I think it is,
Do you think what I think?
I see it,
Do you see it?
I'm not really sure,
I think,
it's a dragon…
green,
with a sharp, crazy bump
and a short tail.
It is a dragon!
It's going
to eat me!
Oh, no!

Jarious Thak, Grade 2
Robert L Stevens Elementary School, CA

I Know Candy

I know candy
Chocolate and vanilla
Sweet and sour
Creamy and runny
I know candy
Bumpy and smooth
Carved and flat
Small and large
I know candy
Lots of colors
Lots of patterns
Lots of holes
I know candy
Minty smells
Sweet smells
Wonderful smells
I know candy
Crunchy sounds of wrappers
Loud sounds of people smacking
Soft sounds of waiting for more

Ashley Ellen Clarke, Grade 3
Horn Academy, TX

Who Am I?

I have two ears.
I have a mouth.
I have four legs.
I have two eyes.
I have four paws.
I have a tummy.
I have a nose.
I have long whiskers.
Who am I?
Am I a bunny?
Am I a goat?
Am I a lion?
Am I a dog?
Am I a tiger?
Am I a fox?
Who am I?
I am a cat!

Tomi Ishola, Grade 1
Kingwood Montessori School, TX

My Dog Tyler

Rolls around all day and night. Also
Plays rope with such delight
Then rolls in bed and sleeps
All night he wakes up as excited
As can be. Then
Goes in his kennel and thinks
He's trapped again but then at
4:00 pm I get home he
Wags his tail ready to go
Get the mail I let him
Out. He stretches ready
To play we go outside
On a walk I walk he talks.
When we get home, he chases the cats
Around. To him something new always
Has to be found. He is a great dog and
He always will be.

Trevor Bielik, Grade 3
Wilchester Elementary School, TX

Spring

Spring has pretty flowers
Spring has April showers.
Spring brings lots of joy,
Spring is for every girl and boy.
It is not summer, it's not fall.
It is not winter, not winter at all!
There are people jogging from breakfast to lunch.
Then they start eating, munch! Munch! Munch!
Then the mommy takes the baby and the baby takes the bear.
Both the mommy and the baby give each other love and care.
Pretty flowers in every size blooming in front of your own eyes.
It's like in the season spring, all the trees and mountains sing!
Instead of winds frosty cold, in this time of year sun is extra bold.
You can plant gardens, you can play ball or don't do anything else at all!
Talk to your mama, talk to your dad.
Make them happy, make them glad.
Feel the wind whispering in your ears,
Telling you give me some happy cheers!
When you want do it, shout out loud!
Spring has come and you're very proud!

Tanvi Panda, Grade 1
Wilma Fisher Elementary School, TX

Sacagawea

Sacagawea is small,
people call her bird woman.

She is a generous woman,
gave her blue bead belt to trade three capes for Lewis and Clark.

She is athletic,
runs fast as a mountain lion.

She is a caring person,
takes care of her family and friends.

She is adventurous,
wanted to travel with Clark, Lewis, and the Corps of Discovery.

She is an American Indian who truly accomplished one of the
most remarkable journeys in the United States.

Dara Lin, Grade 3
De Vargas Elementary School, CA

Christmas

C hristmas is a great holiday.
H ave lots of fun on your time off.
R emember to study even though it's a vacation.
I will miss school very much.
S tay very safe and healthy.
T ime for the Christmas Spirit.
M ake sure you're full of joy.
A pples are good when dipped in caramel.
S ave some cookies for Santa.

Joseph Crenshaw, Grade 3
Midland Elementary School, CA

Flicka

It was summer
I went to the ranch
I found a mustang
In the pasture, in the grass
I said to myself
This is one beautiful black mustang
I saw it bucking and kicking
I felt its fear
As she protected me from that wrecking deer.

Meagan Morgan, Grade 3
Three Rivers Elementary School, TX

Easter

At my church we march.
We hold palms in our hands.
Some people make crosses.
The priest will make a cross on my leg.
I like going to church.

Benjamin Guindi, Kindergarten
Notre Dame Academy Elementary School, CA

Rain

Whether the sky is blue
Whether the sky is not
Whether the ground is cold
Whether the ground is hot
Whether it's Winter, Spring, Summer, or Fall
As long as it's not raining, I like them all.

Robert Carey Karnes, Grade 3
Wesleyan Academe, TX

We Have a Cat
My sister has a cat
That is fat
I have a cat
That scratches my feet
My brother has a cat
That is mean to you
My mom has a cat
That hides
My dad has no cat
Steven Hilts, Grade 3
Warren Elementary School, OR

If I Were an Animal
If I were an animal.
A tiger shark I'd be.
I would live deep in the ocean.
And no one would see me.

I would have good eye sight.
I would get my food by hunting fish.
I would have big sharp teeth.
I hope I'd catch a tasty dish.
Parker Tweedley, Grade 2
Woodcrest School, CA

If I Were an Animal...
If I were an animal.
A kangaroo I would be.
I would jump all around.
Everybody would look at me.

I'd be very good at boxing.
I would be kicking my enemy.
I would live in Australia in the grass.
And eat leaves from a tree.
Joshua Eigenbrodt, Grade 2
Woodcrest School, CA

If I Were an Animal...
If I were an animal.
A dog I would be.
I would be playful and kind.
People would like to see me.

I would be a lab.
A big lab I would be.
I would play all day
And I would be happy.
Katrina Shrago, Grade 2
Woodcrest School, CA

T-Rex
T-Rex
Carnivore, colossal
Combating, chasing, vanishing
He had tiny arms
Tyrannosaurus
Manases Zarate, Grade 2
Dixie Sun Elementary School, UT

The Pool
I like to go to the pool.
It is really cool.
It was much hotter
under the water.
What an amazing pool.
Cecilia Roche, Grade 3
Foothill School, UT

Friends
Friends are good.
Friends are awesome.
What would we do without them?
They're there to help.
They're there to laugh and play.
And always there to be your friend.
Ryan Byrd, Grade 3
Wilchester Elementary School, TX

Animals
Animals
Cute, adorable
Babies are born
Bear cubs, rabbits, deer
Wake from hibernation
Lovely, beautiful
Maya Carranza, Grade 3
A E Arnold Elementary School, CA

Laughter

If laughter makes you want to sing,
Giggles, smiles, last awhile,
'till someone bursts your bubble.
Precious Life is not to waste
You've got to leave a trail.
Laugh, before it is too late,
And smile while you sail.
Tell a joke, or something funny —
Don't just do it for the money,
But for other souls to enjoy.
Maybe you could share a toy,
Maybe write a special story,
Maybe add something glory.
But nothing else that makes them frown,
Or say something that makes them make a mad sound.
If you have an idea, that you want to share,
Don't just keep it in there.
Let your feelings spill out to your friends,
And the laughter and friendship that never ends.
Laughter — is a wonderful thing!

Juliette Rault-Wang, Grade 3
The Nueva School, CA

Hugs

Hugs for everyone and everything. (Even dangerous animals!)
You can hug a shark, but be ready to be a tasty dinner.
You can hug a giraffe, but be ready to fly among the trees.
You can hug a platypus, but be ready to feel unbelievable pain.
You can hug a python, but be ready for a very tight squeeze.
You can hug an ostrich, but be ready to run with lightning speed.
You can hug a kangaroo, but be ready to jump, jump, jump.
But remember if you hug mom and dad, you might just get the best hug in the
    whole world.
Not like the kangaroo with the jolting jump,
Not like the ostrich with the preposterous pace,
Not like the python with the suffocating squeeze,
Not like the platypus with the vile venom,
Not like the giraffe with the sky-high hug,
Not like the shark with the terrible teeth,
I choose to hug my family and friends, because they give me hugs that I love most!

Emily Youngblood, Grade 3
St. Joseph Catholic School, CA

Alligator
Alligator Alligator
Snapping here and there
What do I do
When they are
Coming near,
I don't know, I don't know
I don't know what to do
When they are coming for
You!
Devin Garza, Grade 1
P H Greene Elementary School, TX

Squirrel
Fuzzy flying in the gleaming daylight
nibbling his acorns
jump and squeak
hiding on branches
with a giant fluffy tail
running on trees
running from dogs and foxes
running like speed racer
Go squirrel!
Austin McAlister, Grade 3
Old Town Elementary School, TX

Fish
Fish are small.
Some are big, really, really big.
Short and tall.
Long...not really.
Fat and thin.
Awesome!
Bloop...Bloop!
Camo...poof!
Done...Bloop.
Collin Tippit, Grade 1
P H Greene Elementary School, TX

Gods
Zeus is in charge
of the sky.
Poseidon is in charge
of the seas.
Hades is in charge
of the underworld.
Zeus throws lightning.
Poseidon throws waves.
Hades throws fire.
Thomas Satterwhite, Grade 3
Wilchester Elementary School, TX

Colton
C olton likes to do math.
O ften rides a snowmobile in the winter
L oves his mom and dad
T hree horses he has
O ften does homework
N ovember 12th is his birthday.
Colton Elliott, Grade 1
Spring Creek Elementary School, WY

Animals
Monkeys are expert swingers
Apes don't have tails
Rats are tiny rodents
It is unbelievable
Orangutans are expert climbers
Zach Schreiber, Grade 3
CLASS Academy, OR

Robot
R ocks at making juice
O n the move
B ad sometimes
O n it when cookies are baking
T he robot is a good toy
Adam Harakey, Grade 2
CLASS Academy, OR

Charles the Fish
Charles is my fish
He is red
I feed my fish once a day
I look at my fish
He lives in a fish tank
He is my fish
Katelyn Sumner, Kindergarten
Legacy Christian Academy, NM

Ethan Klein

Ethan sings in the rain.
Talk, talk, talk.
Happy in the sun.
All the people having fun.
Nets are falling.

Keep the cat in the house.
Lots of animals.
Every video game is mine!
In the house now!
Never touch my candy!

Ethan Klein, Grade 1
Kentwood Elementary School, CA

Blue Bird

There once was a good blue bird in a nest
She really loved it for it was the best

One day she had four blue eggs
In two weeks she saw eight legs

She always went outside to sing
For it was her favorite thing

After all this hard work she took a nap
With all her little chicks in her lap

Alyssa Rodriguez, Grade 3
Hamlin Street Elementary School, CA

Friend

I want
my friend back.
Back to my world.
I just want
my friend back
with me,
and
me and him
were good friends.
I would do everything
to get him back.

Kevin Becerra, Grade 2
Robert L Stevens Elementary School, CA

Waterfall

Splash! The water is so fast
it sounds like laughing and as you put
your hand in, on a hot summer day,
you feel like you are in the cool
days of Minnesota. You hear it rumbling
and as soon as you slide down and
land in the lake, like a water slide,
you hear a splash with drips of
water in the air. You feel cool and
relaxed from the laughing voice of
the water.

Michaela Skaribas, Grade 3
Annunciation Orthodox School, TX

Video Games

V ery fun
I love video games
D estiny
E ntertainment
O bsessions

G ames
A wesome
M arvelous
E xciting
S uper cool

Nathan Schulte, Grade 3
Wilchester Elementary School, TX

The Bee

A bee goes from flower to flower.
A bee likes to have lots of power.

The bee likes to be free.
He flies up to the tree.

He is black and yellow.
He lives in a meadow.

It makes a buzzing sound
When it goes round and round.

Olivia Lehman, Grade 3
Hamlin Street Elementary School, CA

Horses

Black, chestnut, white or brown
In the
Stables or the pasture.

A gleaming
Horse so sweet,
Like cotton candy that you love so much.

As pretty as can be,
Like a fresh apple
From the tree.

If you care for her,
She'll care for you, today and every day.
Eileen Gex, Grade 3
Wilchester Elementary School, TX

Rain, Thunder, Then Lightning

Thunder comes
with a boomm
like a cannon ball
getting shot
out of a cannon
then comes lightning
with a big yellow strike
coming out of the sky
like a big yellow laser.
Rain falls down
like teardrops
from a little boy crying.
That's what happens when
it rains.
Jack Kelly, Grade 3
Wilchester Elementary School, TX

Fishing Trip

One sunny day
I was getting ready for my fishing trip.
I headed out,
I caught lots of crabs
But no fish.
The day grew longer
I got a tag,
Then one by one
We pulled tons of fish
In the boat.
We caught so many
We ran out of bait
It turned out to be
A good day after all.
Kevin Harmon, Grade 3
Three Rivers Elementary School, TX

Our Star

You can see my hot gas and fiery flames
    dancing in my soul
And heat pouncing out to planets
    that surround me.
My flaming heat takes about
    eight minutes to capture Earth.
All planets take orbit around me.
If you look at me for long enough,
    you'll be as blind as a bat.
I give some of my light to my friend,
    the moon.
The moon does my job for me at night.
I'm Master of the Milky Way
— The Sun.
Katie MacArthur, Grade 3
Saigling Elementary School, TX

My Nice Sisters

My sisters are nice!
They give me advice!
My sisters are nice to play with!
At the sea...
On the very very sandy sea!
Madeline Olsen, Grade 2
Camino Grove Elementary School, CA

Castles

Castles
Grey, Stone
Towering, scarily above the sky
Mightily protecting
The Fortress
Henry Lowe, Grade 3
Carlthorp School, CA

Penguins
Penguins
Smelly, fat
Eating, sliding, swimming
Eat little fish, squid, and shrimp
Emperor
Elianah Locke, Grade 2
Robinson Elementary School, TX

Cat
Cat
Soft, warm
Loving, kissing, purring
Comes out and plays
Feline
Sofia Vitale, Grade 1
Kentwood Elementary School, CA

Sunny
Our sun is bright
Our sun is shining
Our sun gives us light to see
Our sun gives us energy
The sun is my favorite.
Juan Morin, Grade 3
Three Rivers Elementary School, TX

Penguins
Rock hopper
Aggressive, cute
Diving, swimming, sliding
They live all around the world.
Penguin
Mason Flippin, Grade 2
Robinson Elementary School, TX

Beef Jerky
A fish swimming in the ocean
Rocks lying on the road
Crispy steak that just got cooked
A fish's scales
I love beef jerky! It tastes like salmon!
Levi McGovern, Grade 3
Lolo Elementary School, MT

Kayla
K ind
A t school
Y ellow is cool
L auryn is my friend
A lways playing
Kayla Montejano, Grade 3
St Aloysius Parochial School, CA

Rock Hopper
Penguins
Aggressive, fatties
Laying eggs, diving, playing
Up to 22 inches tall.
Rock hopper
Jacob Harris, Grade 2
Robinson Elementary School, TX

Penguin
Rock hopper
Red eyes, pink feet
Hopping, fighting, eating
Eats tiny squid
Squid-eater
Kobe Baker, Grade 2
Robinson Elementary School, TX

Dad
Awesome
Handsome, playful
Loving, caring, nurturing
Funny, cool
Dad
Sydney Bosarge, Grade 3
Horn Academy, TX

The Whale
Whale
Huge, gentle
Spraying, jumping, diving
Always swimming with its family
Mammal
Maya Hernandez, Grade 1
Kentwood Elementary School, CA

Horseback Riding

I love to go horseback riding on a sunny day,
Up on a hill, in a forest, or near a bay.
I like running and doing obstacle courses
With any one of my beautiful horses.
From their long eyelashes to their lovely tails,
I admire them on and off the trails.
I love the wind rushing through my hair
When we go so smooth and as fast as I dare.
The thumping of hooves is such a rush
Especially when we jump over a large bush.
It's really cool to ride in the rain
Especially with my big Great Dane.
I like to go to the horse races
Where we see them go through their paces.
Horses are fun when they jump around
And when they roll and scratch on the ground.
My horses are so fun and mean so much;
My heart is bigger because of their touch.
My horses make my life complete.
Thank God for horses because they are neat!

Lizzie Artim, Grade 3
St. Joseph Catholic School, CA

The Alphabetic Dinosaur

A Blue
Cuban Dinosaur
Eats Fat
Gorillas
Hungrily Ignoring
Jabbing Kangaroos
Laughing Mysteriously
Now Offering
Purple Quiet
Racing Sneakers
To Ugly
Vile Whales
X-raying Yaks
Zapping
American Boys
Called David

David Hirschhorn, Grade 3
Wonderland Avenue Elementary School, CA

Pokémon

Pokémon are very awesome,
Pokémon are cool,
It's fun to battle,
It's fun to play,
It's also fun to raise Pokémon all day.
Pokémon is tons of fun,
Much better than bakugon or digimon,
Cause Pokémon are so awesome.
So if you're bored or if you're not,
Just play some Pokémon,
It will be fun.

Sean Healy, Grade 3
Wilchester Elementary School, TX

I Love School

I love school
It's so cool
when morning comes
and in bed I drool
Mom wakes me
and I'm off to school
the bell rings
class begins
math, science and recess
then home waiting
for another day of school

Jalen Williams, Grade 3
Russian Jack Elementary School, AK

Sharks

In the deep ocean,
I'm closing my
eyes,
wavy water against my arm,
floating in the cool water.
Something feels funny,
I start to swim
like a Puma,
in the deep ocean.
Stop, stop, please.
I don't want to get eaten!

Adonis Gutierrez, Grade 2
Robert L Stevens Elementary School, CA

Summer

Blue is the color of my pool.
During summer, it's really cool.

Pink is the color of my swimsuit.
It is striped and very cute.

Green is the color of my dress.
Looking for it, I made a mess.

Purple is the color of my shorts.
I wore them to the fishing ports.

Mary-Kate Goff, Kindergarten
Fort Worth Christian School, TX

Springtime

Springtime, springtime,
It's my kind of time.
Birds sing,
Chimes and bells ring.
Spring, spring,
What will it bring?
Like flowers, apples, and more friends.
When you wake up —
Sunshine in your room.
Get out and play,
It's your spring day!

Goddess Cannon, Grade 3
Henry Haight Elementary School, CA

Planets, Planets...

Planets, Planets you are small,
Planets, Planets you are big,
Planets, Planets you are cold,
Planets, Planets you are hot.
Mercury, Venus, Earth, and Mars
Saturn, Jupiter, Uranus,
Neptune, and Pluto you are all.
Sun is not a planet — What is it?
A STAR — Yes, it is.
Planets, Planets, what are these!
Planets, Planets so many of these!

Ibraheem Qureshi, Grade 1
Scholars Academy, CA

Trees

Trees are pretty and shiny
you could not cut down trees
because we won't have any
fruit it is fun having trees
because you could
imagine eating fruit.
Tanya Valdez, Grade 3
Three Rivers Elementary School, TX

Spring

Spring is flowers!
Spring is fun!
Spring is green grass!
Spring is sunny!
Spring is rain!
Spring is warm!
Katie Chambers, Grade 1
Cache Valley Learning Center, UT

King of the Jungle

A lion is the jungle king.
He roars a roar to sing.
Around his neck grows a mane.
He likes to eat meat not grain.
People drive to see lions in the zoo.
They would laugh if a lion said moo.
Maddie Appelhans, Grade 1
Spring Creek Elementary School, WY

Polar Bears

furry, playful
powerful, white, killer
ferocious, huge, tall, soft
Polar Bears
Vanessa Rios, Grade 3
Henry Haight Elementary School, CA

The Moon

The moon shines so bright.
It has a silvery glow.
Good night. Good night moon.
Lily Jensen, Grade 3
Wasatch Elementary School, UT

I Feel the Need for Speed!

I feel the need for speed!!

I feel like a race car
going 100 miles per hour!

Or a mountain lion
trying to catch its prey!!!!!

I feel like a football
flying in the air!

A deer trying to run away
from its Predator...

I FEEL THE NEED FOR SPEED!!
Alyson Elguezabal, Grade 3
C W Cline Primary School, TX

Shark Survival

Sharks
Swift, strong, scary...

Starving...

Swimming, splashing, scanning,
Searching, smelling, sneaking,
Stalking, squirming, swerving,
Smacking, swirling, swarming,
Surrounding, scuffling, shredding,
Swallowing...

Seals, swordfishes, squids...

Surviving!
Lissete Baeza, Grade 2
Dixie Sun Elementary School, UT

Grass

The green grass is tall
The green grass sways in summer air
I play in the grass
Holly Booth, Grade 3
Ygnacio Valley Christian School, CA

Video Games

V iolent characters
I ntense
D iddy Kong is the son of Donkey Kong
E lectronic
O verrated

G ames are fun
A wesome
M arvelous
E xtreme
S kills on the game

Aaron Ha, Grade 2
CLASS Academy, OR

Karoline

Karoline
Smart, fast, faunny
Child of Jirka and Kandi
Lover of my family
Who feels happy
Who needs me
Who gives love
Who fears my scary dreams
Who would like to see my guinea pig
In Czech Republic
Pytlicek

Karoline Pytlicek, Grade 1
Kentwood Elementary School, CA

Spring

Spring is green.
Spring is beautiful.

Spring is flowers.
Spring is swimming in
a cool pool all day

Spring is gentle
rides on horseback for hours.
Spring is running, playing
tag in the front yard all day.

Celeste Bienz, Grade 3
Spring Creek Elementary School, WY

Rainbows

Rainbows,
When it rains
and it's sunshiny,
the sun and rain
make a beautiful rainbow,
as pretty as a parrot.
When you walk to it,
you might see it,
or you might not see it.
I feel like
I'm one of the colors.

Angel Cuevas, Grade 2
Robert L Stevens Elementary School, CA

The Tree

It is fun to sit under a tree
Because there are exciting things to see.

Trees are homes to many small things.
It is where you hear a bird sing.

When I climb up big trees
I can see lots of bees.

Sitting under a tree is fun.
It blocks you from the bright hot sun.

Jonathon Semerjian, Grade 3
Hamlin Street Elementary School, CA

Flowers

I saw some nice flowers in the city.
They were pink and red and oh so pretty.

I know that they need water and sun.
Having a flower is so much fun.

My flower smells so sweet.
It is also a big treat.

I'll never let my flower go.
Not even in the cold or snow.

Parnian Jebraeili, Grade 3
Hamlin Street Elementary School, CA

Blue

Blue is the sea
Blue is the sky
Blue is the color of bright blue eyes

Blue is the ocean
Blue is the wave
Blue is the inside of a very dark cave
Yejin Kim, Grade 3
Wilchester Elementary School, TX

Mr. Quack

There was a Duck named Mr. Quack
Once Mr. Quack was carrying a sack,
Then he found his friend named Zack,
In Zack's sack, were Jacks,
He sold them all
And he became tall,
And then he wanted all his jacks back.
Joseph Stull, Kindergarten
R D White Elementary School, CA

My Hero

My hero was born on Christmas Day.
Nursed her brother night and day.
Started a free school in New Jersey.
Helped injured soldiers without a fee.
She became a volunteer in the Red Cross.
She started the American Red Cross.
My brave and kind hero, Clara Barton.
Pia Shah, Grade 2
Montessori Learning Institute, TX

Dew

Dew in the morning.
Dew at night.
Dew in the grass.

The beautiful dew,
It glistens in the sunshine.
The magical dew.
Savannah Cochran, Grade 3
Wasatch Elementary School, UT

Like a Princess

Dancing ballerina flying through the air,
Pretty as a fairy.
Magic wings and shiny hair,
And a movie star sister.
Queen mother in a castle,
With a purple baby unicorn,
And Daddy loves me too.
Vivian Mai Huong Tran, Kindergarten
Scholars Academy, CA

Everything Is So Beautiful

Birds are so beautiful as fall leaves.
Sky is so beautiful as a clear lake.
Clouds are so white as snow.
Sun is so yellow as a lemon cake.
But at night everything is black
Nothing is bright
It is dark and everything is quiet.
Sparsh Johri, Kindergarten
Scholars Academy, CA

The Cabin

Family cabin
Building campfires
Playing with puppies
Watching out for bears
Beware!!
Hiking, fishing, boating
Fun, fun, fun!
Ryan Delzer, Grade 3
Selwyn College Preparatory School, TX

Land

Land
Land is far away
Land is far from the ocean
Land is far from the sky
Land is far from everything
But it is not far from me
Because I live on land
Faraz Abbasi, Grade 1
P H Greene Elementary School, TX

Stars in the Night

Night is falling, it is dark.
Stars are twinkling
There's a spark.

Here comes the moon, white and bright.
There is a rocket ship
Making trails in the night.

Nocturnal animals come out at night.
Looking for food
They take a bite.

There is a meteor flying by,
Burning up
Through the very dark sky.

Starry night, starry night.
Here and there, far and near.
Many things are in our sight.

Izaac LaBauve, Grade 1
P H Greene Elementary School, TX

Poetry Rocks!

Poetry rocks!
Poetry is fun,
It is my first time.
I really just love it,
But time flew by.
I try to jot down
All my thoughts you know.
I wish time was slower
To let my thoughts grow and grow.
Poetry is hard,
Or that is what they say.
It is pretty easy
Just don't give it a day.
Poetry is soothing,
Poetry is fun,
Poetry is warming,
Just like the sun.

Abhaya Chopra, Grade 3
Horn Academy, TX

Lovely as a Red Heart

I am small as a Chihuahua,
Sweet as a daisy,
Happy and joyful as the color yellow,
Loving as a heart,
Friendly as the number two,
Shiny as a garnet,
And beautiful as a garden.

Alexa Rahardjo, Grade 1
Baldwin Stocker Elementary School, CA

Me

A wesome
S mile
H appy
L ove
Y ou
N oble
N ice

Ashlynn Wied, Grade 3
Faith Academy of Bellville, TX

Shy Emily

I am shy as a bunny,
patient as a blossom,
sweet as the color lavender,
gentle as a cone,
graceful as the number 20,
kind as an emerald,
and friendly as a water drip.

Emily Yu, Grade 1
Baldwin Stocker Elementary School, CA

Aaron the Great

I am adventurous as a dolphin,
dependable as an apple tree,
creative as the color sky blue,
honest as a cone,
trusting as the number 100,
bold as a diamond,
and friendly as ocean water.

Aaron Zhao, Grade 1
Baldwin Stocker Elementary School, CA

Big Sister and Little Sister
Big sister
Nice, helpful
Helping, letting, liking
People, Veronica, Danica, love
Loving, playing, falling
Playful, lovable
Little sister

Trevor Knowlden, Grade 2
Tracy Learning Center - Primary Charter School, CA

If I Was a Flag
If I was a flag my name would be ZAK.
I'd have fifty stars and thirteen stripes.
I'd live next to Providence Hall.
I'd have a pet bald eagle.
I'd be in the Navy.
I'd be a fantastic waving flag in the wind.
But most of all I'd be a United States of America flag.

Zakary Benson, Grade 3
Providence Hall Charter School, UT

Feelings!
Sometimes I feel like a cyclone hitting a boat.
Sometimes I feel like a tornado swooshing houses.
Sometimes I feel like a rainbow shining from the sky, because I'm happy.
Sometimes I feel like a storm cloud blazing from the sky.
Sometimes I feel like a ghost scaring people.
Sometimes I feel like a sticky starfish, sticky like maple syrup.
Sometimes I feel like a star shining from the sky.

Tawfiq Mohammad, Grade 2
Longfellow Elementary School, TX

Cleo
Cleo is my dog she likes it when I am around.
Her coat is like a chocolate bar brown.
I love it when she jumps right up to me and licks me in the face.
I always know when my dog is feeling left out.
My dog is getting larger she is practically humongous!
Most of the time she is laying down but some times she is active.
I always will love that dog no matter what she does.

Zachary Pierce, Grade 3
Wilchester Elementary School, TX

What Purple Is

Purple is ripe grapes on a vine,
Ready to be pressed to bitter wine.
Purple is children climbing the trees,
It is the sound of the still, buzzing bees.
Purple is a happy dog running through the fields,
The sly cat in the bushes, soon to be revealed.
Purple is evening clouds glowing in the sky,
It is the sweet taste of blueberry pie.
Purple is my favorite color!

Luna Adelt, Grade 3
Spring Creek Elementary School, WY

August

August is the month of a little girl's birthday
August is a great feeling

August feels like a sprinkle of water
August looks like sugar plumbs dancing

August tastes like a chocolate covered strawberry
August is a nice bright pink
August is as pretty as a rose, it smells like one too

Amy Djuvik, Grade 3
Wilchester Elementary School, TX

Puppy

Puppy
Soft, beautiful
Walking, running, playing
Always sniffs me at night
Lovely

Emma Sales, Grade 2
Tracy Learning Center - Primary Charter School, CA

Santa's the Best

Santa's big
Santa's red
Santa gives me presents
Every Christmas Day
He is so good and sends Christmas cheer
We like presents and you will get the best this year!

Fernando Gonzalez, Grade 3
St John's Episcopal Day School, TX

Tigers

Dangerous, orange
Black stripes, orange fur, sharp teeth
Carnivore, scary

Manal Siddiqui, Grade 3
Tracy Learning Center - Primary Charter School, CA

Rose

I had a flower that was a rose.
I smell the flower with my nose.
The flower got wet from the hose.

Alondra Chavez, Grade 2
Tracy Learning Center - Primary Charter School, CA

Students

Listens to teachers.
Sometimes does very bad things
To get on the board.

Josiah Adrineda, Grade 2
Tracy Learning Center - Primary Charter School, CA

The Sun

It is blazing hot
It is very far away
Planets orbit it

Veronica Knowlden, Grade 3
Tracy Learning Center - Primary Charter School, CA

Fireflies

Fireflies glowing
They are in the dark blue sky
They shine like the sun

Skylar Tsimmerman, Grade 3
Wonderland Avenue Elementary School, CA

Flying Birds

Big birds in the sky
Falcons soaring in the air
All have a big squawk

Levi, Grade 3
Wonderland Avenue Elementary School, CA

Beautiful Pink

Pink is roses, pink is sunset,
And we all know pink is our big lips!
Don't you think pink sounds like bright pink roses blowing in the breeze?
Or smells like perfume or the nail polish girls wear?
Or maybe it feels like the pink blush in bunnies ears,
What does pink taste like?
Well, of course, pink tastes like sweet candy and juicy watermelon,
I hope you enjoyed my poem of beautiful pink!

Daisy Cano, Grade 3
Marguerite Hahn Elementary School, CA

Kyra

Kind, loving, nice
Sibling of Kedrick, Cassandra, Katelynn, and Corban.
Lover of art.
Who feels passionate about everyone.
Who needs nice people around.
Who gives all she can.
Who fears the dark.
Who would like to see world peace.

Kyra Perkins, Grade 3
Foothill School, UT

A Brave Person

Who fought in the French and Indian War?
Who built a road to Kentucky with 30 men?
Who rescued his daughter from being kidnapped by the Shawnee?
Who was captured by the Shawnee and accepted in their tribe?
Who moved with his family to Missouri?
Daniel Boone!

Arya Sreedharan, Grade 2
Montessori Learning Institute, TX

Stars

Stars are here, stars are there, stars are everywhere
I know why they are in the sky
But I can't tell you why
It will make you cry
And if you cry, I will sigh

Nicholus Taylor, Grade 3
Legacy Christian Academy, NM

Sky and Ground
Sky
Blue, cloudy
Winding, swirling, blowing
Ran, hail, rock, dirt
Pounding, standing, shaking
Brown, rocky
Ground

Brannon Burrell, Grade 3
Tracy Learning Center - Primary Charter School, CA

Teacher and Student
Teacher
Beautiful, helpful
Laughing, talking, smiling
Paper, pencil, book, lunch
Writing, playing, jumping
Nice, friendly
Student

Shanel Nayyar, Grade 2
Tracy Learning Center - Primary Charter School, CA

Gun and Flower
Gun
Hard, loud
Shooting, hurting, dying
Metal, bullets, leaf, pollen
Opening, watering, growing
Pretty, colorful
Flower

Milan Jaspal, Grade 2
Tracy Learning Center - Primary Charter School, CA

Kind and Mean
Kind
Sweet, lovely
Helping, loving, playing
People, animals, bullies, people
Bullying, hitting, beating
Cruel, rude
Mean

Steven Basurto, Grade 2
Tracy Learning Center - Primary Charter School, CA

Winter
Winter
icy, snowy
skiing, snowing, freezing
Olympics, snowman, swimsuits, sun
melting, playing, swimming
burn, hot
summer.

Quynh Trosien, Grade 2
Tracy Learning Center - Primary Charter School, CA

Nonfiction/Fiction
Nonfiction
true, real
exploring, finding, learning
experts, whiz kids, wordsmiths, storytellers
picturing, imagining, journeying
pretend, make believe
fiction

Allyson Baker, Grade 2
Tracy Learning Center - Primary Charter School, CA

Dog/Cat
Dog
fast, strong
racing, playing, sleeping
bones, leash, fur, claws
loving, waking, purring
happy, scratchy
cat

Bryce Campbell, Grade 2
Tracy Learning Center - Primary Charter School, CA

Motorcycle/Bicycle
Motorcycle
fast, loud
speeding, racing, driving
gas, Honda, pedals, basket
pedaling, riding, sitting
slow, little
bicycle

Emiliano Olmos, Grade 2
Tracy Learning Center - Primary Charter School, CA

My Family

I'm going to tell you about my family.
My dad is a lawyer,
My mom runs a business,
And my brother is the cleanest of us all,
The rest of my family is nice
Although they are different,
I will love them forever.
Connor Johnson, Grade 3
Providence Hall, UT

My Best Friend

I had a little dog
That swam in a puddle
He had a house
That he lived in
He didn't try to get out
Of his house
He is my best friend
Samiah Taylor, Kindergarten
Legacy Christian Academy, NM

The Wild Wind

Whoosh goes the wild wind.
Whipping by many tall trees,
Cooling the birds off.

Spreading flower seeds,
Pushing the sailboats along.
Whoosh goes the wild wind.
Kirsten Steele, Grade 3
Wasatch Elementary School, UT

Where I Went

Our journey to Chicago
I was ecstatic, delighted, and marvelous
I felt frightened.
When the airplane started to fly
I was also shy.
Because it was my first time
I will remember when I'm 29.
Alan Delgado, Grade 3
Juliet Morris Elementary School, CA

Ice Cream

Ice Cream
Ice Cream
I had Ice Cream
It is Yummy
It is Yummy
Ice Cream
I had Ice Cream
Jasmine Hernandez, Grade 1
P H Greene Elementary School, TX

Friend

Friend
Nice, Friendly
Caring, Loving, Nice
Great, Fun, Mean, Hurtful,
Rough, Uncaring, Unfun
Wild, Nasty
Enemy
Austin Sample, Grade 3
Horn Academy, TX

Little Turtle

I had a little turtle
His name was John
He accidentally snapped at me
So I put him in the pool
He loves candy
So I gave him some chocolate
And I gave him bananas too
Kylie Thomas, Kindergarten
Legacy Christian Academy, NM

Dangling Dragonflies

A plane gliding across the sky
Tickling feet scampering across your arm
A colorful treasure flying in the air
Glass wings like glass in
a frame
A darting dashing dart
Swish, swoosh, zip, zap, zoom!
Patrick (Brand) Gibson, Grade 3
Lolo Elementary School, MT

Love

Love is when my mom gets me ice cream.
Love is when my dad buys me shoes.
Love is when my brother kisses me.
Love is when my mom puts me in a wonderful classroom.

Malia Le'au, Grade 1
Woodcrest School, CA

Rain Forest

Beautiful, green, snakes
Long, awesome, rainy, humid
Waterfalls, trees, bugs

Nolan Eilers, Grade 2
Tracy Learning Center - Primary Charter School, CA

Flowers

Beautiful, lovely
Colorful, petals, water
Stem, butterfly, nice

Xitlalic Mora, Grade 2
Tracy Learning Center - Primary Charter School, CA

My Dad

My dad is going to come back.
He is going to give me a present.
I think the present is going to be a jet.

Ruben Parvaresh, Kindergarten
Notre Dame Academy Elementary School, CA

Birds

Soft, colorful birds
Blue jays, robins, and eagles
Delicate beauty

Joshua Hernandez, Grade 3
Tracy Learning Center - Primary Charter School, CA

Wind

Petals in the air
Rustling through my long, brown hair
Always in the air

Jasjot Kaur, Grade 3
Tracy Learning Center - Primary Charter School, CA

What Easter Is About

Easter is fun, it brings good cheer,
It is sure to come every year.
But Easter is not about chocolates galore,
It is when Jesus was beaten and sore.
For after all this he was put on the cross,
And everyone thought it was a great loss.
But little did they know that when three days would end,
We would be able to call him our Friend.
They would be rejoicing and having great cheer,
And that is why we celebrate Easter every year.

Hailey Matthews, Grade 3
Home School, OR

Paint

Paint tastes like icky gooey glue,
Yucky and blucky!
Paint feels like sticky liquid,
Gooey and horrible!
Paint smells like stinky markers,
Disgusting and smelly!
Paint sounds like bubbles,
Popping and bubbling!
Paint looks like circles of colors and rainbows,
Beautiful and amazing!

Leah Shepherd, Grade 2
Round Rock Christian Academy, TX

Air

Air sounds like roaring wind blowing something down,
Loud and strong!
Air looks like a ghost,
Nothing and invisible!
Air feels like wind,
Blowy and breezy!
Air tastes like nothing,
Clear and clean!
Air smells like the stuff that is in it,
Food and gasoline!

Joshua Millikan, Grade 2
Round Rock Christian Academy, TX

The Rhythm of the Dolphins

I'm gliding swiftly across the ocean waves.
The sun is setting.
I quietly dive to my BIG home, the sea.
Bubbles surround me.
I'm moving my tail fin to the rhythm of the sea.
As I swim to my flock the sun goes down.
I look up through the glassy top of the ocean and see the twinkling of
an audience of stars.
The waves gently flow up and down.
I'm home.
Another day in the ocean
Another rhythm
Each one different than the one before
Good Night!

Abigail Dewsnup, Grade 3
Providence Hall, UT

Morning

The sweet drift of flowers come,
And the birds sing with grace.
Stillness falls
The only sound is your own thoughts thinking.
Morning is the time of the day when it starts,
When all the animals awaken.

The least bit of commotion
In the house,
Healthy breakfast
PLOP on a plate,
Is eaten with milk
By a person alone.
Morning.

Caitlyn Czinder, Grade 3
Stewart Elementary School, TX

Similes

Shoes are like a warm place for your feet.
Magnets are like sticky glue.
Snow is like a big cold shower when it is hot.
Pants are like clothes for your legs.
A lion is like a fast car.

Elizabeth Trinh, Grade 3
Elder Creek Elementary School, CA

Where I Am From

I am from sparkly crown pins, reading mystery books, and writing in cursive.
I am from long, thin grass that tickles my feet, tall willows with branches dangling around me, and cheetahs running swiftly on a terrain.
I am from warm dumplings on a clean white plate and rice that is as white as snow.
I am from loving Grandpas and caring Grandmas.
I am from an artistic family with dark, black eyes.
I am from "Go to bed!" and "A Mouse with a Bell" after I come home from tutor.
I am from my cuddly rabbit with a pig's snout.
I am from sweet Moon and strong Sangjin.
I am from my parents teaching me how to write in Korean.
I am from old pictures of black and white with my cousins.

Loren Lee, Grade 3
Juliet Morris Elementary School, CA

Rainbows from the Sky

Rainbow is a sticker,
That is sticking on you.
Rainbow is an icy,
That drips on you.
Rainbow is a bag,
That your mom carries in the grocery store.
Rainbow is a crystal,
That you can find.
Rainbow is a kite,
Flying in the sky.
Rainbow is a book,
That you are reading.

Rohan Gnaniah, Grade 1
Round Rock Christian Academy, TX

Chocolate

C ocoa beans make the food.
H ungry stomach growls.
O ver the hill near the house is the candy store.
C andy surrounds the store.
O pen the wrapper.
L ick the chocolate.
A te the bar.
T rash can takes the empty wrapper.
E njoyed the yummy chocolate bar.

Erica Altman, Grade 3
Horn Academy, TX

Can You Play with Me?

Friend,
Friend,
are you going to play with me?
Not today,
said my friend.
Can you?
Can you play with me, Dad?
No, no
I cannot
play with you.
Whooooo
can play
with me?
Can my teacher play with me?
Yes.
My body pops up with joy!
Angelica Toro, Grade 2
Robert L Stevens Elementary School, CA

I Don't Want to Write

I don't want to write a poem
Because I don't
Know what to write about.
I know
I'm writing one anyway
Because my teacher made me.
But,
I write one anyway.
(I know it doesn't make sense.)
I really, really, really, really, really
REALLY
Don't feel like it!
I just don't really
Feel like it...
At all!
Kenzie McKeever, Grade 3
C W Cline Primary School, TX

Mrs. Wenzel

Mrs. Wenzel is a nice and true teacher,
I wish she was a preacher.
Ryan Rives, Grade 1
St Pius X School, TX

Spring

It's Spring. It's Spring.
And what do we see?
We see blue birds
In a big tree.
It's Spring. It's Spring.
And what do we see?
We see yellow butterflies
Flying by me.
Ethan Francis, Grade 1
Woodcrest School, CA

Jellyfish

Jellyfish, Jellyfish,
I love how you sparkle at night,
Big and bright,
But now I have to go,
Sweet dreams little jellyfish,
Good night,
Good night,
Good night.
Haley Evans, Grade 3
C W Cline Primary School, TX

Baseball

Soar ball—Homerun!
Our team needs the win
to move on
To the championship.
This is our last chance.
It is going,
going and it is gone.
Another grand slam!
Cole A. Dutherage, Grade 3
Annunciation Orthodox School, TX

Stars That Twinkle

Stars so bright
that I want to look at it
but I can't
because it's so bright
and I have to go to bed.
Christian Sosa, Grade 3
Old Town Elementary School, TX

My Grandparents

Once my
Grandpa went
To sleep and he
Never woke up.
So he died.
He was a great grandpa.
Still we don't know how he died
And we miss him so much.

But my Grandma didn't die,
And we still go
To the nursing home
To visit her
Whenever we can.
My grandma lives
With a crazy woman
In her nursing home.
When we're there
She talks to herself a lot.
That is very sad.

I still love
My grandparents so much!
Carson Davis, Grade 3
C W Cline Primary School, TX

The Raccoon

The raccoon is in the park.
It goes out when it is dark.

I see the sneaky fine raccoon.
It is looking towards the moon.

He ate my delicious meal.
He is going to pay for this steal.

With his small round short ears
He always can hear very clear.

He eats everything with his claw.
And his sharp claws are very like a saw.
Mehdi Fahimipour, Grade 3
Hamlin Street Elementary School, CA

Leopard and Prey

Fast as a lightning bolt,
 In the African jungle,
Soaring thought the plane.
 It's a leopard dying for its prey.
It sits and waits,
 Mouth open and watering.

Tongue out,
 Jaws open clicking and clacking,
Then deep in the under growth,
He spots his delicious prey.

His mouth drools as he works a few steps
Then he…
Pounced!
And caught his wonderful prey.
Cole Oliphant, Grade 3
Wilchester Elementary School, TX

Wii

Wii
Big, long
Running, flying, riding
Wires, controller, cartridge, TV
Electrifying, controlling, playing
Exciting, helpful
Game
Morgan Nelson, Grade 3
CLASS Academy, OR

My Dog Sophzilla

She is so bad;
But she is so glad.

She chews, chews, chews;
Even on brand new shoes.

She digs, digs, digs;
And comes in looking like pigs.

We love her anyway!!!
Joey Garivey, Grade 3
C W Cline Primary School, TX

Sister

Sister
Precious, funny
Cuddling, sleeping, bossing
An angel showing happiness
Angel

Isaiah Woods, Grade 3
Tracy Learning Center - Primary Charter School, CA

Festus

My dog's name is Festus
He likes to come in our house all the time
He does not like storms because of the lightning
He is brown and wags his tail a lot
He sure does like me

Seth Kitching, Kindergarten
Legacy Christian Academy, NM

Winter

In winter it's so much fun
I like to run.
I like to go to the park,
and I don't like to go in the dark.
I like to play outside in the sun.

Asma Mohamed, Grade 2
Islamic School of Muslim Educational Trust, OR

Pink Flowers

Pink looks like a rose in a garden.
Pink sounds like a little bunny in the fields.
Pink smells like a rose.
Pink tastes like a sweet tart.
Pink feels like a very soft petal in a garden.

Sarah Bradshaw, Grade 3
Providence Hall Charter School, UT

Leprechaun

Leprechaun
Magic, hairy
Lying, pinching, leading
Reminds me of a pot of gold
Irish

Colby Buntin, Grade 2
Tracy Learning Center - Primary Charter School, CA

Kristie Ann Loves Her Cousin
Vanity
It means daughter, clean and smart.
It is the number 3.
It is like light colors in the sky when it rains.
It is when I went to Disneyland with my family.
It is the memory of my cousin Yasminn caring for me
Who taught me to care for others
When she makes me happy and cheerful.
My name is Vanity
It means being gracious, smart and supporting.

Vanity Mounsena, Grade 2
Keone'ula Elementary School, HI

A Daughter
Adaora
It means a daughter, clean, and cute.
It is the number 16.
it is the color of the dark sky.
It is like going to Disneyland when I was a baby.
It is a memory of how my parents were proud of me
Who taught me to be nice and helpful
When they taught me not to be angry and mean.
My name is Adaora
It means that everyone can have hope and faith in people.

Adaora Okeke, Grade 2
Keone'ula Elementary School, HI

Brand
Brannon
It means cool, nice, and awesome.
It is the number 100.
It is like the sun.
It is going to the beach with my family.
It is the memory of dad
Who taught me to be patient and caring
When he makes me wait for the train ride and say thank you.
My name is Brannon.
It means don't be mean.

Brannon Bardago, Grade 2
Keone'ula Elementary School, HI

A Zoo Adventure

The large, black, iron gates creak open at sunset,
and the visitors make their way in.
The huge, white ostrich eggs are in a dirt hole and are about to hatch.
The newly hatched babies' thin legs are slowly stumbling
as they run across the sandy plains.
Tall, yellow giraffes are eating green leaves
by the shimmering, clear, humongous pond.
The snow-white polar bears walk loudly around
sharing different foods with each other.
Joyful blue jays fly high around the peaceful, sunny zoo.
The skinny, brown deer are running on top of grassy, emerald fields.
Wrathful tigers furiously growl as they watch the eager people
staring contentedly at them.
Massive bears seem to murmur things so the excited people hear them
as they watch them caged behind steel bars.
Boisterous people cry happily, "Look!" as they watch
the cheerful animals eat excitedly around the brown, circular rocks.
At last, the tiresome animals slowly go into deep sleep inside their metal cages
while the huge gates squeak closed.

Elena Saviano, Grade 3
The Mirman School, CA

Joy and Peace

Love remembers,
Power and joy and beautiful peace.
In my wonderful heart
There is joy and laughter.
In my magical heart
Love hopes for me
When you pass by.
When I think of fantastic love
I feel peace in me.
So love
Amazing love
Where are you going to give me
Powerful joy and beautiful happiness.
I think magical love changes your behavior
In happy behavior of joy.

Cassandra Franco, Grade 3
Oak Park Elementary School, CA

Football

F lying balls through the air
O n the field players compete
c **O** lossal crowds cheering
T he fans on their feet chanting their team name
B ig hits on the field
A ll over the place
L ike a fight
L ater we go home.

Hasaan Bryant, Grade 3
Horn Academy, TX

Cheetahs and Cats

Cheetahs are fast, sloths are slow
Wow I wonder how fast I can go.
I have a cat, I try to race with him
but my cat always seems to run faster than me
I can never win.
So then I give him a treat,
he snacks on his yummy treat
and he takes a seat.

Savanna Garcia, Grade 3
Goethe International Charter School, CA

Beauty of the Sea

Colors of the sea live, breathe, and flow.
As some things die, other things grow.
Beautiful fish are all around,
Many treasures lay unfound.
Something different is always swimming by
That delights the soul and catches the eye.
Everything goes into one big sea bowl
Where it mixes and makes the beauty whole.

Shahaley Brandt, Grade 3
Foothill School, UT

Mischievous

Mischievous feels like a puma getting ready to pounce on the teacher,
It sounds like kids tattling on each other,
It looks like the teacher has gotten mad at me,
It tastes like a fire getting ready to explode in my mouth,
It smells like hot plastic dripping down the sides of a box.

Kimberly Jettenberg, Grade 3
Klatt Elementary School, AK

Pants

Pants
They help you
Groove
and Move
Dance
and Prance
Hailey Burciaga, Grade 1
P H Greene Elementary School, TX

Flowers

Flowers make me itch
Flowers make me twitch
Flowers make me wise
Flowers make me dive
Flowers everywhere…makes me shy
Flowers make me angry
Brieann Chan, Grade 2
Camino Grove Elementary School, CA

I Know My Cat

I know my cat
The small little animal
The warm purr of happiness
The little meow
That told me before…
I want food!
Travis Wu, Grade 3
Horn Academy, TX

Balloon

Balloon —
Small, purple, round —
Floats
Swiftly, often, outside
Lauren Sanabria, Grade 3
St Mary School, CA

Garden

A garden is fun.
Growing fruits and vegetables
You can grow flowers.
Nate Elizarraraz, Grade 3
Ygnacio Valley Christian School, CA

I Like Carrots

I like carrots,
Orange ones,
Red ones,
And purple ones.

I like carrots,
Thick ones,
Fat ones,
And juicy ones.

I like carrots,
Small ones,
Big ones.

I do like carrots!
Aarti Kalamangalam, Grade 1
Roberts Elementary School, TX

I Can't Write a Poem

Forget it
You must be kidding
It's only one o'clock
My pencil is poisoned
I have Malaria, call 9-1-1
My brain isn't starting
I can't think of ideas
There is an earthquake!
My house crumbled down
My alarm rang
Time's up? Uh-oh!
All I have is this dumb list of excuses
You like it? Really? No kidding?
Thanks a lot
Would you like to see another one?
Shin Kim, Grade 3
Juliet Morris Elementary School, CA

Earth Day

Earth Day is so fun
Many people recycle
Don't fill the landfill
Kendall Fisher, Grade 3
The Mirman School, CA

Rain
Rain falls upon me.
The rain forest is so wet.
Rain helps the plants grow.
Holly Nuño, Grade 2
Our Lady of the Rosary School, CA

Spring
I see frogs jumping.
Trees making shade for the pond.
A small breeze blows in.
Megan Cornia, Grade 3
Beitel Elementary School, WY

My Home
It is a safe place
when it is rainy outside.
I hear the raindrops.
Lance Hovis, Grade 3
Old Town Elementary School, TX

Winter
Hard wind blows through town.
Some people sliding on ice
falling down a lot.
Ethan Sell, Grade 3
Beitel Elementary School, WY

Wonderful Winter Fun
Snow days passing by,
Little children having fun.
And snowmen in sight.
Amy Nguyen, Grade 3
Oak Park Elementary School, CA

Winter
It is snowing hard.
You can't go on the roads now.
It is hard to see.
McKenna Clingman, Grade 3
Beitel Elementary School, WY

A Winter's Day
Snowflakes fall from sky.
Happily children make snowmen.
Soon they go for soup.
Tramina Ngo, Grade 3
Oak Park Elementary School, CA

Butterflies
Butterflies flying
so pretty and colorful.
Flying all day long!
Sadie Campbell, Grade 3
Beitel Elementary School, WY

Princess
Gray and black short fur
Eats a lot and barks a lot
She is my best friend
Cade Weger, Grade 3
C W Cline Primary School, TX

Snow
Snow is fun and cold.
Snow is fun with family.
Snow is very white.
Trey Temsik, Grade 3
Beitel Elementary School, WY

Feeling Music
Guitar strings strumming
peaceful as butterflies and
birds in the forest.
Clifford Dunn, Grade 2
Annunciation Orthodox School, TX

Summertime
It is summertime.
Butterflies are beautiful.
I like butterflies.
Anastasia Wood, Grade 3
Beitel Elementary School, WY

Nature's True Beauty

Spring is the happy season
Spring is the bloomy season
Spring is the season of birth
The season of clearness
The season of the blue
Oh, so blue and clear sky
Seeds grow into trees
Chicks are born from eggs
Animals are born everywhere
Oh, how come no one sees spring
How come nobody takes care of the Earth
Spring is such a good example
An example to take care of the Earth
It is an example of nature and true beauty
Make-up and combs and hair are nothing
Not even close to true beauty
Nature and spring are even better
I love it so much
Spring is my season of birth
It is an example to take care of the Earth
I love spring. Do you?

Ember Nishio, Grade 2
CHEP School - West, CA

Trip to the Mall

A trip to the mall,
Shop, shop, shop!
Pink and black plaid will be fine,
Search, search, search!
When I open the dressing room door,
Swish, swash, swush!
This cute outfit is too big,
Oh man, oh man, oh man!
Finally something my size,
Yes, yes, yes!
As they zip my credit card through the machine,
Cha-ching, cha-ching, cha-ching!
They put my clothes in the bag,
Stuff, stuff, stuff!
When I leave the store,
Success, success, success!

Jordan Crupper, Grade 3
Round Rock Christian Academy, TX

Cookies

Cookies
Round, circle
Eating, munching, crunching
Very hungry on Wednesday
Glad

Sana Siddiqui, Grade 2
Tracy Learning Center - Primary Charter School, CA

Santa

I like to go with my daddy to the mall.
I see Santa and tell him what I want.
I go in my room to sleep.
Santa comes when I'm sleeping.
He brings me toys.

Justin Murray, Kindergarten
Notre Dame Academy Elementary School, CA

Toad

toad
lumpy reptile
peeping, hopping, eating
helpful, load, nocturnal, large
animal

Kathrine Tallent, Grade 3
Lorenzo De Zavala Elementary School, TX

Snack Time

Snack time
Eating, funny
Laughing, talking, chewing
We love to eat snacks at snack time
Crackers

Kaelyn Blackwell, Grade 2
Tracy Learning Center - Primary Charter School, CA

Green

Green is the leaves.
Green is the color of a plump watermelon.
Green is the color of bus 47.
Green is the color of the OLD NAVY writing on my shirt.
Green.

Timothy Isom, Grade 1
Heritage Elementary School, UT

Grandmother

My grandmother died last year,
I used to like to have her near,
I never feared she would go away,
I miss her more every day
Now she is just a memory,
I always knew she loved me.

Sydney W., Grade 3
Wonderland Avenue Elementary School, CA

Every Single Time

Every time I pick up the phone something seems to be
Wrong! What has happened? Is the world gone?
Nothing is right I now have a fright! Things should be good do you think I should
find out what went wrong?
Who has done something really bad? It makes me really sad?
Well I still do not know what happened but it is time for me to GO!!!

Lauryn McClellan, Grade 3
Providence Hall, UT

I Wish

I wish I was a baby girl screaming.
I wish I was a sailor coming home in a row boat.
I wish I was an oak tree blowing in the wind.
I wish I was a hawk flapping its wings way up in the sky.
I wish I was a mist of air.
I wish…

Casey Shultis, Grade 2
Annunciation Orthodox School, TX

Animals

I used to be a plain white egg but now I am a mocking bird flying over the forest.
I used to be a puppy but now I am a 12 year old dog sleeping on a bed.
I used to be a baby narwhal but now I am an adult narwhal swimming
throughout the Antarctic waters.

Parker David Siegel, Grade 3
Annunciation Orthodox School, TX

One Night

One night I went for a nightly walk in the meadow. Animals came, tons of them.
Music! They all dance. The sun came up. They all left. So did I.
But the memory did not.

Emily Etheredge, Grade 3
Warren Elementary School, OR

Maui

On a beach in Maui
Dad got drilled by a wave.
Lucky for him
I made a great save.

He tumbled about
I gave out a shout.
Next thing he knew
I was pulling him out!
Wesley Rich, Grade 1
Troy Elementary School, OR

Flying in the Sky

Flying in the sky,
Is very high,
like a bird
in the sky.
The clouds are smooth,
like cotton.
They look like many shapes, too.
When the dark clouds come,
it turns dark as night.
Mariah Briceno, Grade 2
Robert L Stevens Elementary School, CA

Little Fish

Little fish
is very soft.
Makes me snuggle
on the bed.
A soft pillow
and a blanket too.
Little fish,
Little fish,
will you sleep next to me?
Angelica Gabino, Grade 2
Robert L Stevens Elementary School, CA

Dog and Cat

Little dog and little cat
are playing a game.

Dog and cat were best friends.
They play together all the time.
They play tag and hide and seek.

They always play together,
and they have good fun.
Kelly Yu, Grade 1
P H Greene Elementary School, TX

Easter

E aster fun, makes kids jump.
A fun day appears.
S unny days make kids happy.
T eachers have fun.
E ggs hiding everywhere.
R abbits hopping here and there.
Nikhita Mathur, Grade 2
CLASS Academy, OR

Eagle

White, brown
Flying, gliding, landing
Wings, claws, beak, eyes
Watching, grabbing, eating
Fast, quick
Bird
Vrishank Angadi, Grade 2
CLASS Academy, OR

Spring

Spring is my cat.
Spring is grass.
Spring is flowers.
Spring is swimming.
Spring is bees.
Madeline Odum Shahan, Kindergarten
Cache Valley Learning Center, UT

World of Warcraft

I'm happy
I'm happy
I'm level 33
I love my mom
And she is good to me!
John H. H. Bennett, Grade 3
C W Cline Primary School, TX

Zoo Animals

Giraffes stretch their necks, Stretch, stretch, stretch!
Giraffes eat the leaves oh so high, Munch, munch, munch!
Elephants spray water with their trunks, Squirt, spray, squirt!
Elephants splash with the water below their feet, Splash, splash, splash!
Lions growl at the people all around them, Growl, growl, growl!
Lions prowl around looking fiercely at everything, Prowl, prowl, prowl!
Turtles move so very slowly, Inch, inch, inch!
Turtles eat green moss, Lunch, munch, munch!
Cheetahs run super fast, Zoom, zoom, zoom!
Cheetahs run so fast you can't even see them, Zip, zang, zoom!
Cats are so cute and quiet, Shhh, shhh, shhh!
Cats make graceful sounds, Meow, meow, meow!
Monkeys climb every tree they see, Climb, climb, climb!
Monkeys make silly sounds, Ooh, ooh, aah, aah!
Koala bears are so cute and tiny, Cute, cute, cute!
Koala bears climb trees so high, Climb, climb, climb!
Panda bears are so sweet and cuddly, Cuddly, cuddly, cuddly!
Panda bears are quiet, Silent, silent, silent!
Zoo animals are fantastic, Awesome, awesome, awesome!
Zoo animals are God's amazing creatures, Amazing, amazing, amazing!

Karissa Varner, Grade 3
Round Rock Christian Academy, TX

War

War is an evil above all
Man against man, an unnecessary call
War is when both sides will not win, only fall

War is when families are torn apart
War is what leaves scars on innocent hearts
War is something that is not at all smart

War is when a soldier is on a bloody battlefield
Surrounded by fallen enemies and friends
Wondering if this is his last fight, his end
Wanting to stop the violence, wanting everyone to yield
He stops and wonders what the fight started for
He does not want anyone to hurt anymore
He now understands the uselessness of war
He now understands the uselessness of every war

Rida Mahmood, Grade 3
Islamic School of San Diego, CA

Wolves

Wolves are related to dogs.
Oh and wolves are brave.
Lots of black, brown and gray hair is on their bodies.
Finding a white wolf is lucky.

Jayce Rigler, Grade 3
Providence Hall, UT

A Dog

A dog likes to swim.
He likes to chase cats.
A dog likes to chase bats.
He likes to run.

Diego Gutierrez, Kindergarten
Notre Dame Academy Elementary School, CA

Green Apple, Red Apple

Green apples are sour red apples
are sweet those are so good.
I can't make a choice I love them so much.
I guess I'll have to eat both.

Kevin Edens, Grade 3
Three Rivers Elementary School, TX

I Wish

I wish I was a grown up, so I could get married.
I wish I was Michael Jackson, so I could be a super star.
I wish I was a baby, so I wouldn't have to go to school.
I wish I was Chucky, so I could scare people.

Khalon Nunn, Grade 3
Roosevelt Elementary School, CA

Love

Love is when my dad and mom give me presents.
Love is when my parents play with me!
Love is when my dad and mom read me a story.
Love is when my mom lets me make dinner.

Felix Marecaux, Grade 1
Woodcrest School, CA

The Great Me!
I am tough as sword fish,
clever as a fern,
graceful as the color orange,
calm as a cube,
nice as the number 100,000
honest as a moonstone,
and friendly as a crystal lake.
Arush Puri, Grade 1
Baldwin Stocker Elementary School, CA

The Great Isaac
I am sneaky as a rat,
patient as a cherry tree,
jolly as the color light blue,
cheerful as a circle,
shy as the number one,
funny as a blue diamond,
and happy as a mountain.
Isaac Molina, Grade 1
Baldwin Stocker Elementary School, CA

Miracles
A Miracle is
A moon with bright light
A sunflower rising up
Leaves dancing in the breeze
Whales jumping through hoops
The Earth with its trees and water
A tree's arms holding the wind
Ty Eastman, Grade 3
Coeur d'Alene Elementary School, CA

All About Cecilia
I am friendly as a dolphin,
sweet as a cherry tree,
cheerful as the color rosy red,
proud as a triangle,
carefree as the number nine,
patient as a crystal,
and funny as the ocean.
Cecilia Chiou, Grade 1
Baldwin Stocker Elementary School, CA

All About Savannah Vuong
I am adventurous as a dolphin,
kind as a daisy flower,
entertaining as the color light pink,
fair as a sphere,
funny as the number 100,
nice as an opal,
and friendly as air.
Savannah Vuong, Grade 1
Baldwin Stocker Elementary School, CA

Smart Kylie Montalvo
I am shy like a hamster,
creative as a red rose,
calm as the color purple,
lovely as a hexagon,
honest as the number 100,
bold as a diamond,
and friendly as the ocean.
Kylie Montalvo, Grade 1
Baldwin Stocker Elementary School, CA

The Great Kyle La
I am shy as a hamster,
sloppy as a vine,
even-tempered as the color gray,
respectful as a cube,
ordinary as the number 3,
lazy as gold,
and trusting as candle flames.
Kyle La, Grade 1
Baldwin Stocker Elementary School, CA

Funny Jacqueline
I am funny as a pig,
friendly as a cherry tree,
entertaining as the color pink,
shy as a cone,
kind as the number ten,
happy as a garnet,
and clever as water.
Jacqueline Mu, Grade 1
Baldwin Stocker Elementary School, CA

Thanksgiving
I am thankful for my pets because they are loving.
I am also thankful for good friends
because they play with me and are fun.
I am really thankful for my house
because I have a place to live.
Most of all, I am thankful for my mom and dad
because they help me get through everything.

Benjamin James, Grade 3
A E Arnold Elementary School, CA

What Is a Flower?
What is a flower? Is it something that makes your senses explode with imagination?
Does it let you smell all the scented goodness? Can it make you see all the pretty
colors like pink, blue and orange? Does it make you hear the buzzing of hungry
bees looking for delicious honey? If you feel the softness of their petals you'll
want to keep it forever. When you're walking through the park you'll want to
stay forever, sitting with the flowers just sitting there, asking yourself, "what is a
flower?"

Ellie Ragiel, Grade 3
Annunciation Orthodox School, TX

Christmas Is in the Air
You can smell it in the fresh, damp Christmas trees
that make me think of forests.
You can taste it in the yummy cupcakes.
You can hear it in the
happy children in their homes.
You can see it in the clear, shiny ornaments.
You can feel it in the cool, breezy wind.

James Chung, Grade 3
A E Arnold Elementary School, CA

Dragon
Dragon
Huge, big
Fire-breathing, clawing, smelling
Komodo dragon, leaping dragon, eagle, ptarmigan
Flying, finding, viewing
Wings, beak
Bird

Tesluoch Kong, Grade 3
Creekside Park Elementary School, AK

Spring

It's Spring. It's Spring.
And what do we see?
We see blue frogs
hopping by me.
It's spring. It's spring.
And what do we see?
We see red birds
flying by me.
Jordan Ellison, Grade 1
Woodcrest School, CA

Glasses

Glasses, glasses, hmm,
Which one do I want?
Yellow, red, pink?
I don't know.
Square, circle, rectangle?
Oh, I'll just pick!
I'll get red and circle.
I like these glasses.
Kayla Shipman, Grade 3
Three Rivers Elementary School, TX

Spring

It's spring. It's spring.
And what do we see?
We see brown kittens
Running by me.
It's spring. It's spring.
And what do we see?
We see black puppies
Swimming by me.
Cameron Hunt, Grade 1
Woodcrest School, CA

The Flower Lands

loud,
powerful, amazing,
and happy
flowers a nice
waterfall
Pierre Loch-Temzelides, Grade 2
Annunciation Orthodox School, TX

Football

I like to play football
It's my favorite sport of all
And I make touchdowns
By running with the ball.
When I make a touchdown
The crowd begins to cheer,
I feel very happy
When it's my team name that I hear!
Hayden Overstreet, Grade 3
Warren Elementary School, OR

Penguins

Penguins
Penguins Penguins
Can swim swim
Splash
Penguins Penguins
Can walk walk
Boom
Penguins lay eggs
Kameron Duke, Grade 1
P H Greene Elementary School, TX

Spring

It's spring. It's spring.
And what do we see?
We see white puppies
As pretty as can be.
It's spring. It's spring.
And what do we see?
We see gray kittens
Running by me.
Reyna Barnes, Grade 1
Woodcrest School, CA

fire

explosions
flashing back
to warships
burning forest fires
explosions
Merritt Young, Grade 2
Annunciation Orthodox School, TX

Flowers/Helpers
Flowers
Colorful, small
Smells like perfume
Sunlight, soil, water, shade
Helps get oxygen
Pretty, wet
Helpers
Jennifer Yun, Grade 3
A E Arnold Elementary School, CA

Spring/Water Sport
Spring
Hot, Easter
Animal, sunny, walking
March, egg, baseball, birds
Warm, fruit, vegetables
Swimming, beach
Water sport
David Jeong, Grade 3
A E Arnold Elementary School, CA

Flowers
Flowers,
Gracefully, gorgeous,
Blossom, bud, bloom,
Marigolds, daffodils, tulips, daisies
Hear buzzing sounds,
Sparkling, scented,
Nature
Anusha Basak, Grade 3
A E Arnold Elementary School, CA

Weather/Spring
Weather
Drizzling rain
Sprinkling, pouring, rain
Warm sun is shining
Takes my breath
Bright, cheerful
Spring
Mikaila Campos, Grade 3
A E Arnold Elementary School, CA

German Sheppard Me
Adventurous as a German Sheppard,
clever as a cactus,
creative as the color dark blue,
kind as a heart,
happy as the number 22,
shy as a ruby,
and funny as a breeze.
Isabella Giosso, Grade 1
Baldwin Stocker Elementary School, CA

My Symbols
I am smart as a squirrel,
Gentle as a lily,
Nurturing as the color green,
Loving as a heart,
Orderly as the number four,
Modest as a pearl,
And strong as a tornado.
Elaine Zhao, Grade 1
Baldwin Stocker Elementary School, CA

Luke Mandala
I am playful as a dog,
Funny as a cactus,
Ambitious as the color orange,
Strong as a triangle,
Orderly as the number two,
Courageous as an aquamarine,
And powerful as a volcano.
Luke Youngsma, Grade 1
Baldwin Stocker Elementary School, CA

Happy
I am playful as a horse
Happy as a daisy,
Cool as the color blue,
Kind as a heart,
Orderly as the number four,
Loving as an emerald,
And soft as rain.
Lawrence Sung, Grade 1
Baldwin Stocker Elementary School, CA

I Wish

I wish I had a paint set, so I could paint every day.
That would make me very happy.
I wish I got honor roll every year, so I could be a straight A student.
It would make me very happy.
I wish I could be a teacher.
I could give the students homework and teach them math.
I wish I had a library. I could get books for free and read them all the time.

Alexis Pilgrim, Grade 3
Roosevelt Elementary School, CA

Dancing Butterflies

Fluttering angel glides with sparkling sunlight in the sky
Whistling wind with cold snow falling from the clouds
Flowers blooming so fast with a beautiful bloom
Glittering gems dashing through the green grass
Golden treasure gliding onto delicate red roses
Blasting into the trees
A shimmering creature

Mark Pullium, Grade 3
Lolo Elementary School, MT

Dog and Cat

Dog
Nice, friendly
Barking, chasing, eating
Bones, bowl, tiger, tree
Scratching, meowing, loving
Cute, cuddly
Cat

Kimberly Noriega, Grade 2
Tracy Learning Center - Primary Charter School, CA

Dog

My dog's name is Zim
He knocked over Aiden
He plays games with the cat
He barks a lot
He got a shock collar which does make him bark
The storms freak him out
Zim is my dog

Dante Hernandez, Kindergarten
Legacy Christian Academy, NM

Reading Campaign

W e are so cool.
R eading Campaign we read a lot.
I love my parents.
T ime is going by fast.
I love my family so much even though I don't see them.
N atalie is my cousin.
G eorge is my cousin.

Arisa Nilo, Grade 3
Keone'ula Elementary School, HI

U.S. MILITARY

The U.S. Military protects us.
They help us too.
They fight for us like World War II.
They have battleships, aircraft carriers, and torpedoes.
Planes soar high.
Submarines go down deep.
U.S. Military thank you.

Zarren Oasay, Grade 3
Keone'ula Elementary School, HI

My Shining Star

My shining star is bright and shiny.
It is not too small or too big.
It twinkles above my head.
It keeps me safe and sound.
It gives me a wink and promises me to stay with me.
With my shinning star above my head, I am boosted
with confidence and reach far into my future.

Nuha Pagarkar, Grade 3
Islamic School of San Diego, CA

I See Images

I see images everywhere.
Nature surrounds me; I can't help but to adore its beauty.
I see people, so helpful, so powerful, and so inspired.
I see my family.
They are always there for me.
Regardless on my needs, they always came through for me.
I see the world with all it has to offer.

Sihaam Hussein, Grade 3
Islamic School of San Diego, CA

Easter

E aster is a holiday in spring.
A ll eggs have candy in them.
S ometimes the Easter bunny comes to town on Easter.
T he fun of Easter is finding your eggs.
E very egg is hidden somewhere.
R unning around looking for eggs on the playground.

Defne Alpay, Grade 2
CLASS Academy, OR

Daffodils

I saw a group of daffodils waving with the grass
as the birds sang
I walked among the daffodils
knowing I would keep this memory forever
I closed my eyes and saw the daffodils
the beautiful river and singing birds

Tom Zimmerman, Grade 3
Coeur d'Alene Avenue Elementary School, CA

Pandas

Cute and nice
They eat bamboo
Pandas can be wild
White as snow and black like its nose
Panda's friends are Eva, Aiga, Celena, Kashone, and Annabelle
Good climbers, sleepers and lazy

Annabelle Padachith, Grade 3
Creekside Park Elementary School, AK

Easter

On Easter I find eggs
Red, yellow, and green ones.
On Easter I look at Easter toys.
I wake up my parents early.

Camden Primozic, Kindergarten
Notre Dame Academy Elementary School, CA

Stars

Stars sparkle at night
They are such a delight
Gorgeous at sight

Taryn Mertens, Grade 3
Tracy Learning Center - Primary Charter School, CA

Sky

Clouds sing in the early morning.
The sun walks in the sky for hours.
Air pushes away from the ocean.
Rain kicks its way down to the ground.
Snow touches the ground calmly.
The birds happily fly through the air.
Stars sing when they glow in the night.
The moon sleeps when it is daytime.
Plants jump out of the ground and look up at the sky.
Wind works its way across the country as it blows from town to town.

Fiona Connerty, Grade 3
CLASS Academy, OR

Morning

Knees stretch as they sit down.
Newspapers talk when they're being read.
Tables hold food as you sit.
Coffee dies when you're done drinking it.
Spoons carry food as it runs to the mouth.
Birds sing as you have your morning meal.
Wind whispers as you open your door.
Refrigerators eat when people put food in them.
Rivers pull rocks as they move.
Toothbrushes snore as you brush your teeth.

Danya Abbruzzese, Grade 3
CLASS Academy, OR

Where I'm From

I am from red roses, pine trees, and homework.
I am from the leaping apple tree that gives me the juiciest, shiniest apple.
I am from my mom's tastiest, juiciest salad and from the creamy soup.
From grandmother and grandfather.
I am from brown eyes, black hair, and giant families.
I am from "BRUSH YOUR TEETH!" and "GO TO SLEEP!"
I am from a soft, smooth bear that cuddles me and hugs me every night.
I am from Thea Lee, Andy Lee, and my twin, Vicky.
I am from my sister and me fight for other stuff.
I am from the past fun and adventures that I have done with my family.

Angelina Lee, Grade 3
Juliet Morris Elementary School, CA

Bugs

Some bugs are creepy
Some bugs are slimy
Some bugs are crawly things

Some bugs can chirp
Some bugs can buzz
Some bugs can sing

Some bugs live in grass
Some bugs live in logs
Some bugs live like kings

Some bugs have big eyes
Some bugs have long legs
Some bugs have wings

Bugs, bugs, bugs,
I like bugs no matter what
That's all I'm saying
Luke Hockersmith, Grade 2
Jackson Elementary School, CA

My Dog!

Barks in
His
Cage

We let
Him out
He bolts rapidly
Out
Of
His
Cage

He
Slips
When
He
Turns

How funny he is!
Ethan Hiett, Grade 3
Lolo Elementary School, MT

A Dog Like No Other

Have you met any dog,
that's a perfect fit,
When you see him,
your heart fills with joy.
He tickles your nose
with his wet, moist one,
When he cries for attention,
you comfort him.
He has warm soft hair,
like a bunny's,
Chasing cats,
through the streets,
well,
his heart,
is screaming with joy,
that's,
what I call,
a dog like no other.
Rachel Harkins, Grade 3
Wilchester Elementary School, TX

My Nature Walk

We saw a rose.
It was tied in bows.
It's petals were really
Light. The sun was
Always bright.
The crickets
Were singing.
Morning bells
Were ringing.
So far…if I kept
Them in a jar — it would be
Better. Not for the weather.
When I was riding
My horse I heard all this.
My voice turned hoarse.
They were behind me.
Crickets kept going up a tree.
That's all I see.
Jessica Baskett, Grade 1
St. Joseph Catholic School, CA

Spring
Dew is on the ground.
Newborn baby chicks are chirping.
Farmers plant their seeds.
Ben Brown, Grade 3
Beitel Elementary School, WY

Flute Music
Water in creek.
Inspired by someone playing flute.
High pitch sleep.
Stephen Kelley, Grade 2
Annunciation Orthodox School, TX

Fall
In the smooth fall breeze
leaves are falling from the trees.
Birds are flying south.
Maxx Moore, Grade 3
Beitel Elementary School, WY

Spring
Afternoon shower
We play in the big puddles.
Then we go inside.
Helena Bryant, Grade 3
Beitel Elementary School, WY

Fall
In the fall I race.
Then I jump in the leaves.
Then I bury myself.
Cody Shandy, Grade 3
Beitel Elementary School, WY

Flamingos
Flamingos dancing.
In the water splashing kids.
Flamingos jumping.
Logan Knaub, Grade 3
Beitel Elementary School, WY

The Bad Day
I forgot my homework.
I am late for school.
I missed everything on math.
I only had time to paint half of a flower.
Lunchtime
My stomach hurts.
We had to go to my mom's aunt
Karen's funeral.
It was an awful, very bad day.
Brooke Guymon, Grade 3
Flaming Gorge School, UT

Winter
Snow shivers as you hold it.
Rain jumps when it hits a rock.
Snow forts giggle as you make them.
Ice skates tie themselves.
Ice shakes as you fish.
Snowballs throw as you hit someone.
Books scream as you run.
Snow flakes dance as you catch them.
Valentine cards sing as you open them.
Hot chocolate yells as you sip it.
Isabelle O'Leary, Grade 2
CLASS Academy, OR

Christmas Is in the Air
You can smell it in the
peppermint candy canes.
You can taste it in the
delicious hot cocoa.
You can hear it in the
dashing reindeer.
You can see it in the
twinkling ornament.
You can feel it in the
breezing wind.
Noah Shanahan, Grade 3
A E Arnold Elementary School, CA

The Little Green Frug

The little green frug
is as strange as can be.
It looks very small
but funny to me.
The frug is a frog
but also a bug.
It lives in a house
on a very soft rug.
The little green frug
is nice to you and me.
It swims and flies
it's very nice to see.

Noa Davny, Grade 2
Woodcrest School, CA

Me

S ome
H ow
I got
V oted
A nd said
Y es to

S inging
I love you to my
N ani, who is my
G randmother. Who lives in
H ayward, California

Shivay Singh, Grade 1
Kentwood Elementary School, CA

My Favorite Part of Me!

My favorite part of me
My fat brain!
Thinks
Keeps control
Pumps blood
Zombie without it
Pink
Wrinkly
Huge
Surrounded
My favorite part of me
My fat brain!

Herbert Tompkins, Grade 3
Los Medanos Elementary School, CA

Pretty Red

Red is an apple,
Yummy and shiny.
Red is a bow,
Nice and pretty.
Red is a tulip,
Blooming at spring.
Red is a firework,
Exploding at night.
Red is lip gloss,
All around your lip.
Red is your heart,
Giving joy to God.

Zoey Hill, Grade 1
Round Rock Christian Academy, TX

Football

I want a football,
buy my mom won't let me.
I want a football that is cool,
but my mom won't let me.
So, I asked can I please get one.
She said, "NO!"
So, I asked again and again,
and she said, "Yes!"
You're driving me nuts!!

Kaden Elkington, Grade 3
Foothill School, UT

Spring

Spring is birds.
Spring is warm.
Spring is raincoats.
Spring is rainy.
Spring is baby animals.
Spring is blossoms.
Spring is roses.
Spring is swimming.
Spring is sunshine.

Mark Latvakoski, Grade 1
Cache Valley Learning Center, UT

Snow

Snow here, snow there, snow everywhere
People making snowmen with all kinds of color
People throwing snowballs at each other
White snow, white snow, oh how they love snow!
Snow is cold, snow is freezing...
Ponds, lakes, water turns into ice
Skaters ride on ice and how much fun it is!

John Chen, Grade 2
Camino Grove Elementary School, CA

The Boy with No Feet

There was a boy who I was supposed to meet
He was in a wheelchair, for he had no feet
We were side by side like a marching band
He went off a jump that I thought he'd never land
He soared out in front, right toward the finish
When I finally caught up, I high-fived him and said,
"You did it!"

Brandon Kao, Grade 3
Carlthorp School, CA

Food

P opcorn is tasty and yummy.
O ranges are juicy.
K iwis have seeds in them.
E ggs are yellow.
M angos are yummy.
O ctopus is the best seafood I've ever tasted.
N uts are good for you.

Emma Charvat, Grade 3
CLASS Academy, OR

Food and Things

P opcorn is tasty.
O ranges are orangy.
K lickitat Street is the weirdest street in the world.
E aster is a nice holiday.
M onsters are scary.
O wners take care of their pets.
N oon is lunch time.

Anthony Charvat, Grade 3
CLASS Academy, OR

Football in the Sand
Playing football in the sand.
I can hear the band playing.
I can also hear them saying,
"Go! Go! Go!"
As the quarterback releases the ball,
To someone very, very small
That's me!
I catch the ball,
I run around,
I hit the ground.
Oh my gosh,
I got a touchdown!

Will Janos, Grade 3
Wonderland Avenue Elementary School, CA

Thanksgiving
T hanks to be together
H ave a good Thanksgiving
A round the table, gather and give thanks
N ice people going to the table
K ind people come to our house for Thanksgiving
S licing the turkey
G iving thanks
I nto the turkey we put stuffing
V acation turkey time
I n thanks
N ic has a good turkey
G iving food

Nicolas Duckworth, Grade 3
Lolo Elementary School, MT

Miracles
What is a miracle
a miracle is a cloud flying
or a squirrel getting nuts from a tree
telling me a secret
or the sand touching my feet
or the waves crashing onto the shore
or the stars twinkling like the sun
birds singing to me
or the Earth protecting me

Lourdes Urquiza, Grade 3
Coeur d'Alene Avenue Elementary School, CA

The Sky
The sky is light blue,
It's very beautiful,
There are lots of clouds in the sky.

Alysza Carurucan, Grade 3
Wonderland Avenue Elementary School, CA

Rain
Clear, enjoyable
Wet liquid drips from the clouds
Cold mist fills the air

Nevaeh Haines, Grade 2
Tracy Learning Center - Primary Charter School, CA

Softball
The ball is round.
It is hit on the ground.
It is pitched from the mound.

Emily Yanke, Grade 3
Tracy Learning Center - Primary Charter School, CA

Palm Trees
Swaying in the wind
Feather dusters of the sky
Cleaning all the stars

Nina Williams, Grade 3
Wonderland Avenue Elementary School, CA

Moon
The moon in the sky,
Shines in the dark, starry sky,
What a pretty sight.

Jina Yi, Grade 3
Wonderland Avenue Elementary School, CA

A Spider
In a milking barn
A spider begins to weave
Her beautiful web

Amanda Postman, Grade 3
Wonderland Avenue Elementary School, CA

The Beach
The ocean's waves roll.
The sun shines across the beach.
The fish love the sea.
Diego Kotlizky, Grade 3
Carlthorp School, CA

Rose
Pretty, summer rose
getting bigger as it grows,
the sun looks at it.
Dalila Dris, Grade 3
Goethe International Charter School, CA

Slimy Snakes
Snakes roam up and down
They don't even make a sound
Snakes are amazing
Aaron Abraham, Grade 3
Carlthorp School, CA

Frog
Sitting on a log
Very quiet and gently
Peacefully jumping
Kyle Biedermann, Grade 3
Horn Academy, TX

Spring
Spring is rainy.
Spring is baby animals.
Spring is rollerblading.
Shayde Gilbertson, Grade 1
Cache Valley Learning Center, UT

Tiger
Quietly sitting
Going to attack its prey
So it can eat lunch
Chase Wells, Grade 3
Horn Academy, TX

Spring
Spring is excellent. Spring is warm!
Spring is fun. Spring is fantastic.
Spring is happy.
Emma Larese-Casanova, Grade 1
Cache Valley Learning Center, UT

Turtle
Wonderful slow things
Having fun in the ocean
Slowly swimming fun
M. L. Paige Hernandez, Grade 3
Horn Academy, TX

Spring
Spring is warm.
Spring is flowers.
Spring is rain.
Clayton Conger, Kindergarten
Cache Valley Learning Center, UT

Baseball Cleats
Nike, Adidas
Super sharp cleats hit the ground
Cleats help play the game
Jackson Kelso, Grade 3
Horn Academy, TX

Spring
Spring is fun.
Spring is bees.
Spring is rain.
Jack Knight, Kindergarten
Cache Valley Learning Center, UT

Outside
I love going outside
Feeling the sun shine on me
Loving the cool breeze
Allison Clarke, Grade 3
Horn Academy, TX

Snowy/Sunny
Snowy
Cold, frosty
Sledding, skiing, freezing
Hat, mittens, hot, beach
Playing, swimming, surfing
Fire, swimsuit
Sunny

Gessica Oliveri, Grade 2
Tracy Learning Center - Primary Charter School, CA

Comedy to Tragedy
Comedy
Amuse, mischief
Amusing, clapping, laughing
Teacher, girl, heartache, loss
Distressing, wishing, worrying
Heavy, sad
Tragedy

Romi Tsang, Grade 2
Tracy Learning Center - Primary Charter School, CA

Day and Night
Day
Bright, Sunny
Walking, Talking, Playing
Work, School/Moon, Stars
Sleeping, Relaxing, Resting
Dark, Gloomy
Night

Sara Satoh, Grade 3
Tracy Learning Center - Primary Charter School, CA

Comedy/Tragedy
comedy
light, amusing
laughing, smiling, clapping,
entertainment, mischief, loss, heartache
worrying, wishing, distressing
heavy, sad
tragedy

Christian Silva, Grade 2
Tracy Learning Center - Primary Charter School, CA

Good Night

I sit by my window feeling the hard cold glass on my nose
I see all the lights of the nearby houses turning off
I think about all the people sleeping
And their wonderful dreams
The moon and the stars are doing their jobs
Lighting up the sky at night
And I think about what it would be like to be a star
Helping the moon
And in the morning saying goodbye see you next night
I see the nocturnal animals whispering their relaxing lullabies
And smell the cold fresh air cooling all the people
I hear cars beeping on a lovely night
And I wonder when will I fall asleep, when will it be morning
I take my cold nose off the glass window
And say good night moon
Good night stars
Good night animals
Good night everybody in their cozy bed
Good night world
And I fall asleep

Jonah Braaksma, Grade 3
Coeur d'Alene Avenue Elementary School, CA

The Zoo

The large, iron gates open slowly with a loud squeak.
A yellow bus, parked near the silvery iron zoo gates,
glimmer in the brilliant morning.
An oversized elephant hears the shouting children yards away.
Joyful children see the flamingos gracefully dipping their heads into water,
scooping up the squirmy fish.
Rhinoceroses and hippopotamuses are splashing in their watery habitat.
Two in love lions, inside a dark humongous cave, are cutting up meat
for their three outrageous cubs.
Rock hopping, yellow haired penguins are eating fish by the dozens and
leaving bones in the nooks and crannies of their chilly habitat.
Ooh-oohing monkeys, swinging from leafy branch-to-branch,
are quickly gobbling mushy bananas.
Sharp-toothed alligators, hiding from annoying mosquitoes,
are under the murky swamp water.
As the gigantic bus slowly leaves, and the gates rapidly close behind the children,
the zoo becomes peaceful across all the habitats.

Sophia Winkler, Grade 3
The Mirman School, CA

The Fairy Rainbow
As fairies flutter
in the breeze
all different colors
in the air
form a rainbow
in the sky.
Colleen Dundas, Grade 1
Old Town Elementary School, TX

Spring
In the spring what do I see?
I see plants and a buzzing bee.
Many many animals everywhere.
I see them here, I see them there.
In the spring I play outside each day.
It's so much fun to say yay!
Emad Takhirov, Grade 1
Woodcrest School, CA

The Cold Night
Beautiful stars glowing.
Dogs are howling.
Frost everywhere.
Icicles dripping water.
Meadow covered with snow
Freezing!
Kali Dilley, Grade 2
Sierra Hills Elementary School, CA

Stormy Day
The lightning and rain
Made us stay inside
We could not play
Football, soccer, baseball, or basketball.
John Wayne Castillo, Grade 3
Three Rivers Elementary School, TX

Dogs
Dogs eat any food.
They have different colors.
Dogs are so awesome.
Justice McCray, Grade 2
Robinson Elementary School, TX

Peace
Peace is a seed,
and people are the wind,
which spreads it.
Peace is forgiveness,
and love is the water,
which it is nourished.
Peace is freedom,
the birds fly high,
carrying peace,
by their side.
Peace is God,
and the peacemakers will
be the children.
Peace is the world,
which is wonderful.
Lauren Dodds, Grade 3
Wilchester Elementary School, TX

Fairies
I believe that fairies are real.
Their dust is as sparkly as a star.
They're as gentle as a lamb.

Fairies are real.
They're as playful as a puppy.
Their wings are as pretty as gold.

Fairies are real.
They're as light as a feather,
they're as free as a breeze

Fairies are real.
They're as smart as a whip,
but I think they are as nice as a friend.
Christine Matheson, Grade 3
Foothill Elementary School, UT

Spring
Birds migrate up north
They fly over mountains now
They come to the heat
Jahan Razavi, Grade 3
The Mirman School, CA

If...
the world was soft like a marshmallow
...and everything was hard on the inside

astronauts would swish through the clouds
...and use it like a bouncy ball

Lily Snider, Grade 2
Houston Elementary School, TX

Candy
Candy is very sweet
It is good and neat
It is a tasty treat

And it is fun to eat!

Nelahn Haynes, Grade 3
Tracy Learning Center - Primary Charter School, CA

Basketball
Basketball is fun.
Some people play it under the sun.
The coach says run and shoot it in the hoop.
The blue team almost won, but it went around the loop.
The coach was sad but we were mad!

Mohammad Fraih, Grade 2
Islamic School of Muslim Educational Trust, OR

Syria
Syria Syria come for fun,
There you can eat hot dogs on a bun!
And stay up till 5:00 in the morning!
And then sleep while snoring!
Too much sun!

Noah Wali, Grade 2
Islamic School of Muslim Educational Trust, OR

Clay Clay
Clay clay one day I went out to play.
I can play with clay in a box or with a fox yay yay.
I can play with clay at the park and in the dark.
Clay clay one day I went out to play.
Do you like to play with clay?

Salman Najjar, Grade 2
Islamic School of Muslim Educational Trust, OR

Platinum

Platinum is a card,
In someone's wallet.
Platinum is a crown,
On a king's head.
Platinum are pearls,
In a cave under water.
Platinum is jewelry,
On a woman.
Platinum is a crystal,
In a cave.
Platinum is a snowflake,
Falling down.
Matthew Tweden, Grade 1
Round Rock Christian Academy, TX

Friends

Friends are together when they play,
It always seems to be that way.
They're not the same as jewels or gold,
They're something you can always hold.
When you make a wish,
It won't always come true.
But, when you make a friend,
It will always fit you.
Friends are like flowers.
No two are the same.
If you don't make one,
It is a shame.
Ashlyn Johnson, Grade 3
West Clinton Elementary School, UT

I Spotted Nature

I spotted nature
I spotted it well
And then I fell
Into its arms.

Not long ago
Ever since, I've loved it so
I love the streams that go across it
That come from the faucet,

And I love the smell of mud
That nature makes for bugs.
Madison Scott, Grade 3
Neskowin Valley School, OR

Spring Is Here!

Birds are flying
in the sky.
They are flying
up so high.
The birds don't know
what they found.
They found worms
in the ground.
Children are laughing
really really loud.
Sometimes they see
one big cloud.
Emma Willett, Grade 2
Woodcrest School, CA

Christmas

C oal left in naughty people's stockings
H appy boys and girls opening presents
R inging bells on Santa's sleigh
I love Christmas
S anta Claus is coming to town.
T iny elves building toys
M om sends us to bed
A good time is had on Christmas
S anta eats all the cookies
Jeremy Struzynski, Grade 3
Lolo Elementary School, MT

The Little Green Shark

The shark
so green, blue and red,
how beautiful the scales are
on your head.

The scales on you
are all red, white and blue,
oh, you are so beautiful
to me and to you.
Jennifer Wiley, Grade 2
Harvest Christian School, CA

Light

Light is bright like the color yellow.
Yellow Jell-O is light when you taste it.
If you feel light, you feel heat.
When you pour water on light, it burns.
If you had too much light, you will not sleep.
If you had no light, you will see black.
If an idea came to your mind, light will turn on.
Light is like the sun, so it will last as long as the sun exists.

Iman Mabrouk, Grade 3
Islamic School of San Diego, CA

Working

W orking at school helps you learn a lot.
O ur teachers give us hard worksheets and homework.
R eading is really fun because it helps us understand things and spell.
K ickball is fun but my teacher says "don't forget you still have to do good in
    working."
I like writing as my favorite subject.
N ever stop working after recess and lunch.
G etting a lot of homework helps me a lot.

Symplee Efban, Grade 3
Keone'ula Elementary School, HI

Aloha

Aloha means love,
Love that is like a flower blooming in the summer sun.

Aloha is for showing your ohana (family) love.
You respect your family, and share your aloha.

We sprinkle our aloha to one another, making us a big ohana.
We need to always sprinkle aloha in your heart.

Noelani Helm, Grade 3
Kualapu'u Public Charter School, HI

Haiti

Haiti,
Steamy island,
Destroying shake, running,
Makes me feel super duper sad.
Hurting.

Alayna Mann-Korner, Grade 3
Tracy Learning Center - Primary Charter School, CA

Monkeys
Monkeys
Funny, silly
Swinging, playing, crazy
They like to eat big bananas
Animal

Nicolette Lucatero, Grade 3
Tracy Learning Center - Primary Charter School, CA

Jelly Beans
Jelly beans are like a rainbow.
Jelly beans are mostly blue.
I like black ones.
Jelly beans, one or two.
They taste like yummy gummies.

Zachary Lawton, Kindergarten
Notre Dame Academy Elementary School, CA

Ghost
There once was a boy whose name is unknown
It's said that a ghost took his family and home
And by the way it is said that his house is in Rome
And his ghost has been spotted by Cathedral Dome
That is the story of the boy whose unknown

Isaac Harris, Grade 3
Wonderland Avenue Elementary School, CA

Interesting Pants
There once was a man from France
Who had some interesting pants
But then they fell down
He put on a gown
And scared all the girls at the dance

Leo Viscomi, Grade 3
Wonderland Avenue Elementary School, CA

Zebra
zebra
striped animal
running, escaping, traveling
soft, printed, fast, wild
mammal

Yuliana Garza, Grade 3
Lorenzo De Zavala Elementary School, TX

The Day
The Day is
Fun
The Day is
Cool
It's just like
School
I tell you its
Fun
Just like You!
Hayley DiGiacinto-Grenier, Grade 1
P H Greene Elementary School, TX

The Return
In the winter
when the snowflakes
come down
something is hiding
something profound
with all of her light
and all of her glory
spring will come soon
don't worry.
Emma Latendresse, Grade 2
The Catlin Gabel School, OR

School
I like school.
It is fun.
And I get to do art.
And I like to read books.
And I love the light.
I like my friends.
I like my teachers.
I love my school.
It is fun.
Aadit Agrahara, Kindergarten
Scholars Academy, CA

An Ordinary Day
An ordinary day
Is actually a very special day
You laugh and play
And have a great time
But the best day of all
Is the day you celebrate with your family
You laugh and play with your family
So make a day with your family
A special day
Morgan Vandervoort, Grade 3
Wilchester Elementary School, TX

Lightning
Lightning
Loud, dangerous
Shocking, exploding, burning
It is horribly scary
Electrifying!
Jacob Madsen, Grade 2
Dixie Sun Elementary School, UT

Hurricanes
Hurricanes
Violent, muddy
Hurting, destroying, scaring
Form above the oceans
Cyclones
Miriam Orozco, Grade 2
Dixie Sun Elementary School, UT

The River
The river flows to the ocean.
It is slow or fast.
The river is very useful to life.
The river is peaceful.
The flowing river makes lovable music.
I like the river.
Karan Shah, Kindergarten
Scholars Academy, CA

Robots
R eally helpful
O nly have wires
B oys are harder working robots
O nly nice and never mean
T errible readers
S elf programmed!
Charlie Dunbar, Grade 2
Camino Grove Elementary School, CA

The Night at Dawn

It is very dark.
The moon is very bright.
The dogs bark.
The sky is not light.
The sky is nice and darkish.
All the kites are gone.
The crickets sing their song.
The fish are very quiet.
The stars are very bright.
We all wake up at dawn.

Joshua Brachna-Gonzalez, Grade 2
Tracy Learning Center - Primary Charter School, CA

Where I'm From

I'm from 24 Crayola crayons, product letters, and nature.
I'm from purified water, sand, and veggies.
I'm from rocks, wood, and rubber producing trees.
I'm from egg rolls dipped in soy sauce in a fresh package.
I'm from my grandparents.
I'm from non-zippable mouths to fanciness.
I'm from "Brush your teeth!" and "Put the lotion on!"
I'm from Yoon Kim and Steve Kim.
I'm from a desert camping trip to smelly cat poop.
I'm from my baby blanket to my cloud-soft pillow.

Grace Kim, Grade 3
Juliet Morris Elementary School, CA

Huge Ball of Gas

I am a huge ball of gas,
waving at you from cloudless space.
"Hello," at night is what I say,
and when the morning sun comes,
I slowly drift away...
There are dozens and dozens of me in your galaxy.
Some are forming in seconds,
some will stay in space forever.
I'm a giant, huge ball of burning gas,
I truly am a star.

Piper Hill, Grade 3
Saigling Elementary School, TX

Arianna

A t last you are coming to school
R eads *Amelia Bedelia* and *Judy Moody* books
I ce cream is my favorite
A cts like a singer
N ice to her friends
N ever says no to a challenge
A lways likes to help

M om is her bff
O n Thursday Dad takes me to the bookstore
N eeds lots of kisses and hugs
A ccomplishes all her tasks
R uns like thunder
E ats all her lunch
S its on the rug quietly

Arianna Monares, Grade 1
Kentwood Elementary School, CA

Dolphins

I sit by the sandy shore
And see a ripple pop out of the water like when
The sun comes in the morning. It is not a shark, not a whale...
IT'S A DOLPHIN!

It jumps out of the water
With a silly smile
Laughing with water flowing behind it.
It's gray, it's kind, I wish I had a
Dolphin that was all mine.
At night the waves comfort
The dolphin as it sleeps.

It's more graceful than a fish,
Nicer than a shark, IT'S A DOLPHIN!

Stephanie Muschalik, Grade 3
Wilchester Elementary School, TX

Rain

The rain is falling,
There is a humungous storm,
Lightning and thunder.

Sarah C., Grade 3
Wonderland Avenue Elementary School, CA

What Is a Rock?

What is a rock?
Is a rock a nice home where
an ant can stay warm?
Is it where I can sit when
I'm bored?
Is it what I can throw and see
bounce on the clear lake?
What is a rock?

Katherine Granberry, Grade 3
Annunciation Orthodox School, TX

Teachers

T hey teach lessons
E ducation happens with them
A pples they sometimes keep on their desk
C hildren they teach
H abitats they teach about
E lementary schools most work at
R eading they do
S cience they teach, too

Deziree Parson, Grade 2
Lakeport Elementary School, CA

Oh, Swan

Oh what is a swan?
Is it a graceful and white bird like a
cloud in the sky.
Or its beak so yellow like the sun
shining on any fellow.
Am I as quick as a snake with wings.
Oh what is a swan.

Emeline Birdwell, Grade 3
Annunciation Orthodox School, TX

Soccer

My favorite sport is soccer
Soccer is very fun
You score lots of goals
People are cheering
You on
You get trophies and cupcakes
At the end
Soccer

Allison Still, Kindergarten
Lake Pointe Elementary School, TX

Buzzing Bees

Soldier guarding the hive with his sword
Yellow apples shining in a big puffy tree
Yellow jewels glittering in the flowers
A loud buzz against your ear
Sucking nectar out of a daisy
Sprinting gold over the water
Smoothies shaking in a blender
A soft pillow floating over your head

Sylvia Snyders, Grade 3
Lolo Elementary School, MT

Butterfly

Oh butterfly, oh butterfly!
You're as beautiful as a dragonfly.
And as pretty as a Canadian Goose.
And as handsome as Zeus.
Oh, how pretty you can be.
It's wonderful, can't you see.
Don't you agree with me?
How beautiful you can be!

Divya Cherlo, Grade 3
Kingwood Montessori School, TX

Cheetah

Cheetah
Spotted, fast
Running, eating, jumping
They hunt other animals
Dangerous

Cory Robinson, Grade 1
Kentwood Elementary School, CA

Mommy

My mommy's name is Johanna
She loves me very much
She plays with me and makes me lunch
She has pretty brown hair and brown eyes
She loves me very much

Sydney Moore-Patterson, Kindergarten
Legacy Christian Academy, NM

My Art Journal

I love my art journal!
Every time I am bored I draw.
When I draw,
I feel like everybody in my family
Is watching me
So I have to do my best.
I feel like I can express
My feelings with my drawings,
Like if I draw a flower and it is leaning,
That means I'm sad.
I may not be the best artist
But "Hey I am pretty good for a third grader!"
When I draw I am excited
Because I can't wait until the end
Which is to show it to everybody!
That's the exciting part!
But I think my drawings are amazing
And I love to draw!
My sketches are gray and white.
I like to draw whatever comes in my
Head or I look around and draw what I see.

Lauren Herrera, Grade 3
D P Morris Elementary School, TX

Where I'm From

I am from creamy whipped cream, cold strawberry ice cream, and sticky chocolate
syrup.
I am from black and white pandas climbing onto trees, daisies blowing through
the swift grass,
Sunflowers sweeping through the cold morning sky.
I am from crunchy lumpia, mouthwatering shabu shabu, and from cheesy cheese
sticks.
From grandma and grandpa.
I am from a blabbermouth family, smart-headed family, and a brown haired and
brown eyed family.
I am from "Brush your teeth," and "Be nice to your sister."
I am from my passed away turtle named Alex who used to always play with the
other turtle named Aaron all the time.
I am from Jo, Victoria, Karina, and Kristine.
I am from the time I lost my two front teeth.
I am from my past relatives.

Kianna Rojas, Grade 3
Juliet Morris Elementary School, CA

Rainbow of Love

I think love,
Is a dreaming cloud of spring rain.
In gentle happiness,
Love loves forgiving people
In the country of love,
We welcome love,
Everywhere we go.
Love we enthusiastically love
Changes people's behavior,
In a good way.
When I think of love,
I feel peace in me.

Tasnim Yusuf, Grade 3
Oak Park Elementary School, CA

War

Guns fire
bombs dropping
soldiers fighting for freedom
making sacrifices
tanks firing
trying to survive
but some do die
for America
and for freedom
from this death trap
in the end
a lot are dead

Justin Hinson, Grade 3
Old Town Elementary School, TX

Wonderful White

White is a snowflake,
Falling all around.
White is milk,
Cool and sweet.
White is a veil,
Long and pretty.
White is a kleenex,
When you have a cold.
White is the moon,
Covered in cheese.
White is an angel,
Looking after you.

Jamie Welsh, Grade 1
Round Rock Christian Academy, TX

Purple Monster

Purple is God,
Flashing from the sky.
Purple is hope,
Floating in the heavens.
Purple is a plum,
Very very yummy.
Purple is books,
In your life.
Purple is jam,
So delicious.
Purple is love,
In your heart.

Daniel Tomlin, Grade 1
Round Rock Christian Academy, TX

Laila

Laila is her name,
Barking is her game,
She loves to play ball,
Winter and fall,
She is my little goldkeeper,
Because she is a Golden Retriever,
Every day I love to meet,
When I get home,
I give her a yummy treat!

Rosie Ahuja, Grade 3
C W Cline Primary School, TX

My Dog

My big dog is mean.
I hate my big dog.
Giant is his name.

He licks me too much,
and jumps on me.
I'd like to push him
Into the sea.

Miguel Rodriguez, Grade 3
Foothill School, UT

Helen Keller's Life

At a young age,
Ill with scarlet fever
Sadly became blind and deaf.
Annie Sullivan
Helen's teacher,
Her companion, a supporter.
Helen was taught
To write, to speak,
To read with Braille.
When older, she attended Radcliffe College.
After, she wrote books and
Gave speeches around the world.
Ms. Sullivan passed away
When an eye operation failed.
Polly Thomson stepped in.
Years passed,
Polly died after falling sick.
Alone was Helen, but,
Helen continued on until 1968
When a heart attack
Took her life.

Laura Chansavang, Grade 3
De Vargas Elementary School, CA

Teachers

Teachers stare you in the eye,
And they snap at you when you talk
Unexpected. You always have to sit up
Straight and you never get play time.

Teachers laugh when you fall out of
Your chair, and if you laugh, it's straight to the
Principal's office. Even the principal won't
Smile or at least laugh.

But at Wilchester, teachers never stare,
They don't snap at you when you talk,
Teachers love to laugh and smile a lot,
And you are never blamed. I think…

Wilchester is the school for me!!!

Victoria Camden, Grade 3
Wilchester Elementary School, TX

My Dog Macey

Make it stop!
She's driving me crazy!
She is fun to play with,
But she drives me nuts.
When I have to go to sleep at night
She stretches her legs out
Kicking me in the back.
She kicks me off the bed
Onto the floor.
But I stay on the floor
So it won't happen again.
I just fall asleep on the floor.
It's driving me crazy!
Make it stop!

Jarrett Allen, Grade 3
C W Cline Primary School, TX

All About Black

Black is shoes,
You wear on your feet.
Black is charcoal,
Smoking in the fire.
Black is a jet,
Shooting in the sky.
Black is a cat,
Cuddling on you.
Black is a panther,
Pouncing on its prey.
Black is a storm,
Thundering all around.
Black is a chair,
Soft and fluffy.

Ethan Anderson, Grade 1
Round Rock Christian Academy, TX

Karate

Karate
Teacher, student
Fighting, learning, blocking
I like my lessons
Kung fu

Patrick Young, Grade 3
Ygnacio Valley Christian School, CA

Basketball

I like basketball.
I like to shoot hoops.
Shoot!
Pass!
Run!
That's my sport.

Jalen Gibson, Grade 1
Longfellow Elementary School, TX

Chef

Chef.
I like cooking cake.
Baking,
flipping,
and giving.
That's my hobby.

Aurelia Mickens, Grade 1
Longfellow Elementary School, TX

Math

Math oh math you are so great.
Your big A pluses I appreciate.
Math oh math you are so great
I could watch you all day,
But one thing I can't do
Is tie my shoe.

Reagan Kopplin, Grade 3
Three Rivers Elementary School, TX

Music

Energetic
steady, rhythm
movement, running
sailboat, sadness

Luke Poirot, Grade 2
Annunciation Orthodox School, TX

Fall

Crunching leaves in the rain
milky skies and mist come
fall is the right place to be.

Melissa Taylor, Grade 3
St Raphael School, CA

Mirror

How many days does it take to look in the mirror and do the right thing?
How many days will it take to be nice?
How many days will it take for a dove to fly across the sky?
How many days will it take to know that being a different color is ok?
How many days will it take to be nice to each other?
Just think about what it feels like to you
So just do the same to the others
So just think…think…think…
And do what you want them to do to you
So treat others how you want to be treated!

Nicole Golenberg, Grade 2
Laurence School, CA

Cookie Cake

Cookie cake tastes like sweet scrumptious treats,
Sugary and tasty!
Cookie cake smells like fresh baked bread,
Delicious and delectable!
Cookie cake feels like goose bumps,
Lumpy and bumpy!
Cookie cake sounds like rice krispies,
Crunchy and munchy,
Cookie cake looks like a sweet treat to eat!
Luscious and terrific!

Allie Cermak, Grade 2
Round Rock Christian Academy, TX

My Baby Brother

My baby brother
Always keeps me up.
He screams.
He always eats and eats.
My baby brother sleeps and I can't play with my friends.
My baby brother is so cute.
He loves to look at the panda.
He loves the ladybug too.
My baby brother —
I love you!

Ernie Carrillo III, Kindergarten
Notre Dame Academy Elementary School, CA

My Feelings

When I laugh, I am on fire.
I am calm like water...shhhhhhh.
I am lonely like a lonely cub.
I feel jumpy like a kangaroo!
When I am a shy tortoise, I hide in my hard shell.
I am dizzy like a dizzy dolphin.
When I am happy, I feel like a jumpy fish.

Cielo Serna, Grade 2
Longfellow Elementary School, TX

My Feelings

Sometimes I feel like a pretty princess telling all my people what to do.
Sometimes I feel excited, like a big marshmallow bouncing up and down.
Sometimes I feel mad, like a volcano erupting.
Sometimes I feel proud, like a balloon popping!
Sometimes I feel like a star up in the sky.
Sometimes I feel lazy, like a statue just standing all day.
Sometimes I feel scared, like when I go in my closet.

Rhemi Herron, Grade 2
Longfellow Elementary School, TX

Black Is...

Strong like a king who rules the world
A wild, strong tornado whose breezes move strong
A hurricane that spins faster and faster
The dark sky of midnight
The scary things that come out!
The early dawn that starts to shine as happiness rises
And the darkness is powerless

Jada Barham, Grade 3
Lolo Elementary School, MT

Zooming Dragonflies

Sparkling wings zooming by the clouds,
Colorful gems gracefully fluttering in the wind.
Beautiful flowers gliding in the sunlight.
Fluffy clouds flying in the soft breeze.
Nice and colorful puff balls with the feeling of flowers.
Balls of color in the summer air.
Nice graceful snowflakes in a nice soft flower bed.

Ailey Robinson, Grade 3
Lolo Elementary School, MT

Fishing

I like to fish
And put it in a dish

I have a fishing pole
I like to fish in a hole

You get to catch a lot of fish
They taste good in a dish
Sam Bingham, Grade 3
Cache Valley Learning Center, UT

A Bird

The sound of a bird is:
sing
twitter
peck
peep
tweet
chirp
fly
Celyne Luong, Grade 3
Elder Creek Elementary School, CA

My Best Friend

I look at you and I feel so good.
I do whatever you say.
I do I do I do.
Please believe me when I say I do.
When I go to bed you help me go to sleep.
You do you do you do.
You rattle when I shake your head.
But you are my stuffed kitty cat.
Maria Crema, Grade 3
Edward Byrom Elementary School, OR

Pig

Pig
Fat, bumpy
Laying, resting, twisting
Always really, really dirty
Hog
Leah Abitante, Grade 1
Kentwood Elementary School, CA

Summer

S un is bright this season.
U nder cover in water fights.
M ighty kids are jumping around.
M & M's being eaten in the sun.
E ntire school year is over.
R eally really fun.
Cooper Jackson, Grade 3
Spring Creek Elementary School, WY

Pearl

P uppy
E ntertaining
A wesome
R eally cute
L oving
Kate Faris, Grade 3
Horn Academy, TX

Recess

Recess
Wild, crazy
Fun, friends, free
Good, great, amazing, awesome
Recess
Brady Patterson, Grade 3
Horn Academy, TX

Little Brother

Vaughn
Cute, soft
Laughs, smiles, cries
He bangs his toys
Baby
Miles Butler, Grade 3
Selwyn College Preparatory School, TX

Snow

The snow seems to follow wherever
I go
It truly covers me from
head to toe.
Hunter Heisz, Grade 3
Carlthorp School, CA

The Beautiful Sea
The beautiful sea,
Is as light as the blue sky,
Look at the fine waves.

Sharon Hahsong Nah, Grade 3
Wonderland Avenue Elementary School, CA

Tornado
Carries everything
Tornadoes pick you up high
Spins you around

Colton Duke, Grade 3
Tracy Learning Center - Primary Charter School, CA

Massage
Rubbing and patting
Very beautiful music
Laying and resting

Armina Moshiri, Grade 3
Tracy Learning Center - Primary Charter School, CA

Nature
Wind, flowers, and birds
bees collecting pollen too
grass, spiders, and more

Tyler Gore, Grade 2
Tracy Learning Center - Primary Charter School, CA

Butterfly
Flying, spotted, cute
Soaring through the sky like wind
Eating, laying eggs

Meghan Timm, Grade 3
Tracy Learning Center - Primary Charter School, CA

Sun
orangy, round, sun
beautiful, bright, bursting, sun
yellowish, big, hot, sun

Alondra Camarena, Grade 2
Tracy Learning Center - Primary Charter School, CA

The End

What you are reading will end it will end when you have read it
It is oh so very sad that everything must end sometime
So I must say good-bye to you
I have to say we all have a dying day.
Even our books and toys must end when they are old and loved
It is the same with everything but the worst with life
The poem must end the toy will be passed on
But when a loved one goes the end has come
The end is the end so...
The end

Sydney Kurland, Grade 3
Wonderland Avenue Elementary School, CA

Camaros

Camaros are fast.
Hop in, you want to
Go for a ride? I turn
On the engine. I put
It in drive. Here we go
For a ride! I push the
Gas pedal. And we're
Off, Vroooom!
The engine roars
100 MPH.

Aron Bartlow, Grade 3
Wonderland Avenue Elementary School, CA

This Is White to Me

White is the spirit of someone passing,
It is the color of the heavens above,
White is the sound of a little whisper in your ear,
One that you can hear,
White is the color of a reflection in a mirror,
When no one is there,
White is a heart that's all ripped apart,
White sounds like a beautiful voice that sings,
There are a lot of things white,
But for now, this poem's got to go out of sight!

Elijah Tovar, Grade 3
Marguerite Hahn Elementary School, CA

Welcome Love

I think love
Is lovely freedom.
Amazing love always wears peaceful kindness.
In my wonderful heart
I care about my careful family.
So love amazing love,
Where are you?
I'm in a different world.
I think love changes
Wherever I go.
In the peaceful country of love
All kinds of love
Are welcome.

Jennifer Lagunas, Grade 3
Oak Park Elementary School, CA

Going to the Pool

Splash splash
The pool is going to be great
I can't wait
"When are we there, mom?"
"In five minutes."
"Really, I can't wait."
"We're here."
Yay!
Splash! Splash!
The pool s*p*a*r*k*l*e*s
I can't wait to go in
Splash
The pool is great.

Ellis Kim, Grade 3
Wonderland Avenue Elementary School, CA

Ocean Blue

I see an ocean
It is blue, I see an ocean blue.
I was happy to see the ocean blue.
I went home and drew the ocean blue.
I sailed on a boat on the pretty ocean blue
Soon I found a whale toy in the ocean blue.
I was so happy to see the ocean blue.

Chaitanya Bhat, Grade 1
Scholars Academy, CA

Friend
Friend
Football, basketball
Giving, playing, helping
He is fun!
Brian
Legend Morris, Grade 1
Heritage Elementary School, UT

Sunset
Oh, sunset, oh sunset
Up in the sky,
You are like oranges
I think you're beautiful
The way you shine brightly.
Kendra Garcia, Grade 3
Three Rivers Elementary School, TX

Brown
Brown is the color of my teddy bear.
Brown is my hair.
Brown is trees.
Brown makes me feel great!
Brown.
AnnaBelle Williams, Grade 1
Heritage Elementary School, UT

Hole
I see a hole
In the ground
It looks like a crater
Or a prairie dog's house
That can be home
Brandon McCann, Grade 2
Mosaic Academy, NM

Math and Baths
I like math and baths
My house has a dirt path
We have a bird bath in our yard
Do you like bubble baths?
I always take a steam bath
Brittaney Stetson, Grade 3
Legacy Christian Academy, NM

Nature
R eally pretty.
O hh ahh makes people amazed.
S mells really good.
E xcellent is the word for roses.
S uper red.
Kiera Mallory, Grade 3
Keone'ula Elementary School, HI

Funny
giggly and goofy
happy and goofy
I feel funny
jumpy and wiggly
crazy with a k
Harrison Windmiller, Grade 3
St Raphael School, CA

Colors
Red is a flower.
Yellow is a banana.
Black is a dog.
Green is grass.
Colors.
Angelina Naakai Perez, Grade 1
Heritage Elementary School, UT

Red
Red is a stop sign.
Red is a kite flying high in the sky.
Red is the flag waving.
Red is fun.
Red.
Christopher Dieguez, Grade 1
Heritage Elementary School, UT

Kitten
Kitten
cute, furry
playfully jumps high
loves lots of attention
Feline
Kali Crume, Grade 3
Warren Elementary School, OR

One of a Kind

I had a dog
And he had a lot
Of extra skin
And he was so
Funny and sweet.

He was one
Of a kind!

But one night
We came home
And he was
Lying on the floor
And breathing
Very deeply
And we took
Buck to the vet.

He was dying.
He was
My best friend.

And I love
And miss him.
Emily Manahan, Grade 3
C W Cline Primary School, TX

Treasures

I like treasures.
Makeup treasures
Rock treasures
Stuffed treasures
Any kind of treasure.
Treasures in the box
Treasures on the beach
Treasures in a pocket
I like treasures
Art treasures
Birthday treasures
Book treasures
I like treasures.
Elise King-Gribb, Grade 1
Spring Creek Elementary School, WY

Puppies Forever

Puppies, puppies, puppies,
Who doesn't like puppies?

Cute, cute, cute,
Puppies,
Soft, playful, sweet!
One, two, three,
Let's see more!

Puppies, puppies, puppies
Never go
Because,
I love you!

Never go puppies!
Never get extinct!
I'll never lose you puppies,
I'll always love you puppies,
As long as you stay
With me!
Katherine Young, Grade 3
C W Cline Primary School, TX

Holly

I have a cat named Holly
She is cute and jolly

My cat is black and white and is so sweet
She sleeps on my lap and is very neat

She attacks my dog and my feet
And also my fingers under a sheet

I love her a lot, I'm glad she's my cat
I am scared though she will get fat

Holly has a toy mouse
That she carries around the house

She chases my sister and me
She watches the birds and the bees
Ashley Baughman, Grade 3
Warren Elementary School, OR

Icicle
I cy
C old
I ncredible
C overed in sparkles
L ovely
E nchanted
Skyla Smith, Grade 3
Cache Valley Learning Center, UT

Butterflies
Butterflies inside
Standing on the edge, praying
Time to take the jump
I will spare my flight
It's a flight that has fright
But will make me bright!
Saphiana Zamora, Grade 3
Connally Elementary School, TX

Ballet
B eautiful ballerinas
A mazing grace
L eaping
L eotards — black and pink
E veryone claps
T oe shoes
Sarabeth Cooley, Kindergarten
Reid School, UT

Spring
In the spring what do I see?
I see flowers sprouting at me.
Flowers, flowers, what do you see?
I see people picking up me.
People, people, what do you see?
We see floating lily pads swishing by me.
Violet Josephson, Grade 1
Woodcrest School, CA

Spring
Spring is grass.
Spring is rain.
Spring is fun.
Spring is flowers.
Spring is bees.
Spring is baby animals.
Emilia Borecki, Grade 1
Cache Valley Learning Center, UT

The Flag Waves
The flag waves and I wave back
I see and the sea sees me
The waves move so gracefully.
It makes me feel sad in my heart.
It sounds like memories flying by.
The flag waves and I wave back.
Madelyn Sheffield, Grade 2
St John's Episcopal School, TX

Tiger Shark
Tiger Shark —
Cool, mean, messy —
Swims,
Everywhere, today, and away
Ralph Contreraz, Grade 3
St Mary School, CA

Fish
Fish —
Royal, blue, yellow —
Gliding
Swiftly, at night time, everywhere
M. Fernandez, Grade 3
St Mary School, CA

Thunderstorm
I came from the world
My real name is thunderstorm
I crackle and crash
Clara Biles, Grade 3
Selwyn College Preparatory School, TX

The Fat Cat
There is a cat
That is so fat
Because he ate a rat.
Mia Hedman, Grade 1
St James Episcopal School, TX

My Dog Ringo

My dog Ringo is a Golden Retriever
Or should I say my best friend. Ringo has brown
Sparkly eyes that shine like the stars, a healthy body
That will make him strong when he grows up, and
Floppy ears that go floppy, floppy flop, flop.

Ringo is 4 years old, his birthday is on St. Patrick's
Day; better wear some green or else pinch! Ringo has
Golden soft fur and can do a wonderful snuggle.

I also think Ringo is the best swimmer ever and best
Of all he has a big loving family that loves him very
Much, I love you Ringo.

Madelyn Perdomo, Grade 3
Wilchester Elementary School, TX

Fourth of July

Fourth of July, Fourth of July, don't go away,
Today is a good day.
You'll see fireworks in the sky
And even see ribbons around so high.
Stars appear in the sky
As bikes pass with ribbons
Everything is nice
As the moon is out
Even though it's dark in the sky
Don't go away.
Fourth of July is fun
Make sure you don't run.
Fourth of July, Fourth of July, don't go away.

Son Pham, Grade 1
Scholars Academy, CA

School

School school school is fun
I really love to play and
When I play I say hooray
I like the monkey bar, and our
School is not that far. I like
Math, and when I go home
I take a bath.

Lana Athashim, Grade 2
Islamic School of Muslim Educational Trust, OR

Owen Stodder

O wns a PSP
W rites neatly
E njoys video games
N ever wakes up early

S leeps in a bunk bed
T eases his little brother
O wns a wallet
D rinks milk
D reams to be a basketball player
E arns a dollar every week
R uns with his dogs

Owen Stodder, Grade 1
Kentwood Elementary School, CA

The Borse

The large brown borse
is as strange as can be.
It lives in the grasslands
sometimes by a shady tree.
The borse is an omnivore.
it eats grass and meat.
The borse roams the grasslands,
but doesn't like the heat.
The borse can run
as fast as a horse.
If you really wanted to
you could ride the borse.

Lauren Lee, Grade 2
Woodcrest School, CA

The Beach

The Ocean is blue.
The houses are big.
The sand is soft.
The shells are hard.
The waves are fun.
The dolphins play.
Clamming is fun.
We hunt for shells.
We walk the pier.
We swim in the ocean.
I play with my cousins.
I love the beach!

Anna Kampp, Grade 3
St. Joseph Catholic School, CA

Art Penguin

I saw a penguin
So handsome and smart
And somehow he made art!
He got some ice and threw
It on the ground.
And with his flippers
He gave it a good pound.
He spread it around in parts
And there you go he made art!
His art it was a picture of me!
And when I saw it
I jumped full of glee!

Jeremiah Green, Grade 3
Mission Bend Christian Academy, TX

Music

My feet hear the music,
and they start to move
up and down.

The rhythm of the beat,
makes my feet jump and shake.
It's all in the music.

I love Music!!!

Hector Ramirez, Grade 3
Foothill School, UT

Christina

C ool for
H elping a
R eally good friend
I ntelligent
S weet and sour
T alkative
I ncredible at math but
N ot perfect
A truly cool person

Christina Watson, Grade 3
Horn Academy, TX

Baby Brothers
B ooty shakers
A lphabet do'ers
B ut as cute as buttons
Y oyo breakers

B lubber containers
R ug rats
O verrated
T humping
H at wearing
E xhausting
R ambling
S uper brothers
Macy Alexander, Grade 2
Giddings Elementary School, TX

Miss Richards
M agnificent Richards that is really smart
I ntelligent Richards that is funny
S he smiles a lot
S he is splendid at art

R ichards is awesome at math
I ntelligent reading Richards
C hildren like Richards
H ow exciting she is
A wesome at everything
R ichards really rocks
D oing intelligent
S tuff that we can't do
Jezreel K.K. Johnson, Grade 3
Keone'ula Elementary School, HI

Spring
I see the pansies blooming,
I hear the birds chirping,
I smell the nectar of the flowers,
I touched a moth I caught yesterday,
I taste candy from my Easter Basket…

I know it's spring.
Micah Matthews, Kindergarten
Home School, OR

Mr. T-Rex
Mr. T-rex what do you do?
Mr. T-rex how are you?
Mr. T-rex what do you say?
I always look for food all day!
I am really fine!
I always say, Roar!
Morgan Robertson, Grade 1
Woodcrest School, CA

Spring
Spring is finally here!
I can see California poppies blooming.
I can hear blue jays singing happy tunes.
I can smell my mom baking a coffee cake.
I can taste peaches and lemons.
I feel the fresh air around my body.
Jennifer Rivera Lamborn, Grade 2
Woodcrest School, CA

All About Me
Scary and cute as a coyote,
Strong as a maple tree,
Enduring as a diamond,
Friendly as the number two,
Sharp as an emerald,
And fast as a waterfall.
Denny Han, Grade 1
Baldwin Stocker Elementary School, CA

Turtle
Turtle —
Green, slow, small —
Moves
Quietly, later, around
Maya Evensizer, Grade 3
St Mary School, CA

Spring
Spring is here
Sunshine shines
Water flows
Sterling York, Grade 2
Whale Gulch Elementary School, CA

Peanut

I have a new horse,
that lives with my aunt.
He likes to eat peanuts.
I told him he can't.

So I'll name him Peanut,
so he won't be sad.
Now he likes oats.
That's not so bad!
Lauren Fischer, Grade 1
St Mark's Day School, TX

My Turtle

My wiggly, squiggly turtle
is loving and so kind.
He goes with me to school
I hope he learns to mind.

He never, ever says he's bored.
He even likes my friends.
I hope the way he plays with me
never, ever ends.
Mackenzie Stewart, Grade 1
St Mark's Day School, TX

Ocean

Ocean
Roaring waves
Pounding, crashing, rumbling
Reaching up the beach
Sea
Owen Lassally, Grade 3
Carlthorp School, CA

Garden

I like gardening.
I grow food.
Digging,
Planting,
Giving them water.
That's my hobby.
Katilyn McElroy, Grade 1
Longfellow Elementary School, TX

The Platasaurus

The platasaurus
is really green.
it is a dinosaur
that can still be seen.
The platasaurus
has a big roar.
Sometimes it likes
to do much more.
It likes to eat
lots of meat.
It also likes
to have a treat.
Luke Talamantes, Grade 3
Woodcrest School, CA

Coral Reefs

C oral
O cean animal
R efuge to other animals
A parrot fish eats it
L ots of colors

R eef
E ats starfish
E ventually dies
F eels soft and hard
S alt water
Lindsy Smith, Grade 1
P H Greene Elementary School, TX

Home

Staplers bite paper when being stapled.
Refrigerators yell as they shut.
Clocks run as the second hand moves.
Newspapers get beat up as we crush them.
Trucks walk into the garage.
Erasers fight pencils.
Tables carry plates and forks.
Closets give kids their coats.
Coats jump on kids.
Computers sleep when shut off.
Caleb Morita, Grade 2
CLASS Academy, OR

What Is Weather?

What is weather?
Is it mother nature's feelings?
Is it seasons going back and forth?
Is it what excites a weather woman?
Is it thunder, lightning, rain, hail, snow and the sun?
What is weather?

Alexandra Herrera, Grade 3
Annunciation Orthodox School, TX

The Big Ball of Light

I contain x-rays, photons, and electrons.
My light can travel at almost 187,000 miles per second.
One million Earths could fit in me if I were hollow.
The moon and I can play hide and seek during eclipses.
My little buddy, Mercury, is constantly at my side.
I am the Sun.

Laura Fisher, Grade 3
Saigling Elementary School, TX

My Fabulous Pup

My fabulous pup is only six months,
She looks at me like a duck,
She begs,
She whines,
But most of all she shines.
The other dogs look and say she is very pretty,
I know she likes to rest in bed,
But she always falls off and bumps her head,
Then she looks at me and cries,
I say "Poor puppy don't whine."
Although she is so cute,
She leaps in my arms and says
"Ruff ruff,"
I love my little girl,
But she is also growing up.
She is too big to play rough with me,
But she will always be my little girl.

Britlyn Osborne, Grade 3
D P Morris Elementary School, TX

Extreme Hedgehog
Hedgehogs are awesome, cute, and fast.
The Hedgehog is super extreme.
Hedgehogs are prickly, cool, small, ratlike, and chubby.
Hedgehogs are awesome.

James Henry Ray, Grade 3
Annunciation Orthodox School, TX

Hippopotamus
The hippopotamus is big.
He is special
Because God made him.

Marissa Gendy, Kindergarten
Notre Dame Academy Elementary School, CA

Baseball
One batter up, bam!
A single, bam one more hit
First inning is done
Caesar Bedell, Grade 3
Horn Academy, TX

Lion
It's fast with its feet
It has a super loud roar
It eats gross, weird meat
Jake Beinart, Grade 3
Horn Academy, TX

Love
Love is peace
Love is kind
Love is slowly losing your mind
Nia Ojo, Grade 3
John Cabrillo Elementary School, CA

Cows
Cows, they eat a lot.
Cows love the meadow.
Cows, cows, they love eating grass.
Brandon Garcia, Grade 3
Montessori Academy of North Texas, TX

I Don't Care
I don't care
If my closet
Is messy!

I don't care
If my brothers
Mess up my room.

I don't care
If I
Make a spill.

I don't care
If my brothers
Call me names.

I
    Just
        Don't
            Care!
Brianna Parr, Grade 3
C W Cline Primary School, TX

I Hear
I hear the trees swaying
In the gentle breeze
I hear the fire bird
Andrew Robison, Kindergarten
Mosaic Academy, NM

Puppies
Oh puppies so cute!
So warm and fuzzy!
So playful and joyful!
So come on and buy,
The most cutest and vivacious puppy of all,
Puppies for your life
Maha Ali, Grade 3
Annunciation Orthodox School, TX

Index

Author Autograph Page

Author Autograph Page

Author Autograph Page

Author Autograph Page

Author Autograph Page

Author Autograph Page